THE DYNAMIC LAWS OF PRAYER

Other Books by Catherine Ponder

A PROSPERITY LOVE STORY
A Memoir

THE DYNAMIC LAWS OF PROSPERITY

THE DYNAMIC LAWS OF HEALING

THE PROSPERITY SECRET OF THE AGES

THE DYNAMIC LAWS OF PRAYER

THE HEALING SECRET OF THE AGES

OPEN YOUR MIND TO PROSPERITY

DARE TO PROSPER

THE SECRET OF UNLIMITED PROSPERITY

OPEN YOUR MIND TO RECEIVE

THE PROSPERING POWER OF PRAYER

The Millionaires of the Bible Series:

THE MILLIONAIRES OF GENESIS

THE MILLIONAIRE MOSES

THE MILLIONAIRE JOSHUA

THE MILLIONAIRE FROM NAZARETH

THE DYNAMIC LAWS OF PRAYER

Previously Released as
PRAY AND GROW RICH

by

Catherine Ponder

DeVorss Publications
Camarillo, California

The Dynamic Laws of Prayer
Revised and enlarged edition
Copyright © 1987 by Catherine Ponder

Previously released as **Pray and Grow Rich**
Copyright © 1968 by Catherine Ponder

ISBN-10: 0-87516-583-4
ISBN-13: 9780875165837
Library of Congress Catalog Card: 86-72267
Sixth Printing, 2009

DeVorss & Company, Publisher
PO Box 1389
Camarillo CA 93011-1389
www.devorss.com

Printed in the United States of America

CONTENTS

PART I

SIMPLE METHODS OF PRAYER

That Can Bring Dynamic Results to You!

One prays with the mind. Why prayer has miracle power. Prayer makes you irresistible to your good. Nothing dull about prayer. The overall benefits of prayer.

How a businesswoman got out of a rut. Nothing dull or complex about dynamic prayer. Your *universal* God power can bring results. Your *indwelling* God power can bring results. Why prayers go un-answered. Pray first instead of last. Prayer attracts a millionaire investor. The path to instant good. Prayer is soul-stretching. No strain in prayer. When your prayers grow stale. The variety of prayer. Oriental and Western prayer methods are reversed. Prayer will teach you its secrets.

Prayers of protection can affect crops and weather. Protection prayers put out fire. Prayer can protect in war. Your angel-protectors. Angels of prosperity and healing. Divine protection is promised mankind.

Affirmations produced the author's first book. Prayer begins with words. The powerful results of affirmation. Why verbal prayer is necessary. The psychological value of verbal prayer. Verbal prayer brings quick financial help. Powerful types of affirmation. *First:* The prayer of talking directly to God. *Second:* The prayer of asking. *Third:* The prayer of asking for direct guidance. *Fourth:* The decree of divine intelligence. *Fifth:* The decree of divine love. *Sixth:* The decree that God's will is being done. *Seventh:* Decrees of the divine plan. *Eighth:* The decree of divine order. *Ninth:* The decree of blessing. *Tenth:* The prayer of faith. *Eleventh:* The prayer of divine restoration. Write out your decrees. Prayers of decree in summary.

PART II

ADVANCED METHODS OF PRAYER

That Can Bring Dynamic Results to You!

Not just for ministers. From the sublime to the ridiculous. How prayers for this book were answered. From nothing to everything. Increased good for you.

Psychologists know about miracle consciousness. Ancients knew how to activate spiritual consciousness. How to activate your miracle consciousness. The Christ Mind. The power in the Name, "Jesus Christ." Call on the Name Jesus Christ. Write out Jesus Christ prayers. Picture Jesus Christ. Behold the Christ in others. How to behold the Christ in yourself. How inviting the Christ within heals one. How to invoke the peace of Jesus Christ. How to affirm the finished works of Jesus Christ. Ways to invite the universal Christ presence. How a sophisticated woman was healed. How the forgiving power of Jesus Christ works. The miraculous power in the name Christ Jesus. The white light of the Christ. Invoke the Christ consciousness through the words of Jesus. Release your miracle power.

The history of concentration. The incredible power of concentration. A housewife's deliverance from trouble. The necessity of concentration in prayer development. Induce concentration through list-making. Your *first* list: What you want to eliminate. How a businessman's elimination list brought success. Your *second* list: What you want. A healer's success formula. Top executives prove power of list-making. Your *third* list: thanksgiving. Induce concentration through picturing. "Prayer in pictures" can be turning point to results. How a businesswoman experienced a happier life. How the author brought about completion. How a college professor got another degree. How a slum family "graduated" from their tenement. Imaging creates, then concentration hastens results. Induce concentration through decree. Verbal prayers are "mantras of power." Not too old for a job. From "rags to riches." Induce concentration through secrecy. A woman healed herself through concentration. Inner concentration. How to develop your inner powers of concentration. How to concentrate regarding troublesome people. The art of concentration develops slowly.

His secret weapon for success. Meditation provided guidance. Meditation prospers. Meditation heals. The difference between concentration and meditation. Two reasons for meditation. The author's meditation experience with this chapter. *First:* How to meditate for inner renewal. No hurry in meditation. *Second:* How to meditate for guidance. The mechanics of meditation. Sacred texts for meditation. The author's meditation text for accomplishment. For healing, protection and forgiveness, meditate upon the Psalms. The Psalms brought freedom from a troublesome job. Deliverance from trouble. Why some people cannot meditate. Do not feel guilty. Why meditation usually has not been taught in the churches. The dangers of meditation. To meditate upon evil is destructive. Why a housewife got negative results from meditation. The past and future can be seen in meditation. The fruits of meditation. "Dry" periods in prayer are normal. The precious balm of prayer.

The secret of all attainment. Why the lack of silence is abnormal. What happens in the prayer of silence. How one boy grew up to realize the power of "sitting in the silence." How to get spiritually ready for the silence. The truly great people in history practiced the silence. Silence is in every element of nature. The healing power of the silence. Silence healed those who had been hospitalized. Informal methods of practicing the silence. An advertising executive reaped the rewards of silence. The practice of the silence can bring more friends. The triumph that only silence can bring. The prospering power of the silence. Know when to rest your case! How to formally practice the silence. The fruits of the silence.

How a human relations problem was resolved. How to identify with the prayer of realization. Healing of breast came through realization in prayer. Spiritual prediction coming true. Realization: the prayer of holy telepathy. Ask for inner assurance of answered prayer. Receive guidance by dwelling on the subject. Affirming guidance gets results. An inner feeling is the secret of effective prayer. Various prayer methods can bring realization. The author attained realization through the prayer of concentration. Realization may come casually. How prayer was tested in scientific experiments. How others got results through realization. After realization, then what? Realization makes results real.

The author's introduction to prayer groups. The author's early prayer partners. The power of prayer partners. Why prayer groups are powerful. How prayer groups function. The power that comes from praying with others. Praying for your enemies. Select prayer groups with care. Prayer partners versus prayer groups. Letting go brings fulfillment. Being on a prayer list brings promotion. The personal benefits of participating in a prayer group. A prayer group's experiences with divine love. The help that prayer groups and prayer partners can give organizations. The success secret of first-century prayer groups. Should families pray together? Prayers for spouses can bring results. The effectiveness of prayers at a distance. How to meet "dry periods" in prayer effectively. When to conclude a prayer group. The greatest strength of our time.

The price of answered prayer. How to "seal" your good and make it permanent. Pray, then pay. How to gain freedom from a narrow, pinched existence. The vast benefits of tithing. The power of a success covenant. Discipline perfects. An invitation from the author. A special note from the author.

PART I

SIMPLE METHODS OF PRAYER
That Can Bring Dynamic
Results to You!

Introduction . . . .

PRAYER IS WHERE THE ACTION IS!

Prayer is receiving more consideration today than at any time during the past thousand years. Why? Because prayer is where the action is!

A young man with a grave problem was asked by his minister, "Have you prayed about it?" He answered, *"Prayed?* This is no time to pray. It's time to *do* something!"

To pray is to *do* something—the most important "something" you can first do about any problem.

Why?

Because prayer is thé only action you can take that truly makes things different—from the inside out.

This is true because physical action releases the weakest form of energy, whereas mental and spiritual action release the highest form of energy.

Prayer deals primarily with the states of mind and

3

laws of mental activity that rule your world. Prayer
changes your mentality; it first changes your thinking
as it calms, uplifts and renews you. This is one of the
purposes of prayer — to change your thinking, which in
turn changes your world.

But prayer goes further. There is another reason for
all the shouting about the "power of prayer."

*Prayer releases the highest form of energy in the uni-
verse, as it links you with a God energy, which is your
source.* When this happens, prayer "turns you on"!

How?

*When you pray, you stir into action an atomic force.
You release a potent spiritual vibration that can be
released in no other way. Through prayer you unleash
a God energy within and around you that gets busy
working for you and through you, producing right
attitudes, reactions and results. It is your prayers that
recognize and release that God power.*

You may not feel the force of prayer because it oper-
ates at a higher vibration than that ordinarily felt by
man. In fact, prayer releases an energy that is usually
too fine to be recorded physically.

Nevertheless, as you pray you expand mentally and
spiritually so as to become big enough in consciousness
to *receive* a larger flow of the divine energy generated
through prayer. Prayer is not only asking and communing — *prayer is also receiving.*

A skeptic once insisted that he did not believe in the
power of prayer. When asked if he had ever prayed,
he replied that he had once. On that occasion he was
lost in a deep forest and could not find his way out.
He had been there several days and was beginning to
feel the pangs of starvation. He said that in his "weak-
ness" he prayed.

"Then God *did* answer your prayer, or you would not be here," exclaimed his acquaintance.

"No," replied the skeptic, "God did not answer my prayer. A couple of hunters came along soon afterward and showed me the way out."

This man did not understand that his prayer had been answered, and that the hunters were the human agency through which God's work had been done. Nevertheless, through the act of prayer, he had for a moment recognized the God power within and around him, and had thereby contacted and released it to produce results for him. He had not only asked, but also received.

ONE PRAYS WITH THE MIND

In recent times we've heard much about "the power of thought" as well as about "the power of prayer." These two terms are linked. They are twin powers. The mind is the connecting link between God and man. Prayer is a method of thought that links God and man. One prays with the mind.

Some authorities claim that what it usually takes a person six hours to do could easily be accomplished in only one hour by a person who knew how to pray and meditate first!

A man who practices daily meditation recently proved it, as he often has. He had been given three writing assignments which he was expected to complete in a single day. At first, he was tempted to panic just thinking about the task before him—one that would take the average journalist several days at best to accomplish satisfactorily.

Then he quieted his mind, prayed and meditated for an entire hour. During this meditation time, ideas for all three writing assignments quietly flowed into his conscious mind. He then proceeded with the tasks and completed them in a few hours without the usual "blood, sweat and tears."

An engineer with grave responsibilities on a large project had only one method for solving his engineering problems. When they arose, he always retired to his private office and sat quietly behind his desk, meditating and praying for guidance. Always the answer came as the right ideas or the perfect solution cropped up.

One day one of his employees, a young "jet set" engineer right out of college, asked the secret of this engineer's phenomenal success. When informed, this young man replied incredulously, "You mean you *just* pray and meditate and the answer comes?"

The root meaning of the word "man" is "one who looks up." Some psychologists claim that man uses only about 1/10 of 1 percent of his energies and powers, because he does not live up to the root meaning of his name: He does not look up, nor does he look within, often enough. It is sad to realize that perhaps all but 1/10 of 1 percent of man's forces are wasted because they are expressed outwardly instead of inwardly. But something can be done about it!

WHY PRAYER HAS MIRACLE POWER

Scientists tell us that there are no mistakes — only the working of higher laws not commonly understood.

Actually there seems to be one set of natural laws for the physical world and another set for the invisible world of mind and spirit. The laws of mind and spirit are so much stronger that they can be used to accentuate, neutralize, or even reverse the laws of the physical world. *The act of prayer seems to set off the working of those higher laws.*

Prayer can get the job done—when nothing else can.

Why is prayer so powerful? Why can prayer accentuate, neutralize or even reverse the laws of the physical world?

Because *through prayer, you tap the operation of higher laws of supreme mind and spirit. Through prayer you release a spiritual force which shatters fixed states of mind that may have caused much havoc in your world.* Your imprisoned thoughts and pent-up negative emotions go free and dissolve, as a higher energy floods your being and your world.

Indeed, *the energy and power released in prayer help you to "crash through" the negative thought strata that had previously bound you to all kinds of problems.* Thereafter, the impossible becomes possible. Your ships come in. So-called miracles occur. It is then that you realize that prayer *did* overcome the usual "laws of nature" and accomplish what they said couldn't be done!

If prayer were commonly understood and practiced by mankind universally, the dreaded things of this world—crime, disease, poverty and war—could become ancient history. You can begin helping to eradicate these universal ills, as well as a score of personal ones, as you begin deliberately developing your prayer powers described in this book.

PRAYER MAKES YOU IRRESISTIBLE
TO YOUR GOOD

Perhaps you are thinking that prayer has not yet made your dreams come true or your ships come in. That is because the art and science of prayer are not accomplished in one giant step nor in one dramatic act. Prayer is a continuous practice which should be applied to the little as well as to the big things in your life.

Does this sound dull? Well, it isn't. If you have thought so, you do not know what you've missed!

Prayer can be supremely exciting. Once, when I was praying for guidance about my teenage son's future, Air Force planes flew overhead so low that they interrupted my prayer time. When it happened on two separate occasions, I realized this apparently was the answer. Within a matter of weeks, my son had decided to delay attending college and had enlisted in the United States Air Force.

Prayer also has a sense of humor at times. Once when I was trying to get guidance about whether to accept a lecture invitation in the state of Indiana, a college band near my apartment suddenly started playing "Back Home Again in Indiana" so loudly that it roused me from my prayer period, and I took that as intuitive guidance to go to Indiana to lecture. It proved to be the right thing to do.

Dr. Billy Graham once said, "The man who has never discovered the power of prayer in a spiritual sense has never really lived." I believe it! And as you apply the prayer methods described herein, you will believe it, too.

Once you get the workings of it, there is a certain

indescribable fascination about prayer; an unforgettable, irresistible quality, an exuberant and exultant feeling that draws you back to it again and again. As you turn within to its power more and more, you discover you are carrying within your own being a portable paradise which you can contact anytime anywhere, regardless of what is happening around you.

There is a quaint saying among the Pennsylvania Dutch, "The hurrieder I go, the behinder I get!" Prayer slows you down to get real traction. Prayer gets you in the mood to receive your good. Prayer gives you a taste of heaven, and it tastes good! (The word "heaven" means "expansion" and the practice of prayer expands both you and your good.) St. Francis of Assisi, who loved to pray in a cave, described prayer as "a heavenly sweetness."

Your soul gets twisted out of shape when you battle life, people, circumstances. Prayer takes away your spirit of fuss, gives you a gentleness of pace. One of the most obvious signs of the person who prays is the quiet way he is able to maintain his equilibrium in the grip of circumstances, until those circumstances finally lose their grip on him!

One cynic has said there is nothing so unattractive as a prayerless woman. Allow me to be even more cynical: There is nothing so unattractive as a prayerless person, because his prayer-less-ness has demagnetized him to the blessings of life.

When you pray you quiet your mind, body, emotions, vibrations. Prayer gives you a sense of peace and tranquillity that are attracting powers. In one way or another, prayer makes you first more attractive, and then gets busy attracting your good to you. Yes, *prayer makes you irresistible to your good!*

NOTHING DULL ABOUT PRAYER

A lot of dull things have been written about prayer, but you will not find any of them in this book!

If prayer has seemed a dull practice to you in the past — a practice that you regarded as fine for sweet ol' ladies and innocent children but one that just did not work for you — it was probably because you simply did not know how to pray. There's more to prayer than mumbling a few self-conscious words that you know never reach the ceiling.

When you pray with your conscious mind only, just a fraction of your total mind prays, and you get only a fraction of the results due you through prayer.

The purpose of this book is to acquaint you with all the fascinating ways you can pray: through relaxation, denials, affirmations, concentration, meditation, the silence, realization, thanksgiving. Regardless of your life situation, you will find there is always a way you can pray — to suit your mood and circumstances — a method that gets the job done. There is no better way to secure all the blessings of life, which are your divine heritage.

After studying the favorable effects prayer had on his patients, world-famous doctor and scientist Alexis Carrel, M.D., once promised: "If you make a habit of *sincere* prayer, your life will be noticeably and profoundly altered." But you must be sincere in prayer. You should pray the way you make love — *with everything you've got!* One plain-spoken theologian has described this method as "passionate praying." Truly, as you study the dynamic laws of prayer herein described, you will find yourself getting into the act of prayer more and more.

THE OVERALL BENEFITS OF PRAYER

Prayer will then turn on the action of God's goodness within and around you. As you persist in developing your various prayer powers, *it will dawn on you that prayer is where the action is;* that prayer *has* "turned you on" and you will undoubtedly have the results to prove it. But whether or not the sure-fire answers to prayer come through right away, you will become convinced of its necessity in your life from the peace of mind and deep soul satisfaction you experience which, in turn, lead to every outer blessing.

When this happens, you will no longer complain, "Why all the shouting about the power of prayer?"

You will be one of the enriched "shouters"!

CATHERINE PONDER

P. O. Drawer 1278
Palm Desert, CA 92261
U.S.A.

THE SHOCKING TRUTH ABOUT PRAYER

— Chapter 1 —

Once when there was a storm at sea, a distressed passenger on a great ocean liner rushed up to the ship's captain and asked, "How serious is this storm?"

"It is so serious, madam, that only prayer can save us."

"My gracious!" gasped the woman. "Has it come to *that?*"

The shocking truth about prayer is that most people are afraid of it. They would rather go down with the storms of life than pray their way out of them.

Why?

Probably because of their *sheer ignorance* of the most fascinating force in the world.

Prayer *is* such a fascinating power that once it gets your attention, it will not let you go. Because of its fascination, the spirit of prayer is easier caught than taught. Once you've tapped this power it becomes a steady pressure, demanding attention and expression in your life.

You may even find yourself become a "prayer addict," because you will find you have to have it for real victories. Prayer will sustain, uplift and renew you as nothing else will. Prayer will calm, satisfy and fulfill you as nothing else can.

The shocking truth about prayer is that as a spiritual being, made in the image of God, a little lower than the angels, *you have dynamic prayer powers within you!* Through developing these prayer powers, you renew your mind and body, calm the storms of daily living, and you may even completely transform your life with unexpected good.

An additional shocking truth about prayer is that there is nothing complicated about it. There are simple ways in which you can begin to employ and *enjoy* the power of prayer. Indeed, there are far more ways to pray than you've dreamed possible, each of which is a delight.

The word "dynamic" has the same root as the word "dynamite." That which is dynamic is powerful, forceful, filled with energy, and leads to change. That which is dynamic tends to blast you out of a rut!

A "law" is a principle that works. The word "law" also suggests a desire for order in one's life. And the word "prayer" means "communion" with God and His goodness.

Thus, *the dynamic laws of prayer* are dynamic principles *that work;* they are laws of mind and spirit that are powerful, forceful, filled with energy, and that lead to vast improvement in your life as they help you make common union with God and His goodness. Furthermore, they are far more easily contacted and executed than most folks realize. Emerson went so far as to say we are already "begirt" with these laws *which execute themselves!* In his Essay on "Spiritual Laws" he declares:

> The lesson is forcibly taught . . . that our life might be much easier and simpler than we make it; that the world might be a happier place than it is; that there is no need of struggles, convulsions, and despairs, of the wringing of the hands and the gnashing of the teeth; that we miscreate our own evils. We interfere with the optimism of nature. . . . We are begirt with laws which execute themselves.[1]

How wonderful to have this awareness of good come effortlessly into our lives — that as we make contact with these powerful laws of mind and spirit, they can execute themselves.

HOW A BUSINESSWOMAN GOT OUT OF A RUT

A businesswoman felt she had gotten in a rut in both her business and personal life. Though she was busy, she was also bored. Finally she talked about her problems with a friend, who said, "Prayer is the one thing that can blast you out of the rut you are in." The friend then asked her to begin decreeing for five minutes every day: "OF MYSELF I CANNOT DO IT, BUT THE CHRIST WITHIN ME CAN AND IS PERFORMING MIRACLES IN MY MIND, BODY AND AFFAIRS HERE AND NOW."

---

1. Ralph Waldo Emerson, *The Writings of Ralph Waldo Emerson* (New York: Random House, 1940).

Within a week, electrifying changes began taking place. Old conditions and relationships quickly faded away. Suddenly new doors opened in her career which soon led to a happy new personal life as well. The miracle power of prayer had worked.

You will discover, with this busy career woman, that developing your dynamic prayer powers is the most important thing you can do, regardless of what else is on your agenda. A well-developed prayer consciousness will lead you to everything else: peace of mind, health of body, success in your affairs, and all-round happiness.

Prayer is the "package deal" to successful living! A schoolteacher once declared, "As I develop my prayer powers I've got it made, because everything else in life will then come." Prayer is the one supreme instrument given to man by God for all attainment.

NOTHING DULL OR COMPLEX ABOUT DYNAMIC PRAYER

A shocking truth about prayer is that there is nothing complex about it. There is nothing "ho hum" about prayer. It is the most soul-satisfying experience in which you will ever get involved. Instead of being dull, it becomes an exciting process.

The history of prayer shows that man has always prayed. One of the first things primitive man did was to pray for food and for protection. Even unevolved man realized the necessity for, as well as the natural-ness of, prayer.

It has only been since man has become more "civil-ized" that he has decided he was too sophisticated to pray; thus he has named prayer a mysterious, complex process. (Quite contrary to popular opinion, the really sophisticated people of this world *do* pray. They even get sophisticated results! I was once a guest at a dinner party given in an exclusive club by the widow of a Texas oilman. The main conversation at dinner was how this elegant, world-traveled woman had recently experienced a marvelous spiritual healing through using definite prayer techniques. Her prayer method was discussed in detail over dinner among a gathering of "highbrow" guests. And so I repeat: The really sophisticated people of this world do pray and they even get sophisticated results!)

Prayer can again become a simple, satisfying experience of renewal and enlightenment for you as you realize the various ways you can pray effectively for the riches of life, and all that goes with them.

Many people hesitate to pray because they do not understand the nature of God. Since the word "prayer" means "communion," the purpose of prayer is to commune with God, whose nature is supreme good. To pray is to make common union with all good.

If you think of God as a stern, spiteful, puritanical old man sitting off in the sky, severely judging you, then why pray? Why complicate matters further by trying to make contact with that kind of being? If you still think of God as having a split personality of good and evil, then it is understandable why you would have little desire to make common union with such a being in prayer.

The sign in front of a church recently read: "Our God is not dead. Too bad about yours!" Of course, God is not dead. God as love, God as spirit, God as supreme good, cannot die. But let's hope the limited concepts of Him are dying out of man's consciousness.

YOUR *UNIVERSAL* GOD POWER
CAN BRING RESULTS

Theology has long taught that God is both immanent (within) and transcendent (universal), though mankind has usually thought of God only as transcendent—out there somewhere far away. One theologian has described the people who believe in God-immanent as the "God-withiners," and of the people who believe in God-transcendent as the "God-beyonders."

God as transcendent is the universal God presence that is everywhere evenly present. You become attuned to God's universal presence when you affirm, "THERE IS ONLY ONE PRESENCE AND ONE POWER IN THE UNIVERSE, GOD THE GOOD, OMNIPOTENT." You can bring that universal presence into your life by affirming: "THERE IS ONLY ONE PRESENCE AND ONE POWER IN MY LIFE (or IN THIS SITUATION, DIAGNOSIS, PERSONALITY, OR APPEARANCE)—GOD THE GOOD, OMNIPOTENT."

Does such a prayer sound rather high-flung for producing practical results in your life? Well, it isn't, as you will see by the following cases.

A businessman overcame ill health, financial failure and family difficulties by daily dwelling upon the prayer, "THERE IS ONLY ONE PRESENCE AND ONE POWER IN MY LIFE—GOD THE GOOD, OMNIPOTENT." At the time he began making this prayer statement, both he and his wife were in ill health. They had spent much money on various treatments, but still suffered. This man had gone from one job to another, and had never found his true work. Their only child had been a problem.

As this man began to affirm only God's goodness in his life, things began to improve. Nothing spectacular happened, but he could see that omnipotent good was becoming more evident. This encouraged him and gave him courage to persevere in claiming God's blessings.

First, his wife's health improved. Soon they were both able to give up the expensive drugs and health treatments so long prescribed. As he continued affirming the good, he was offered the kind of job he had long desired. The way opened later for him to buy this business, which had been his dream. His business prospered in ways he could not have foreseen. Their child matured and found work that challenged and satisfied him. He later married and settled down to a harmonious, successful way of life.

This businessman has continued to keep this prayer statement where he can see and use it daily: "THERE IS ONLY ONE PRESENCE AND ONE POWER IN MY LIFE — GOD THE GOOD, OMNIPOTENT."

A famous London metaphysician who had much success in protecting men in war, did so through dwelling upon the universal God presence. Often he would decree, "THERE IS NOTHING BUT GOD." His explanation for his success in prayer was this: "Instead of praying for or spiritually treating the persons, I spiritually treat myself; that is, I try to get out of my own mind the false ideas of God and man that have been ingrained therein by years of false training. If I can get my realization of God clear, the person is healed (or protected) instantly."

Spiritual healer H. B. Jeffery used a similar technique, as pointed out in his book *The Principles of Healing*.[2] The prayer statement he often gave those seeking healing was, "I LIVE, MOVE AND HAVE MY BEING IN GOD, AND HE WORKS IN ME TO WILL AND TO DO HIS GOOD PLEASURE." Dwelling upon the universal God nature has often healed the sick and troubled.

A writer named Mary Austin developed cancer and was given a year to live. She chose to go to Rome to spend the time studying early documents of Christianity. She became so absorbed in her studies that she lost all fear of cancer. One day she realized the cancer was gone. By her study of the nature of God and other religious themes, healing had come. In another instance, a person was healed after praying over and over, "THERE IS NOTHING BUT GOD."

YOUR *INDWELLING* GOD POWER
CAN BRING RESULTS

God is also immanent or within you. This is the God-nature which Jesus tried to point out to all mankind. It was to this indwelling spiritual nature that Paul referred as man's "hope of glory" (Colossians 1:27). Job described it as a "spirit in man" (Job 32:8).

When you realize that God is not only the universal spirit of good filling all the universe—but that God is also within you—and that it is this indwelling God-nature you are contacting, developing and bringing alive in prayer—then you can see that there is no need to strain or reach out.

---

2. H. B. Jeffery, *The Principles of Healing* (Fort Worth: Christ Truth League, 1939).

You have your own indwelling Lord who longs to help, inspire and guide you. This indwelling Lord is interested in every detail of your life. You can pray to this indwelling Lord about everything that concerns you—from finding a parking place on a busy street to the healing of a supposedly incurable disease.

WHY PRAYERS GO UNANSWERED

Many peoples' prayers are not answered because they do not know about this indwelling Lord. They are straining to try to get the attention of a supposedly far-off God, who may or may not be interested in their problems (or so they believe). It can be frustrating to try to pray to that kind of God, and it is little wonder that many people don't even try.

The shocking truth about prayer is that there is no strain or frustration in true prayer because when you pray you are making common union with the God-nature of supreme good *within* you. *In true prayer you turn within, not without!*

A grandmother told her grandson that God was within him. The little boy wanted to believe this, but it was a new idea to him, so he doubtfully mused, "If God is within me, what is He doing? Is He just lying down in there?"

It often seems that our indwelling God-nature has been lying down on the job because we have not known how to make common union with this innate goodness. *Actually God is far more willing to give than we are to receive. A loving Father wants our prayers answered. He wants our dreams (which are really His dreams for us!) to come true. He has no higher way of expressing*

Himself than through His own image and likeness—
man. The problem has not been that God didn't want
to give man greater good. The problem has been that
man did not know how to receive it. Prayer is the
missing link. Through prayer man opens his conscious-
ness to receive the fullness of God's blessings. Prayer
is receiving.

The ancients knew the age-old secret: that God is
within. In the original Sanskrit the word for "prayer"
was "pal-al," meaning "judging oneself as wondrously
made." This is among the highest forms of prayer, to
recognize yourself as being a wondrous expression of
God, and then to commune with that inner God-
nature. (Later chapters instruct you how to do this.)

What a thrill it is to realize that God is within. A
six-year-old girl attended a church for the first time.
When her father, a doctor, met her after Sunday
School to escort her to the church service, she seemed
to be on "Cloud Nine." When her father asked how
she had liked it, she replied dreamily, "It was wonderful!"

"Honey, what was so wonderful about it?"

"Daddy, I found out where God is! He's out there in
the trees, grass, animals, and world just as I've always
known. But Daddy, God is also *within* me and I can
talk with Him there any time I want to!"

The turning point came in George Fox's life in 17th-
century England when he made this same discovery:
that God is a living spiritual presence, revealed within
the soul. Having learned this, he developed such spiritual power that his very presence caused his followers
to "quake" and tremble. Thus began the Quaker (Society of Friends) religion. George Fox often described
God as "the teacher within."

Sixteen centuries ago the Roman monk Augustine
declared he was amazed that men should go abroad
to gaze upon wonders while passing by the greatest
wonder of all—their own God-given divinity—which
he described as a "crowning wonder." St. Augustine's
advice was: "Retire into thyself, for Truth dwells in
the inner man."

PRAY FIRST INSTEAD OF LAST

The shocking truth about prayer is that when you
have a need, you can always be shown how to meet
that need, if you pray about it first instead of last;
whereas you can do many things on the human level
and still the need will not be met when you have neglected to pray about it first.

A businesswoman had a severe sore throat which
drugs had not cleared up. One night she attended a
small prayer group and asked the group to pray for the
healing of her throat. Their prayer for her spoken in
unison was this: "YOU ARE NOT POWERLESS TO CLAIM
YOUR GOOD. NOTHING CAN HOLD YOU IN BONDAGE, YOU
ARE FREE WITH THE FREEDOM OF SPIRIT. YOU FREELY
CLAIM YOUR HEALING NOW."

The businesswoman spoke these words aloud, too.
Within twenty-four hours, her throat was completely
healed. (For an explanation of health problems in the
throat area, see the chapter on "Power" in the author's
book, *The Healing Secrets of the Ages*.)[3]

*Prayer is the most practical thing in the world. Pray
first instead of last!*

---

3. Published by DeVorss & Co., Marina del Rey, CA 90294.
Rev. ed. 1985.

THE SHOCKING TRUTH ABOUT PRAYER

PRAYER ATTRACTS A MILLIONAIRE INVESTOR

During the depression years, a businessman who knew about the power of prosperous thinking as well as about the power of prayer took a bankrupt business in Los Angeles and made a fortune from it. Years later he sold the business and retired. But the man who bought this thriving business was not a prosperous-thinking-or-praying man, and in a few years he was losing money.

Several of the salesmen and employees who had worked with the first man and had watched him build the business into a million-dollar one finally asked the new owner to invite the former owner to show him how he had built the business through spiritual methods. In sheer desperation, the new owner reluctantly agreed to do so.

The retired millionaire set to work by coming into town and renting a room at a downtown hotel, for the sole purpose of being left alone to do intensive prayer work about the situation.

He soon learned that several hundred thousand dollars had to be raised quickly or the business would close. Every morning he called in the owner and salesmen to talk with them about the power of prosperous thinking. (See the author's book *The Dynamic Laws of Prosperity*[4] for simple techniques in developing prosperous thinking.) When they mentioned the need for several hundred thousand dollars, he would quietly say, "It will come, and in time."

For nine days he remained in his hotel room praying for guidance, affirming prosperity, instructing the

---

4. Published by DeVorss & Co., Marina del Rey, CA 90294. Rev. ed. 1985.

employees in prosperous thinking, and generally *building a spiritual consciousness through which his prayers for this business could be answered.*

Finally, on the ninth day, when he went into the hotel dining room for dinner, he felt guided to chat with a man he found sitting alone at a nearby table. Though strangers, they discovered that they had mutual friends in New York and Los Angeles. They had read many of the same books, and used many of the same ideas through prayer and prosperous thinking to build successful businesses. Before they parted that first night, the man from the East asked the millionaire if he knew of a good place to invest some money, explaining that he had a son-in-law who wanted to come West, and he was looking around for him.

In a few days it was all settled. The rich man from the East brought not only his son-in-law and money into the previously failing business, but also brought his own wealth of spiritual knowledge and experience. The owner who had let the business go down willingly sold his own interest at a profit and got out. The salesmen kept their jobs and the business was once again in the hands of prosperous-minded, praying people. Of course it again prospered.

As for the practical results that prayer wrought in this situation, the man from the East explained he had intended to go to San Francisco to look around, but that he had suddenly felt guided to go to Los Angeles. He had also intended to look leisurely for a business in which to invest, perhaps taking months to decide upon one. But while in prayer, he had gotten the feeling he should get to Los Angeles at once. He had planned to go to a certain hotel upon arrival in town, but on the plane he had talked with a man who had strongly recommended he check into the hotel where, unknown to him, the millionaire was praying.

Furthermore, he had made all these decisions only after the millionaire had checked into the hotel and during the nine days he was holed up in his room in prayer. As the former owner had prayerfully looked to a rich, loving Father for guidance, and had made rich affirmations, they had literally brought to him a rich man and rich results.

During the nine-day stay in the hotel one of the prosperity affirmations he had declared daily was this: "THE INFINITE MIND IS MY REAL RESOURCE AND I AM UNLIMITED BECAUSE GOD IS UNLIMITED." An equally powerful prayer when confronted with desperate circumstances is this: "I AM SPIRIT, WORKING WITH MIGHTY, POWERFUL, SPIRITUAL FORCES. THE DEMANDS OF SPIRIT MUST AND ARE BEING MET NOW."

This man proved that prayer is the most practical thing in the world. Pray first instead of last! If it's good as a last resort, it's far better as a first resort.

THE PATH TO INSTANT GOOD

Many people doubt that their prayers have any power, so their idea of prayer is to pray only in an emergency—the prayer of desperation. The pilot of a large trainer plane radioed his ground control station as follows:

"One wing sheared off; landing gear gone; visibility fifty feet; cargo dynamite. What are your instructions."

Quickly from the radio tower came this message:

"Now repeat after me, 'Our Father who art in heaven, Hallowed be Thy Name. Thy kingdom come . . .'"

Many people are like that man in the radio tower; they think prayer is only for emergencies, whereas, *if people prayed more, there would be fewer emergencies to meet, and those would be met victoriously.*

Prayer is an art and a science. The dictionary describes an "art" as "a skill"; also as "human ability to make things happen." The dictionary describes "science" as "knowledge which is gained by systematic study and practice."

Prayer, then, is the studied and practiced skill or ability to cause good things to happen in one's life through contact with one's own indwelling Lord.

This explains why some people seem to have prayer-power and others do not. Those who do not, pray only in an emergency, if at all. They wait until they are coming in for a crash landing before it occurs to them to ask God's help.

It is good to practice the presence of God just as you would practice music. Practice makes perfect in the art of prayer, just as in developing any other skill. It is easy to do this because the more you practice the art of prayer, the more enjoyable and satisfying it becomes, and the more fascinated you become with both its mystical and practical value. After a while, you find yourself "going within" on a moment's notice any time, anywhere — making contact with your own indwelling Lord, which then brings peace, renewal and right results. *Prayer is the path to instant good!*

PRAYER IS SOUL-STRETCHING

Has prayer sometimes led you down a dead-end street of no results, rather than up that victorious path to instant good?

Prayer is soul-stretching.

When your prayers have not been answered, perhaps it is because your soul was being stretched big enough to accept that answer.

Maybe you've heard the story about the young minister who went home to visit his parents for the first time after having taken his first church. His parents expected glowing reports of his work. When his mother asked, "Son, has your ministry grown much since you took it over?" he honestly replied, "No, but I have! I have had to grow to try to make it grow." That young man was getting his soul stretched.

When your prayers seem not to be answered, it is often because the answer is going to be bigger and better than you had anticipated. So keep on praying, in order that you will be big enough in consciousness to be able to accept the desired blessings when they come!

This is the time to affirm: "I AM OPEN AND RECEPTIVE TO GOD'S GOOD IN EVERY PHASE OF MY LIFE NOW. I AM OPEN AND RECEPTIVE TO GOD'S GOOD AS IT MANIFESTS IN EVERY PHASE OF MY LIFE NOW."

I recently asked a famous minister, who enjoys all the blessings of life in abundance, the secret of his success. He replied that early in his career he began daily declaring: "I AM OPEN AND RECEPTIVE TO GOD'S BLESSINGS IN EVERY PHASE OF MY LIFE NOW." He has continued this prayer practice over the years with abundant results of health, wealth and wisdom.

At times when you pray you may not get what you pray for; yet you pray not in vain. Though things do not always change as you wish them to when you pray, one thing is sure: *You change!* Always some change is wrought in the invisible that is needed and that leads to life's answers.

When your prayers are not immediately answered,

it is often because you have been trying to limit God's good in your life.

You have probably been unconsciously saying, "Not Thy will, but mine be done. Put it here, Lord." Your prayers thus go unanswered until you unconditionally surrender and say, "Lord, You know best. I know Your will for me is greater good than I can possibly imagine. I now let go and let this prayer be answered in Your highest and best way. I now let go and let Your unlimited good flow into this situation or condition."

You may be sure that under all conditions, irrespective of your seeming needs and desires, lasting good will come to you when you ask only that God's good will manifest in your life. *If each of us abandoned ourselves fully to God's good will, the world would again become a Garden of Eden.*

The shocking truth about prayer is that all prayers are answered by our loving Father. Whenever a prayer seems to remain unanswered, you can be sure that somewhere there is a closed door between you and the Infinite Giver. *Always, desire in the heart is God tapping at the door of your consciousness, trying to get you to accept greater good in your life.* Instead of pushing aside your desire as impossible of fulfillment, declare: "I AM RECEIVING. I AM RECEIVING NOW. I AM RECEIVING ALL THE GOOD GOD HAS FOR ME, AND GOD HAS UNLIMITED GOOD FOR ME NOW!"

When your prayers have not been answered, look within and ask to be shown how to remove the block.

NO STRAIN IN PRAYER

People often become discouraged in prayer because they struggle to pray in certain ways for which they are not yet ready. Often they feel that unless they are able to pray as some advanced soul prays, their prayers cannot have power.

How foolish. *The simplest prayer can be answered.* A little eight-year-old girl heard a lecture I gave on prayer and said afterward: "I know all about the power of prayer and it works. Last week my dog left home and was gone two days. He had never done that before and I was afraid he would never return—until I remembered the power of prayer. Then I went out, sat in my swing and prayed for him to come home. In a few minutes my dog came running into the yard and was very glad to see me."

You unfold in prayer power gradually, normally, naturally as you are ready for it. You do not have to strain. In fact, strain defeats prayer. Even though your growth sometimes seems gradual, even slow, that is the normal way. Forced growth can bring a negative reaction. All spiritual advancement comes in phases of normality.

There is nothing strange, odd or abnormal about prayer power. It is an easy, natural, normal process. You can always get results, right where you are, at your present level of understanding through prayer. *You have all the prayer power you need right now to meet life victoriously!*

A troubled housewife was nervous and sleepless. Upon telephoning her minister she was asked to affirm, "THE PEACE OF JESUS CHRIST IS POURED OUT UPON ME NOW, AND I AM RELAXED IN MIND AND BODY." As the minister declared these words for her over the telephone, this tense woman relaxed and peace came. But hours later she again became nervous and frightened.

Though she had never had any faith in her own prayer power, she now felt forced to depend upon it.

Groping for the right method, she finally just gave up and said, "Not my will but Thine be done, dear Father." A great sense of peace again enfolded her and she relaxed into a deep sleep.

Through this experience she learned a great truth: *You already have all the prayer power you need to meet life victoriously right now, regardless of the problem. It's just a matter of getting down to business and using the prayer power you already have.*

WHEN YOUR PRAYERS GROW STALE

As you develop your prayer consciousness, if your prayer powers seem to grow stale — if you have periods when you do not seem to be able to pray effectively or even pray at all — do not be discouraged. These are often periods when your prayer consciousness is changing and expanding. A digestive process, a purification, is taking place. You may feel uncomfortable, with an indescribable feeling of being "crowded" deep within your being, so that it is hard to make inner contact. A cleansing process is at work, crowding out and dissolving old negative emotions.

As your prayer powers come alive within you, they cleanse the deeper levels of your subconscious mind. As those old thoughts and feelings rise to the surface of your conscious mind, that is when you feel a "crowded" sensation because a deep change, a deep healing is taking place.

After this purification process is over, you will again be able to pray effectively, but perhaps in a different way, on a deeper level. *There are degrees and levels of prayer to meet your needs at the various levels of your life experiences.* The 16th-century mystic, St. Teresa, described this progressive unfoldment in prayer in her celebrated book *Interior Castle,*[5] with each degree or level of prayer being compared to a separate room in the house of the soul. She compared the soul's growth through prayer to that of a silkworm that becomes a butterfly.

Thus, as you develop your prayer powers, you go through various degrees and levels of prayer to other degrees and levels of prayer. That is why one type of prayer does not always satisfy you; nor will it always work for you. That is why you need to know the various methods of prayer described in this book and how to invoke them.

If prayer has not proved so triumphant in your life as you feel it might, perhaps it is because you have not realized all the various ways you can pray. At times one method of prayer seems right. At other times, this same prayer method just doesn't work. When your prayer methods seem to have lost their power, that can be a good sign! It may indicate that you are growing spiritually, mentally, emotionally, and that you are ready to "try your wings" through another type of prayer.

THE VARIETY OF PRAYER

No two people pray exactly alike. Prayer is personal. Prayer is individual. You should not be alarmed if your prayer methods are completely different from those

---

5. E. Allison Peers (trans. and ed.), *Interior Castle,* by St. Teresa of Avila (Garden City, N.Y.: Image Books, Doubleday & Co., 1961).

of your family or friends. Often a husband and wife pray completely differently, yet each is satisfied, each makes spiritual contact.

A businessman told me that he prays verbal prayers of denial and affirmation. These are his methods of prayer and he has experienced marvelous results in health and prosperity from them; his wife, on the other hand, practices prayers of meditation and the silence. These methods have been equally effective for her.

There are many levels and degrees of prayer to meet the spiritual needs of many types of people, all in various levels of spiritual understanding. *The saints and mystics of old were very powerful in prayer, yet no two described their prayer experiences in the same way. Neither do we!*

ORIENTAL AND WESTERN PRAYER METHODS ARE REVERSED

The Oriental method of prayer teaches that relaxation and control of the body, cleansing of thought and emotions, deep breathing, followed by turning inward and practicing concentration, meditation and ecstatic union with one's divine self are all steps of prayer that must come first. Then only in the advanced phases of one's prayer development — after one has mastered all these phases — does one have the ability to manifest things or to immediately realize one's desires.

Jesus' method was just the opposite: Ask, seek, knock, and results shall come. He constantly prayed and manifested immediate results of healing and prosperity for his followers, though He emphasized praying for spiritual blessings, too.

In a sense, both views are right. It seems normal that the Orientals, with their detachment from things and materiality and with their slowness of pace, would place more emphasis upon developing the deeper phases of prayer first. Yet most beginners in prayer would find this bewildering to try! Certainly if someone had informed me years ago when I began my quest into the power of prayer that I had to learn to relax and control my body, cleanse my thoughts and breathe properly, control my thinking, then learn to concentrate, meditate and practice the silence *before* getting my prayers answered, I would have said, "Forget it."

Jesus' method of showing people how to pray and manifest things, or get outer results, right away is usually a more acceptable method for convincing one that prayer works.

Perhaps Jesus knew that once one gets things through prayer, or once one is convinced prayers regarding people and things have power, one becomes so awakened to the prayer powers within him that the fascination then grows and he wants to go deeper into prayers of concentration, meditation, the silence and realization. However, our materialistic Western mind somehow likes to be convinced and shown the power of prayer first with things, people and events.

Thus the prayer methods described in *Part I* begin with the Western approach to prayer: how to get immediate results. These chapters describe prayer methods through which you reach God, and through which your prayers have beneficial influence upon yourself, as well as upon things, people and events, as you learn prayers of relaxation, cleansing, and decree.

Part II of this book describes methods through which God can reach you in the deeper phases of prayer:

concentration, meditation, the silence, and realization. The prayer of giving and the use of prayer partners are also described as spiritual methods for getting your prayers answered.

PRAYER WILL TEACH YOU ITS SECRETS

The shocking truth about prayer is that it will teach you its own amazing secrets as you study the various methods described herein. As you practice the types of prayer given early in the book, this will prepare you for the deeper methods of prayer that will unfold naturally within you and which are described later in the book.

Learning the various methods of prayer that are described will give you a whole new perspective on the subject. You will realize there are yet ways and methods through which your prayers can be answered!

You will discover that you have more dynamic prayer powers than you had previously dreamed possible. Perhaps this is the most shocking truth of all about prayer —and about you!

WHEN YOUR PRAYERS HAVE NOT BEEN ANSWERED

— Chapter 2 —

There are those who say, "Why pray? Prayer is a farce. My prayers have never been answered." Yet there are others who can attest to a long list of answered prayers. If God ever answers prayer, He always answers prayer, being the same God. Therefore, if there seems to be any failure of principle, the trouble is not with God, but with the one who prays.

There is also a belief among many people that when their prayers have not been answered, it is because God has said "no" to their prayer requests.

Prayer is no farce. And God never says "no."

God always says "yes"—but to the highest desires of your heart—not to the surface, limited ones. Most of us can recall times that we prayed limited, selfish prayers that did not get answered, and how grateful we were later.

Since God always says "yes"—but to the highest desires of your heart—there is often much you need to do to clear out false beliefs and negative emotions, in order to make way for your prayers to be answered.

When it seems that your prayers are not being answered, it is usually because there is something *within* you that is blocking the answer—some limited idea or negative emotion.

Prayer often has to work amazing results *in* you before it can work amazing results *through* you and *for* you. So often after we've prayed, we've been inclined to snap our fingers and expect instant results. Often if we did get an instant result in prayer it would not last because we would not have changed sufficiently to accept and retain the answer.

If you refuse to let prayer work in you, changing you deep within, then you stop prayer from working *for* you. *There must be an inworking before there can be an outworking.*

After praying, you must be ready to change and change and change. The change must be within your own thought and feeling nature, so that you will be big enough in consciousness to accept the answer for which you are praying—probably in a more expanded form than you had in mind.

Most people who complain that their prayers have not been answered fall into a certain mental and emotional pattern: They are people who are too rigid in their outlook on life. They need to give a little in their attitudes. They need to unbend mentally; they need to stretch emotionally. They are too set in their thinking. They are not willing to change the inner, so that God can change the outer phases of their lives.

They are like the woman who prayed earnestly for a healing of her eyes. Yet every time she came to church

she would say (almost triumphantly): "I notice that
Mr. and Mrs. Smith haven't been attending church
lately. What's wrong?" Or she would complain that
the temperature was either too hot or too cold in
church that morning. Always something was wrong.
This lady unconsciously looked for what was wrong
rather than what was right in life, and so she was not
an open, receptive channel for her prayers for healing
to be answered.

As with this woman, rigidity in our outlook on life
and mental resistance to people and conditions often
keep our prayers from being answered. We must be
willing to change the inner so that God can change
the outer phases of our lives.

HOW TO "GROW" INTO THE ANSWER

So often we miss our answers to prayer because we
insist upon an immediate result, rather than being willing to grow into it. We want every good thing at once —
"instant good" — before we have unfolded to the point
of receiving it, so we miss the answer. We are not yet
ready to receive it.

It will encourage you to know that spiritual giants
such as Abraham and Isaac had to wait from twenty
to twenty-five years to get some of their prayers answered. Abraham waited twenty-five years for the birth
of his son Isaac. During that time he realized that God's
delays were not denials and that, as promised, God
would fulfill in His own time and way. Meanwhile,
Abraham had to cleanse his thinking of fear, doubt
and bitterness and grow into answered prayer. The
birth of Isaac was that answer.

Later Isaac had to learn this same spiritual lesson.

After twenty years of married life, his wife Rebekah was still childless. Her barren condition caused her to be reproached by the daughters of Canaan, and her childlessness was also a trial to Isaac's faith. Finally Isaac prayed anew and Jacob was born. Still later, Jacob waited twenty years before receiving the blessings of the Lord, though he worked hard in the meantime to redeem himself from his mistakes. So Abraham, Isaac and Jacob learned a great spiritual lesson: that God does not hurry the fulfillment of His plan, but answers the great desires of men's hearts in His own time and way.[1]

Thus, when you pray, do not insist upon immediate results or rewards. *They will come as and when you are ready to receive them.* The Greek philosopher Epictetus said, "No great thing is created suddenly. If you tell me that you desire a fig, I answer you that there must be time. Let it first blossom, then bear fruit, then ripen."

The prayer you want answered is the prayer of the whole man: spirit, soul and body . . . the one that will satisfy your whole being. It may or may not be what you cry out for in a moment of pain or desire. The only thing you have to be concerned about when you pray is that you grow big enough in consciousness to receive and maintain the answer to your prayers when it comes.

Many people are not willing to do this so they stop the answers to their prayers completely and then bitterly complain that God has let them down.

---

1. The success secrets of Abraham, Isaac and Jacob and their mental attitudes that led to answered prayers are shown in the author's books *The Prosperity Secrets of the Ages* and *The Millionaires of Genesis*, both published by DeVorss & Co.

WHEN YOUR PRAYERS HAVE NOT BEEN ANSWERED

The mystics of old had a three-part formula for getting their prayers answered. Their three mystic steps to answered prayers were: (1) Purification, (2) Illumination and (3) Union.

How often we try to bypass that first step of purification and rush on to get illuminative guidance and then attempt to make union with results.

That famous 16th-century Spanish priest, St. John of the Cross, described the purification periods through which we must pass to answered prayer as "the dark night of the soul." In my book *The Dynamic Laws of Healing*,[2] you find this cleansing experience described as "chemicalization, a healing process." The steps in chemicalization or soul-cleansing are therein explained.

OVERCOMING BLOCKS TO ANSWERED PRAYER

Purification, the first step in answered prayer, works through forgiveness. When your prayers have not been answered, there is someone or some experience of the past or present that needs to be forgiven by you. Forgiveness is purification. Forgiveness dissolves the mental and emotional blocks between you and answered prayer. (More about this in Chapter 4.)

The very pain you suffer, the very failure to demonstrate over some matter that touches your life deeply, may rest upon just this spirit of unforgiveness that you harbor toward the world in general or toward someone in particular. You must release it to get ready for answered prayer: "I RELEASE THIS TO A LOVING FATHER,

---

2. Catherine Ponder, *The Dynamic Laws of Healing* (Marina del Rey, Calif.: DeVorss & Co., 1966).

WHO PERFECTLY HEALS IT NOW, AND I GET READY FOR
ANSWERED PRAYER!"

The thoughts that most frequently work ill to you
and stop your prayers from being answered are thoughts
of criticism and condemnation. If you are criticizing
or condemning anyone, you are keeping your own
prayers from being answered. Where there should be
an open channel in your thinking, there is a big grudge
blocking the way to your good.

FORGIVENESS BRINGS RESULTS

In my book *The Dynamic Laws of Prosperity* is the
story of a man who appeared one cold winter day for
my counseling. He was in pain, out of work, lonely,
unhappy, just "down and out" in every way. One of the
most critical people I have ever met, he hated the politicians in Washington and blamed them for all his
problems.

After realizing his spirit of unforgiveness could be
the cause of his many problems, including finances,
this sick man agreed to join me in humbly speaking
words of forgiveness and to stop all his name-calling.

A few months later when he paid me another visit,
this man had changed so much that I did not recognize
him. Cleaned up and healed of the pain in his body,
he had gotten a wonderful job and a fiancée, whom
he brought along for me to meet. They were later
married, and there was little he desired in his life that
he did not eventually get.

*This man proved that getting results in prayer de-
mands that anger must be overcome.* It simply is not
possible to get any results worth talking about, or even
to exercise much prayer power in the way of healing,

unless and until you have gotten rid of resentment and condemnation toward your fellow man. Until you are prepared to rid yourself of such critical emotions, your prayers will go on and on being unanswered.

HOW TO DISSOLVE NEGATION
WITHIN YOU

To dissolve resentment declare often: "CHRIST IN ME NOW FREES ME FROM ALL RESENTMENT *TOWARD* PEOPLE, PLACES OR THINGS OF THE PAST OR PRESENT. CHRIST IN ME NOW FREES ME FROM ALL RESENTMENT *FROM* PEOPLE, PLACES OR THINGS OF THE PAST OR PRESENT. I MANIFEST MY TRUE PLACE WITH THE TRUE PEOPLE AND WITH THE TRUE SURROUNDINGS NOW."

The reason that forgiveness is the first step to answered prayer is because it cleanses your mind, body and affairs, and gets you ready to receive your good. A fine cleansing prayer to use daily is: "CHRIST IN ME IS MY FORGIVING POWER."

For those whom you wish to forgive and by whom you wish to be forgiven, affirm: "CHRIST IN YOU IS YOUR FORGIVING POWER." For all involved, affirm: "CHRIST IN US IS OUR FORGIVING POWER. CHRIST IN THIS SITUATION IS ITS FORGIVING POWER. THE CHRIST IN THIS SITUATION PRODUCES THE PERFECT FORGIVENESS NOW."

Every marriage counselor, minister, prison official, psychiatrist, psychologist and worker in the mental health field has known persons whose lives were blighted and problem-filled because of unforgiveness. These problem-filled people held grudges, were in bondage to hate, and had plans for revenge, all of which boomeranged upon *them*.

When you find yourself saying, "It serves him right,"

or "She got just what she deserved" — watch out! This is an attitude that can stop *your* prayers from being answered. *Holding to such a grudge is like holding to a hot coal. It will burn you again and again until you let it go.*

Fear, doubt, worry also close the door to answered prayer. *Your hurts stand in the way of answered prayer.* Do you dwell on wrongs and mistreatments, and carefully preserve them in your memory? You must have the courage to loose them and let them go. Excuses, self-pity, blaming another for your problems, all stand in the way of answered prayer.

Prayers of forgiveness from and toward those who have abused you or who have persecuted you are the highest form of prayer, yet the hardest. But they are also the most rewarding and soul-cleansing! For this purpose affirm often, "I PASS FROM PREJUDICE, HATRED OR CONDEMNATION TO GENTLE, FORGIVING LOVE."

The love of God simply cannot enter a bitter, hardened, unforgiving heart, whereas prayers of forgiveness break down walls and barriers to your good, often instantly, and so are well worth the soul effort they demand of you. *Forgiveness is the secret formula for answered prayer!*

HOW HER LIFE WAS HEALED, PROSPERED AND HARMONIZED

So often people who complain that their prayers have not been answered are those who are not doing their part by observing daily prayer periods. They want their prayers answered, yet they are not even attempting to make daily contact through which they can be. This is as inconsistent as wanting their doctor to heal them when they haven't even made an appointment to see him!

There once was a lady whose condition of arthritis steadily worsened in spite of fine medical treatment. There were also inharmony and financial problems in her life.

One day, while browsing through her Bible for guidance, she noted that almost every passage she read talked about prayer. It was then that she realized she had not been taking time daily for prayer, meditation or spiritual study. She had not made spiritual contact nor become a channel for answered prayer.

From that day forward she made prayer and meditation a part of her daily schedule. As she did, things first became harmonious in her home life. Regarding financial matters, she soon received a letter informing her that certain insurance and salary benefits, which had previously been withheld, would now be paid her on a monthly basis.

As she continued with her daily prayer periods, the pain diminished, new strength and vitality were generated. A whole new life gradually opened to her as she persisted in observing those daily prayer periods. Eventually she was completely free of this supposedly incurable disease. Prayer had healed her.

God always says "yes," but we have to make contact with Him before that answer can appear. Daily prayer opens the way. There are people who say you can pray anytime, anywhere, informally—that you do not have to go formally to God. In a sense they are right. But if you were trying to contact an important person, wouldn't you extend the courtesy of an appointment?

The 13th-century German mystic, Meister Eckhardt

said, "God is bound to act, to pour himself into thee, as soon as He shall find thee ready."

In the little pamphlet *God Has the Solution*, Emmet Fox explains:

> God can do anything. It is never too late. There is always an answer even when we cannot see it. When praying, ask yourself bluntly if you really expect an answer to your prayers. Do you really expect what you pray for? Could you accept it if it came?
>
> If you are not sure, then it's better to pray for faith, and release the problem to God. Pray for the divine solution and for the right arrangement of your affairs. Then leave the details to God. *If you feel you have not received an answer to your prayers, then pray for understanding.*[3]

SAYING "NO" BRINGS ANSWERED PRAYERS

Often a person's prayers are not answered because he scatters his forces so that he dissipates the spiritual power accumulated in prayer, and there is no channel through which his prayers can be answered.

After you pray, learn to say "no" to unnecessary things, people and activities in your life. Conserve your time and energy more, so that your prayers can get answered. Do not pray and then dissipate that prayer power through endless activities with needless people.

One of the first things a praying person learns is to say "no" to activities and people who would fritter away

---

3. Emmet Fox, *God Has the Solution* (Unity Village, Mo.: Unity School of Christianity).

his time and energy, thereby keeping his prayers from being answered.

There is a certain inner discipline that goes with getting one's prayers answered. Nobody places this inner discipline upon us but ourselves. I have seen many potentially fine people just never make the grade spiritually and never get their prayers answered because they had not learned to say "no" to the unnecessary people and events in their lives.

As you expand and uplift your thinking, you change. The people and activities of your life should often change, too. What was perfectly right at one period in your life is no longer right, because there is something bigger and better trying to open to you. You have outgrown the former good.

But if you do not give up the lesser first, the greater cannot come through. Then you complain that your prayers have not been answered. Yet no one stopped the answer but yourself. Learn to say "no" if you want your prayers answered.

As long as you scatter your forces, frittering away your time on unnecessary people and events, you will have to go on paying a high price for your folly, and that high price is unanswered prayer.

Dr. Emilie Cady has explained in her famous book, *Lessons in Truth:*

> Every person should take time daily for quiet and meditation. In daily meditation lies the secret of power. No one can grow in either spiritual knowledge or power without it. You may be so busy with the doing, the outgoing of love to help others, that you find no time to go apart. *Doing* is secondary to *being*. When we are consciously the truth, it will radiate from us and

accomplish the works without our running to and fro.
If you have no time for this quiet meditation, make
time, take time. You will find there are some things
better left undone than that you should neglect regular
meditation.

You will find that some time is spent every day in
idle conversation with people who just run in for a few
moments to be entertained. If you can help such
people, well. If not, gather yourself together and do
not waste a moment idly dissipating yourself to gratify
their idleness. You have no idea what you lose by it.[4]

A previously unglamorous housewife, whose life suddenly took on better health, an inner radiance and
beauty, increased job benefits for her husband, success
for her only son, and even a sudden, vast financial inheritance from a totally unexpected source, was be-
sieged with requests for her success secret. It was simple:
"I learned to say 'no' to the lesser. Through spending
more time in prayer and spiritual study, I got ready for
the greater good I desired. It came."

*Until you learn to say "no" to the lesser, your greater
prayers will never get answered.*

ANSWERED PRAYER WILL NOT BE RUSHED

The shocking truth about prayer is that many people
pray in the correct way, but then are in too much of a
hurry for results. When results do not immediately
appear, they lose heart and complain their prayers
haven't been answered.

---

4. Emilie Cady, *Lessons in Truth* (Unity Village, Mo.: Unity
School of Christianity, 1894).

If you sowed seeds today, the harvest would not be available tomorrow, would it? Of course not. A certain amount of time, *an orderly unfoldment* of events, would first be expected.

This is true of prayer, too. God is just never in a rush. He knows our wants before we ask him.

God does not violate the orderly arrangement of events. Instead, He withholds the next development until order is first established in the present situation.

In my book *The Healing Secrets of the Ages* is the story of a schoolteacher who had prayed and prayed for life's blessings. She was in ill health, dangerously overweight, out of harmony with her family, and unable to keep a job.

Finally a spiritual counselor visited her in her home and discovered the basic cause of her many ills: Her house, as well as her outlook on life, was in a state of total confusion. The counselor pointed out to this unhappy woman that God does not violate the orderly arrangement of affairs to answer our prayers. Instead, He withholds the next development until order is first established in the present situation.

Grateful to know the cause of her difficulties, she got busy bringing order into her thinking and environment. As she daily affirmed, "DIVINE ORDER IS NOW ESTABLISHED AND MAINTAINED BY THE POWER OF THE INDWELLING CHRIST," restoration of her health, family happiness, and professional success gradually took place.

This schoolteacher came to realize that you must live as normally as possible when you are trying to get your prayers answered. Do the next logical thing to bring order into your life. Then hold up your head and keep going. Do not give into the problem. Do not waste time worrying about "what people will say." Let them think or say what they will. Go your way in peace, affirming "divine order" every step of the way.

CLEANING UP YOUR LIFE CAN LEAD TO ANSWERED PRAYER

You must clean up your life if you truly want your prayers answered. The "skeletons in the closet" that you think no one knows about have got to go!

It is useless to pray for benefits, protection, financial supply, guidance and instruction when all the time you are doing those things which you know are not right in the sight of God or man.

An attractive businesswoman developed a mysterious disease in her feet and legs, which the finest of doctors, including specialists at the Mayo Clinic, had been unable to heal. They could find no organic reason for her health problems.

Meanwhile she had many of her friends praying for her healing—all to no avail. What her physicians and prayer friends did not know was that she had been having an affair with a married man for years, and the subconscious guilt generated from it had affected her health and his.

She needed to have the courage to clean up her life. God was withholding the next development until order was first established in the present situation. Many people are like this attractive woman. They refuse to clean up and clean out their lives. They refuse to let go the lesser and trust God to give them their greater good. Meanwhile their prayers go unanswered and their problems mount.

In still another instance, a successful but lonely

businesswoman longed to be happily married. She had long indulged in a life of compromise, going from one illicit love affair to another, reasoning that these transient experiences in love were better than none at all.

Finally realizing she was neutralizing any hope of answered prayer by her immoral actions, she vowed to clean up her life, which had been dissatisfying and frustrating at best.

As she deliberately closed the door on old relationships former, nicer, friends came back into her life. One day they introduced her to a fine widower. She soon married him and he gave her a lovely home and the life of peace, contentment and emotional security she had longed for. But none of these desirable blessings had appeared until she courageously cleaned up her life.

This lady discovered like Joshua of old that sin had to be put away (Joshua 7:20) before her prayers could be answered. The Bible is filled with illustrations of the bitter experiences that come upon man when he persists in being disobedient to the divine will. Often a cleansing or purging has to take place, as in the case of Joshua's disobedient soldier, Achan, before Joshua's prayers for victory were answered.[5]

Remember that there is no hurt or harm to yourself or to others in answered prayer. If your prayers are not being answered, it may be that their answer would harm someone involved. Clear your mind by asking honestly, "Is this desire for answered prayer obedient

---

5. See Chapter 6, "When Your Prosperity Is Withheld," in the author's book *The Millionaire Joshua* (Marina del Rey, Calif.: DeVorss & Company, 1978).

to the divine will? Will this prayer hurt anyone if answered? Is this desire in accord with God's will for everyone involved? Is it for the Lord's own purposes?" Dedicate your prayers to God's good will and to His high and holy purposes, and a lot more of your prayers will then be answered, though they may surprise you by being answered in a far higher and better way than you had anticipated or would have dared hope!

PERSISTENCE IN PRAYER BRINGS A DRAMATIC HEALING

Many people do not get their prayers answered because they do not persist. It pays to be persistent! It is the "praying through" attitude of Jacob, his "holy boldness" of vowing "I will not let thee go, except thou bless me" (Genesis 32:26).

Some years ago, a man in New York City visited a spiritual counselor, asking for help with a supposedly incurable skin disease. The counselor assured this discouraged man that nothing was incurable with God. This man suffered great pain in his back; a part of his mouth and the lobe of one ear had been eaten away.

The counselor asked this suffering man to go home and spend three days in persistent prayer, believing he would be healed. During this time he was to take no medicine or food, but was to fast and pray. He was instructed to spend four hours a day meditating upon some healing affirmations given him. The balance of the time he was to study the healings of Jesus in the Four Gospels.

The affirmations he used four hours a day for three days were these:

"I NOW CONSECRATE MY MIND AND BODY TO GOD. I AM NOW WILLING AND READY TO GIVE UP FALSE IDEAS ABOUT MYSELF AND OTHERS. I KNOW THAT GOD HAS FORGIVEN ALL MY MISTAKES. I NOW SEE MYSELF AS GOD SEES ME, WITH HIS RADIANT LIGHT FILLING EVERY CELL OF MY BODY. I AM CLEAN, PURE, HEALTHY, FREE. I THANK GOD FOR HEALING POWER. I THANK GOD FOR FULFILLING THE DE-SIRES OF MY HEART. I THANK GOD THAT I AM WHOLE, FREE, WELL NOW AND FOREVER."

This man was persistent in prayer. Three days later when he returned to the counselor, he had been healed. The lobe of his ear and his mouth were free from the disease. The pain was gone. As with Jesus, who healed the epileptic, this man proved, "This kind can come out by nothing, save by prayer" (Mark 9:29).

HOW TO MEET ONE DAY AT A TIME
VICTORIOUSLY

If your prayers have remained unanswered, begin now asking God again, but in a different way. Ask God for the wisdom, courage, strength to live just one day at the time. Pray to be able to meet just the present day, the present experience, victoriously. Stop strain-ing and reaching out to tomorrow's challenges.

Ask God unhesitatingly for that which you need for the next twenty-four hours. Stop straining about next week, month or year. Day by day, ask for God's help to live that moment victoriously. As you do so, the miracle of answered prayer will unfold in your life as never before.

God always says "yes." The answer *will* come. The blessing will appear as you persist in prayer and quietly grow into the answer. Let your understanding of Eternity begin with the Eternal Now.

THE FRINGE BENEFITS OF PRAYER

If your prayers seem a while in being answered, that is an indication there will probably be fringe benefits accompanying the answers to your prayers. When your prayers make long voyages, they come back laden with cargoes containing more blessings. It seems that when God keeps you waiting for an answer, He gives liberal interest for the interval you may have had to wait.

There once was a young man who became very ill. His mother was informed there was no hope of recovery from a medical standpoint. To complicate matters, he was also an alcoholic. But friends continued praying for his healing.

One day his doctor left town for a vacation and the case was taken over by another physician who believed in giving massive doses of vitamins to his patients. As the sick young man began absorbing these large doses of vitamins, not only was he healed of the physical condition that had been considered hopeless, but the desire to drink left him, too. Healing of alcoholism proved to be the fringe benefit to his mother's prayers.

When your prayers seem not to be answered, that is the time to affirm "the divine idea," "the divine plan," "your true place" in life: "I AM A DIVINE IDEA IN THE MIND OF GOD, AND I AM NOW GUIDED INTO MY TRUE PLACE. I LET GO EVERYTHING AND EVERYBODY THAT IS NO LONGER A PART OF THE DIVINE PLAN OF MY LIFE. I NOW EXPAND QUICKLY INTO THE DIVINE PLAN OF MY LIFE, WHERE ALL CONDITIONS ARE PERMANENTLY PERFECT."

A businessman, nearing retirement age, had been without work for some months because his former employer had gone out of business. Prayers offered by himself, family and church friends seemed of no avail, until one prayer group began declaring for him: "JOHN BROWN IS A DIVINE IDEA IN THE MIND OF GOD AND IS NOW GUIDED INTO HIS TRUE PLACE. JOHN BROWN NOW LETS GO EVERYTHING AND EVERYBODY THAT IS NO LONGER A PART OF THE DIVINE PLAN OF HIS LIFE. JOHN BROWN NOW EXPANDS QUICKLY INTO THE DIVINE PLAN OF HIS LIFE, WHERE ALL CONDITIONS ARE PERMANENTLY PERFECT." He was soon quickly offered a series of jobs in the executive category for which he had longed, one of which he immediately recognized and accepted as his "true place." It proved to be so.

OTHER PROVEN TECHNIQUES THAT CAN BRING ANSWERED PRAYER

When you pray, you must be willing for everyone involved to be just as much benefited from your prayers as you wish to be. You must be willing for your enemies as well as your friends to be blessed. You must be willing for everyone, no matter who they are or what they have done to you, to receive an answer and a benefit, not just yourself. There is no hurt in answered prayer! Unselfishness is the hidden key to answered prayer.

Furthermore, *praying for others causes your own prayers to be answered!*

A teacher of judo had sprained her foot while teaching a class. Her doctor put her on crutches and informed her she would be unable to walk for at least two months.

Having a full schedule of civic and church activities, as well as heavy family responsibilities, this young matron did not feel she could accept this well-meant diagnosis. On Tuesday night, after having sprained her foot the day before, she attended on crutches a prayer group whose members prayed for her healing. On Thursday night when she could not sleep, she remained up most of the night praying—not for her own healing, but individually for each name on her long prayer list. The following Sunday—less than a week after her accident—she attended church, minus the crutches and bearing no sign of a limp. The only irregularity was that she wore flat-heeled shoes rather than the higher-heeled pumps usually worn. She felt that her complete healing came the night she had spent praying for others.

When you have prayed for a long time for certain prayers to be answered and they seem not to have been, that is the time to decree "divine completion": "THIS IS A TIME OF DIVINE COMPLETION. IT IS DONE. IT IS FINISHED. IT NOW MANIFESTS, IN THE NAME OF A LOVING GOD."

Then, whether your prayers seem to be answered or not, just continue to "seal" the answer by declaring often, "THANK YOU GOD FOR ANSWERED PRAYER."

Thereafter, *let go and trust.* Dare to observe "a Sabbath" or a resting period from trying to manifest results. As you do, you will discover that the Lord never said "no" to your prayers. Instead, the answer comes under "divine timing."

THE PRAYER OF
RELAXATION

— Chapter 3 —

People who complain that it is hard to pray are people who do not know about the prayer of relaxation.

When you practice the prayer of relaxation you learn how to "pray easy." Many folks think that the prayer that gets results is just the opposite—the prayer that "prays hard." As in everything else—"easy does it."

Perhaps you have heard the story about the Catholic girl who fell in love with the Protestant boy and wanted to marry him. Since they had different religious backgrounds, the girl and her mother agreed to pray about the situation. The first week after they prayed, the young man passed by their church. This was encouraging. The second week after they had prayed, he not only passed by it, but this time he looked in. The third week he went in and sat down. The fourth week, as their hopes of answered prayer were mounting, he stated he had talked to their priest; and the fifth week he announced he had decided to join their church. But alas, their sixth week of prayer for this young man brought a surprise. The girl lamented, "Mama, we prayed 'too hard.' Now he's going to be a priest!"

The prayer of relaxation helps you do just the opposite—"pray easy." The prayer of relaxation helps you become open and receptive to your good. This happens because your objective in prayer is not to fight against conditions, but rather to commune with God in anticipation of the good you would like to experience in your life. The prayer of relaxation has definite effects upon the body, too. Tests show that up to 75 percent of the pain which exists when a person is tense and jittery vanishes when he relaxes.

A tense businessman was concerned about a desperate business problem. When he wrote to a prayer counselor in our organization, she advised him to give his problem "the light touch," explaining that to give it the light touch would be to give it the "touch of life." They suggested he do this by practicing prayers of relaxation. As he learned to "pray easy," the turmoil in this man's life subsided. Solutions came.

When it seems your prayers have not been answered, if you review how you prayed, you may discover that you just never relaxed; you never released the problem or condition that bothered you to God in prayer. You tried to pray in a tense way and you only held onto, rather than releasing and getting release from, the problem. Without realizing it, you may have fastened yourself to the problem:

Dr. Emmet Fox once explained in his booklet *The Mental Equivalent:*

THE PRAYER OF RELAXATION

> The great enemy of prayer is a sense of tension. . . .
> Tension in prayer is probably the greatest cause of
> failure. . . . The mind always works inefficiently when
> you are tense.[1]

Perhaps you are apt to take yourself, other people,
and life in general too seriously. The mystics spoke of
"attachment in detachment." *In prayer it is good to
detach yourself from people, places and things for a
while.* Otherwise you become too concerned. When
that happens, your attention and inner forces flow
outward and dissipate. You can become tense, rigid,
losing your balance. That tension can become a habit.
But when you deliberately practice detachment and
relax your grasp, your inner forces are then reconnected with your source. You function at a higher rate
of vibration and the blessings of the universe then flow
to you — instead of from you.

A minister who is famous for helping people develop
their prayer powers once explained:

"I have had many cases of people who had strong,
powerful minds, and who had reached a place in their
spiritual unfoldment where it seemed impossible for
them to get their prayers answered. An examination
into the consciousness and habits of such persons revealed that their mental and spiritual work was done
under strain. They were invariably anxious or tense,
rarely relaxing, with the result that they generated
inharmonious energy and constructed such an inharmonious wall around themselves that they were en-
closed in it as in an invisible shell. This prevented them
from demonstrating the very things they desired and

---

1. Emmet Fox, *The Mental Equivalent* (Unity Village, Mo.:
Unity School of Christianity).

for which they were working, even straining, to realize mentally and spiritually. Just as soon as this wall of inharmony and strained thinking was dissolved, the things they desired came to them. These people were taught how to relate affirmations of relaxation and peace to deep breathing. This practice always brought desirable results."

TO RELAX IS THE FIRST STEP IN PRAYER

The word "relax" means "to loosen" and "to release." When you practice the prayer of relaxation, you learn how to "loosen" and "release" your problems, so that they can be resolved.

You also learn how to loosen your mind and body, to let the activity of the Holy Spirit—the whole spirit of God's good—work in, through, on, and round about you. When you are relaxed you gain power because you become an open, receptive channel for the power of the universe to flow in and through.

Perhaps you are thinking, "But that *is* the problem. I cannot relax. I cannot turn loose."

You have not turned loose because you have not known how. We hear much these days about the desire for relaxation. People pay hundreds, even thousands of dollars for tranquilizing drugs, exercise classes, psychiatric treatments, and for exotic vacations in faraway places, all in an effort to relax.

Yet one of the simplest methods of relaxation is one that costs nothing but a little time and practice. It is one that people generally know nothing about and would underestimate at first glance as "too simple to work"—the prayer of relaxation. However, this method proves all-powerful for health and release from nervous strain, as well as a delightful way of getting one's prayers answered, when practiced for even a little while.

And so I repeat: You have not turned loose because you have not known how. There is a way! As you practice the prayer of relaxation herein described, you will find yourself turning loose more and more. Relaxation *will* come, first in mind, then in body. You will be filled with a power greater than your own, so that tense striving will cease. Problems will be resolved. "Easy does it" will become your theme song for successful praying and successful living.

The prayer of relaxation should be the beginner's method of prayer, as well as the first step in all methods of prayer.

HOW TO TUNE IN TO A UNIVERSAL POWER

The prayer of relaxation is truly the easy method of prayer, because in the prayer of relaxation you just do "what comes naturally," by turning within and relaxing both mind and body. When this happens, you then tune in on the magnetic or cosmic current of the universe which pulsates through your whole being, as well as through the whole universe, constantly. However, until you become still, quiet, relaxed, you are not aware of this pulsating, magnetic, power-filled current and its tremendous vibratory energy which longs to fill you and your world with its good.

There is no limit to what you can accomplish through relaxing and becoming attuned to this magnetic current within and around you. The Buddha taught that, through using this current, a man could become so peaceful that nothing could ever hurt him again. Confucius taught that by using this God-force, man would no longer say unkind words to, or perform unkind deeds upon, his neighbor. Job spoke of this magnetic current as a "spirit in man" (Job 32:8). Jesus described it as "the kingdom of God within you" (Luke 17:21). Paul thought of it as "Christ in you, the hope of glory" (Colossians 1:27).

Modern scientists describe it variously as electrical energy, an innate intelligence, and as an atomic vibration of light that fills every cell of man's being. Occultists have long described it as "the white light of spirit" in man, and traditional churchmen refer to it as the Holy Spirit or Holy Ghost.

I first became aware of this inner magnetic current when I attended a spiritual retreat for the first time several decades ago. There in an atmosphere of peaceful, prayerful relaxation, this universal current came alive in my body. Its activation within me almost frightened me out of my wits. It seemed especially strong in my hands and I recall carrying my right arm around in a peculiar upright position as though it were in a sling for days, until an enlightened soul explained what was happening to me. Since that time, as related in my book *The Healing Secrets of the Ages,* this universal current has served as a healing power flowing through me to my readers in the words of Truth found in the pages of my books.

Regardless of the name you give it, this magnetic current may be contacted and released through relaxation. Through the practice of deep breathing and deliberate relaxation of the mind and body, you tune in to this magnetic current which flows through, within and around you. Through regular practice, you can attune yourself to the magnetic forces of the universe, which will renew, inspire and uplift you in mind, body and affairs.

Through practicing the prayer of relaxation, you will find yourself tuning in more and more to an inner stillness you have never known before. In that inner stillness is all the power, energy, and guidance you will ever need or desire. In that inner stillness you will receive spiritual manna from heaven in whatever earthly form best suits your needs. Once you have "tasted" that heavenly inner stillness and partaken of its manna, you will never again be satisfied without it. You will find yourself returning again and again in prayer to partake of that heavenly communion, to taste its sweetness and peace, and then to experience its earthly benefits as increased health, wealth and happiness in your outer world. Like St. Francis of Assisi you may even be tempted to retire to a cave to pray often, so as to be overcome by "the heavenly sweetness" of prayer.

PRAY IN THE BODY

The importance of including the body in prayer cannot be overemphasized. You must pray *in* the body, rather than straining to reach outside of it in prayer. The body is the third part of the trinity of spirit, soul and body. The body *is* the sacred temple of the living God and should be included in your prayer development.

Only as man is able to pray *in* the body, causing it to relax and become an instrument of the universal life current, can his prayers have power and be answered. *Any method of prayer that bypasses the body also bypasses the way to answered prayer.*

Not only in the formal act of prayer, but also as you

go about your day, say to your body often, "RELAX, LET GO, LET GOD." However, do not let the informal acts of prayer take the place of formal ones. Sometimes people say, "Oh, I do not have to take time formally to pray. Since God is omnipotent, I can pray silently as I work and play." Such misguided souls cheat themselves of one of the greatest experiences in life: The act of formal prayer.

Your first duty in prayer is to bless your body and help it to relax. Sometimes the mind gets so anxious about what it wishes to do that it tends to neglect the body. The mind is often inclined to reach out so much, especially when one is praying, that the body is neglected and suffers. *Pain and suffering can be a means of drawing the attention of the mind back into the body.* Often the pain begins to subside and even to disappear when one turns his thoughts inward into every part of the body, telling it to relax, loose, let go.

The body is like a child. It needs constant praise and appreciation. When you try to push and force the body to do your will, this produces tension and pain. But the act of praise and blessing causes it to relax and cooperate.

Your body needs your attention and your love, and it awaits your mental instructions. Give your thoughts of love and appreciation to your wonderful body temple. It is precious to you. Your body is an instrument of the mind, which enables you to live on this earth plane. You need to let the spirit of God take hold of your mind and set it doing its perfect work in the body.

Stop crucifying and start resurrecting the body as an instrument of your divinity. For this purpose, declare often: "I AM CALM, SERENE, RELAXED."

As you relax the body more and more, gaining control of it, you are then able to become less conscious of it in prayer, and to go deeper in consciousness into the more advanced prayer levels of meditation, the silence and realization. *The prayer of relaxation leads into every other method and type of prayer, and must always come first.* Over and over in developing your prayer powers, return to the prayer of relaxation. It is both the beginning and the advanced method of prayer.

FIRST STEP IN PRAYER OF RELAXATION: SPEAK TO YOUR MIND AND BODY

When you sit down, kneel down, or lie down to pray, your first conscious act of prayer should be to speak to your body, as though it were a little child, telling it to relax. Your body is filled with intelligence and its cells will actually hear your decrees for relaxation and will respond. You will be amazed how the body will take you seriously and follow your instructions. Say, "YOU NOW RELAX AND LET GO. YOU NOW RELAX AND LET GO ALL TENSION, STRESS, AND STRAIN. YOU ARE NOW RELAXED IN MIND AND BODY."

Then declare in a more personal way, "I NOW RELAX AND LET GO. I NOW RELAX AND LET GO ALL TENSION, STRESS AND STRAIN. I AM NOW RELAXING IN MIND AND BODY. YES, I RELAX AND LET GO."

Get your thoughts right down into your body by turning your thoughts inward, within the body, as you gently instruct the body to relax. You may need to say to it a number of times, "RELAX, LET GO, LET GOD." If you do not feel relaxed after telling the mind and body to let go, perhaps it is because you have not let go enough. Relax all you can. Then relax some more. Keep on relaxing more and more. From the top of your head to the tip of your toes, go through your body, telling it to relax. When anxious thoughts try to gain your attention, tell them to "RELAX, LET GO, LET GOD." Let go and then let go some more.

HOW TO RELAX YOUR EMOTIONS

After telling the body to relax as a first step in the prayer of relaxation, then quiet your thoughts and emotions by declaring to them, "BE STILL. BE STILL AND KNOW THAT I AM GOD."

Many busy people have attested to the fact that these words of the Psalmist make a fine prayer for producing a relaxed mind and body, or a relaxed atmosphere in which to work. Say often to your mind, body and affairs: "BE STILL AND KNOW THAT I AM GOD. BE STILL AND KNOW THAT I AM GOD AT WORK IN THIS SITUATION. BE STILL AND KNOW THAT I AM SUPREME GOOD AT WORK IN THIS SITUATION NOW."

A businessman once told me that he found this method to be a remedy for sleeplessness. After retiring at night, if his mind still seemed wide awake, attempting to go over and over business problems, he would say to it, "BE STILL AND KNOW THAT I AM GOD. BE STILL AND KNOW THAT I AM GOD AT WORK IN THIS SITUATION." Invariably this method worked. He relaxed into restful sleep and awakened in a peaceful, confident state of mind.

In the prayer of relaxation, think of surrendering your entire world to a loving Father—spirit, soul, body, relationships, financial affairs, spiritual understanding. Say to yourself, "I RELAX IN MIND AND BODY. I FEEL THE PEACE OF GOD. I REST IN HIS LOVING PRESENCE."

Then as taught in the Delsartean philosophy, just "decompose," mentally as well as physically, by dropping from the mind all thought of being crowded or pushed. Dwell upon the words of the prophet, "Not by might nor by power but by my Spirit, saith the Lord" (Zechariah 4:6).

A PROFESSIONAL WOMAN HEALED
THROUGH RELAXATION

A professional woman had become tense and nervous over various family matters. Her mind was filled with agitation and her body with fatigue, as well as with vague but definite pain. A heavy schedule faced her in her work, so that she did not feel free to take the time for an exhaustive medical examination. She realized, also, that the tense state of her mind had undoubtedly caused the physical symptoms and if she could clear the tension from her mind and body, the pain could subside.

She began to practice daily the prayer of relaxation. In her prayer time she would breathe deeply and say, "I RELAX, LET GO, AND LET GOD." She would place her hands on the area of the body that was in pain, declaring these words of relaxation.

Often she would decree: "I AM FREE FROM TENSION, STRESS AND STRAIN. I SURRENDER MYSELF ENTIRELY TO GOD. I AM AT PEACE IN MIND AND IN BODY. FROM THE TOP OF MY HEAD TO THE SOLES OF MY FEET, I FEEL RELAXED. I AM CALM, SERENE, RELAXED. I FEEL GOD'S PEACE FILLING MY MIND AND BODY. I REST IN GOD'S GOODNESS."

When tension would try to overtake her during her busy days, she would say, "RELAX, LET GO." As she dwelled much upon prayers of relaxation, her whole world responded. Her body seemed less fatigued, the pain diminished considerably within only a few days, and then gradually faded away completely. Her business life became more relaxed and harmonious, as did her entire outlook on life. Harmony, order, and peace became more and more evident as she continued to dwell on prayers of relaxation.

How often problems of health, human relations, and finances work out quickly and quietly for those who practice the prayer of relaxation, as they declare to those problems: "I RELAX. I RELEASE YOU. I LOOSE YOU. I LET YOU GO. I LET GOD HEAL YOU IN HIS OWN WAY. I FREE YOU TO THE PERFECT SOLUTION." *Sometimes it is a surprise and a jolt to your ego to find that your problem remained with you because of your fierce, tense, possessive hold on it. The prayer of relaxation produces freedom wherever it is needed, and then the divine solution can come!*

SECOND STEP IN THE PRAYER
OF RELAXATION: BREATH

As you loosen the mind and body by telling them to relax, you then want to make prayer contact with your own indwelling God-nature. Job explained how to do this: "There is a spirit in man, and the breath of the Almighty giveth them understanding" (Job 32:8).

Breath is very important to prayer. The word "breath" and the word "spirit" have the same root meaning in all languages. It is through the breath that you make contact with the spirit. *The God within (immanent) and the God without (transcendent) are united by breathing!*

The ancient Greeks believed that there was a creative or ruling spirit within man, which they called the "breath." Socrates was the chief advocate of this theory. The Greeks looked upon man as a "breath being" and any illness of man was diagnosed as a disturbance of his spirit in his breath.

The ancient people advised people to breathe outward, to entirely empty their lungs of breath, and then draw in the breath with some affirmation of good. When they breathed outward again, they had only a healing breath going through their bodies and affairs. *The ancients believed that your breath is vitally connected with your happiness! They felt that all despondency and depression could be overcome by breathing in and out words of praise.*

When you speak words of relaxation to your mind and body and then deliberately breathe deeply, you unite your spirit, soul and body. You unite your conscious mind (located in the front forehead), your superconscious mind (located in the crown of the head), and your subconscious mind (located in the chest and abdominal region).[2]

When you relax and take a deep breath, this unites all three phases of your mind power, bringing them together at the top of the lungs, where the conscious and subconscious mind activities meet in prayer. As you bring these mind activities under your thought control in the area of the breath, you then have real power for prayer and meditation, for it is in that area

---

2. See the author's book *The Healing Secrets of the Ages.*

of the body that you literally "feel" the activity of spirit as it works to dissolve problems lodged in the subconscious mind, thereafter producing peace. (More about this prayer method in the chapter on meditation.)

You actually pray through your breath. You can tell when your prayers have been effective, because of the peaceful feeling that will permeate the lungs-breath area, clearing up negative emotions, producing peace in the entire chest-heart area. It is then that you know your prayers have been answered on the inner plane and that the outer results will manifest in due season. (See the chapter on realization.)

After a good prayer period, you find you can breathe more freely. The burdens seem lifted from the subconscious breath-area in the body. Your feeling nature is uplifted, renewed, peaceful, filled with new power.

As you practice the prayer of relaxation, you will find that instead of breathing from the top of your lungs, you will breathe more deeply. As you continue to practice relaxing the body in prayer, you will find yourself breathing from as deep in the body as the abdominal area.

You will discover that deep breathing relaxes your body and gives you mental and spiritual powers previously unknown. Deep breathing in prayer seems to awaken your intuition, telepathy and deeper prayer powers, such as meditation and the silence. Your extrasensory perception powers will come alive, too, without any effort on your part. You will know things about the past, present and future which no human voice ever reveals to you.

Thus deep breathing helps you to relax so that your good can come on through into visibility. Deep breath-

ing adds to your health, improves your looks, opens your mind and affairs to success.

As you develop your prayer powers, not only will you find yourself breathing more deeply without realizing it. You will also crave fresh air, which will quickly revitalize you within and without.

When your prayers have not been answered, and you are trying to realize greater good, do a lot of deep breathing. Then relax, and release your desires, saying, "I RELEASE THIS TO THE FATHER. I LET GO AND TRUST."

HOLY BREATH—WHAT IT MEANS

Job spoke of the "breath of the Almighty." Sometimes it is good to declare: "THE BREATH OF THE ALMIGHTY NOW GIVES ME UNDERSTANDING ABOUT THIS." Or "THE BREATH OF THE ALMIGHTY GIVES ME NEW LIFE."

This "holy breath" is to the intellect what air is to fuel, as it lifts the weight of human problems off the soul, warming it with the fires of divine love, the warmth of which permeates man's whole being, healing it with peace.

God created man with this "holy breath" according to Genesis 2: "And the Lord God breathed into his nostrils the breath of life; and man became a living soul."

Elijah apparently had developed this "holy breath" for healing because when he placed his mouth upon the mouth of the dead child, life was restored (II Kings 4:34).

Jesus attempted to awaken fully the spiritual consciousness of his disciples when he "breathed on them and said unto them, 'Receive ye the Holy Spirit'" (John 20:22).

Paul revived Eutychus after he had been killed by falling from a balcony, apparently by exercising "holy breath healing" (Acts 20:10).

The mystics of old felt that this "holy breath" was the pure breath of the Almighty; that it was filled with universal life energy which could heal incurable diseases or incurable situations; and that it longed to pour itself forth through receptive man. However, experiencing the "holy breath" isn't something you do mechanically or mentally. It simply happens to you and through you as soon as your prayer development allows it entrance. You will become aware of it in times of quiet, prayerful, relaxed meditative periods.

Prayer, generally, might be described as a sort of spiritual breathing which will cause the soul of man to live again, just as physical breathing, mechanically induced, has caused the body to live again.

THIRD STEP IN THE PRAYER
OF RELAXATION: PEACE

Remember that when you pray, you turn your attention within by speaking words of relaxation to your mind and body, and by breathing deeply. Your good is within your indwelling God-nature, and you are trying to release it through the prayer of relaxation. You are then ready to take the last step in the prayer of relaxation: You are ready to speak the word of "peace" to your mind and body.

As you keep relaxing and breathing deeply, you can gain a sense of peace by saying to any noisy, racing thoughts, or any upset emotions, "PEACE, BE STILL." *You can control the body as well as the mind by speaking words of "peace" to it.* Say often whether it seems to be so or not, "I FEEL THE PEACE OF GOD. I REST IN HIS PEACE."

It is good to dwell upon the phrase from that old hymn, "PEACE, SWEET PEACE." *The mystics have long known that the consciousness of peace in prayer is the forerunner of victory, of healing, and of answered prayer.* The peaceful state of mind is the powerful state of mind. It is the healing state of mind. In the word "peace" is every element of good.

In the consciousness of peace is released all the blessings of life which man seeks: health, abundant supply, a full and replete life, talents, strength and happiness. Peace includes every good thing that is possible to the human being.

If you can get into and remain in a peaceful state of mind, you become a receptive channel for every other rich blessing in life. This is true because peace releases a strong vibratory force, which is teeming with life and recharges one quickly. Establishing peace interiorly has been known to heal diseases.

In my book *The Healing Secrets of the Ages* is the story of the businessman who had smoked for years to the detriment of his health but had been unable to terminate the habit until he attended a religious lecture on "peace." On his way home, he reached for a cigar and suddenly realized that the realization of peace received at that lecture had dissolved all desire within him to smoke. The habit had simply fallen away. There was not a minute's nervous distress or emotional reaction—only a great sense of freedom and gratitude. This man never smoked again.

St. Francis of Sales, in his devotional writings of the 16th century, gave this advice:

> Strive everywhere and in all things to be at peace. *If trouble comes from within or without, receive it peacefully—without excitement.* If we must needs fly from evil, let us do it calmly, without agitation, or we may stumble and fall in our haste.
>
> Let us do good peacefully, or our hurry will lead us into sundry faults. Even repentance is a work that should be carried out peacefully.

LAST POINTS ON PRAYER OF RELAXATION

So you have the three easy steps to be practiced in the prayer of relaxation:

First, speaking words of relaxation to mind and body; *second,* breathing deeply; *third,* dwelling upon words of peace for your whole being. It is a simple and delightful practice.

Last points include these: Do not practice the prayer of relaxation for long periods of time when you first begin to pray daily in this manner. Instead make your prayer periods short (and sweet). Practice makes perfect in prayer, as in anything else.

Do not try to perfect your prayer powers at the very first sitting. Do not try to force the unfoldment of any of these methods of prayer. If you do not relax and become as peaceful as you would like at the first prayer attempt, do not become concerned. Prayer is an art and a science and must be practiced as any art or science in order to be perfected. You should daily practice developing your prayer powers just as you would practice music or the development of any other talent.

The main point is to go back to the prayer of relaxation day after day for just a little while. You will become fascinated with its quiet power in your life; you will begin immediately to feel better and you will gradually note the development of a more tranquil, happier state of mind, as well as vast improvement in your health and in your relationships with others.

Many beginners become discouraged in prayer because they try to pray for long periods when they are not yet mentally trained or emotionally prepared to do so. Keep your prayer periods short, so that your mind does not wander and so that you do not become "heady" in your prayer efforts. This would only cause tension — the very thing you started praying in the first place to overcome!

Remind yourself often: "I DO NOT PRAY TENSELY, ANXIOUSLY, OR HEAVILY ABOUT ANY SITUATION. INSTEAD, I PRAY ABOUT ALL THINGS WITH A LIGHT AND EASY TOUCH."

"Easy does it" where your prayer practice is concerned. Give it the light touch, the relaxed thought. Prayer is meant to be a delightful, satisfying, uplifting experience. When you give the practice of prayer the light touch by practicing short periods of prayer and relaxation daily, you quickly come to enjoy it and look forward to the quick lift it will give you. The more you enjoy your daily prayer periods, the more prayer power you will seem to have and the more easily the blessings you long for will begin to flow to you.

It is then that you will know what Tennyson meant when he promised, "More things are wrought by prayer than this world dreams of."

THE PRAYER OF CLEANSING

— Chapter 4 —

In recent times we have heard much about the power of positive thinking. It is a great philosophy that has helped millions to better their lives. But if your prayers have not been answered, almost in spite of your positive thinking, it may be that you haven't used prayers of cleansing *first* to unblock hostile emotions and buried resentments which must be cleared out before positive thinking can be permanently effective. Even the Bible said new wine was not to be placed in old bottles (your old attitudes).

If people around the world knew about the prayer of cleansing and used it faithfully, they could revolutionize their lives for all kinds of good in a matter of only hours!

The ancient mystics felt that the development of prayer power always began with purification, which eventually led to illumination and finally to union. The initiates of Dionysus, the mystery cult of the Greeks, felt so strongly about it that they observed "rites of purification."

How often most of us have tried to skip that *first* phase of prayer — purification — as we attempted to race on into illumination and union; and how often we have complained bitterly that illumination and union continually evaded us.

The Bible is filled with cleansing symbology used by the Hebrews of old. Their acts of sacrifice, renunciation, repentance — even their "wailing wall" — were all symbols of inner cleansing, release of negative emotions, and purification of their thoughts and emotions.

Life is a constant purification process. However, purification is nothing to be feared! If you try to bypass that purifying process, you stop your good because you have not cleansed your mind and emotions to receive it. The prayer of cleansing gets you ready to receive your good.

Famous prayer authority Friedrich von Hugel once said that it is your own fault if you do not get purified in this life! Dante described the gradual cleansing of the soul in his *Purgatorio.* The pray-ers down through the centuries have described it as "the purgative way."

Thomas Aquinas spoke of the seven deadly sins of the mind and heart of man which must be cleansed in this "purgative way." Perhaps he knew about the ancient belief that there were seven layers of the mind that needed constant cleansing. Modern metaphysicians speak instead of the "seven senses" that must be cleansed as man takes up the spiritual life: his five human senses, and his two superhuman senses of intuition and telepathy.[1]

Bible symbology might have been referring to cleansing the seven layers of the mind, or of cleansing the seven senses of man, in the story of the leper Naaman, who was healed after following Elisha's instruction to wash in the Jordan River seven times (II Kings 5). After making grave mistakes David cried, "Purify me. . . . Create in me a clean heart, O God; and renew a right spirit within me." His "cry" became the famous "Psalm of Cleansing" known as the 51st Psalm. Jesus might have been describing man's experiences on "the purgative way" when he spoke of the necessity of cleansing the inside of the cup first so that the outside of the cup might become cleansed also (Matthew 23:26).

Most people turn to prayer at a time when their lives seem filled with evil. Though they do not realize it, they are in the mystic process of purification. They are on "the purgative way."

Though it seems uncomfortable, this "purgative way" is a healthy process of soul-cleansing in which negative thoughts, feelings, and memories rise out of man's subconscious mind to the surface of his conscious thoughts, feelings, and relationships, and seem to present him with problems of evil.

Through meeting these experiences of evil, man learns lessons that are necessary for his growth and understanding. Although he seems in the midst of an evil experience, when he learns that it is a purifying

---

1. See Chapters 14 and 15 of the author's book *The Dynamic Laws of Prosperity.*

process and dares to invoke the prayer of cleansing, he can then turn that experience of evil into one of good.

And so I repeat: *Purification is nothing to be feared. It is a healing process, and the prayer of cleansing is master of purification. It is a joyous process that can always lead to better things!*

THE "LESSON" OF EVIL

Evil is not a "problem" but a "lesson." It is an experience in purification. *An understanding of this purification process through which the soul passes is a first requirement for one on the pathway of prayer.*

It is not enough to pray to God to remove evil appearances from your life. You must find out *why* they are there, and *what* lesson you are to learn from them. Cease fighting and resisting evil. Pray for the humility and patience to learn the lessons evil is trying to teach you.

All evil is corrective. It becomes a teacher to those who are willing to learn. Those evil experiences did not begin somewhere outside yourself, but within your own secret thoughts and feelings. There within you they can be erased as you invoke the prayer of cleansing. Then, as you learn the lesson those evil experiences have to teach you, they will fade away.

Concerning evil experiences you probably wail, "But I did not know any better." Of course you didn't. There is no evil in the universe which is not the result of ignorance, and which would not, if you were ready and willing to learn its lesson, lead you to higher wisdom and then vanish. When men remain in an evil experience which does not pass away, it is because they are not willing to learn the lesson that it came to teach them.

He who would shake himself free of evil must be willing and ready to undergo a disciplinary cleansing process, through which he gains new wisdom and strength that can lead him to abiding happiness. However, this disciplinary, cleansing process is not hard or difficult but has to do with invoking simple prayers of cleansing as described in this chapter. His "lesson" in evil having taught him what he needs to know then dissolves, having served its purpose. *Thus nothing is evil that brings forth good!*

THEY INVOKED THE PRAYER OF CLEANSING THROUGH DENIAL

The *first* thing you wish to do in the midst of a "lesson" in evil is to cleanse your mind of any fear you have about it. *If you want your prayers answered you must often turn from evil appearances and cleanse your mind of any fear about them by saying "no" to them.*

This you do through the prayer of denial, in which you deny that the problem has any power over you as you simply say "no" to it.[2]

This gives you a sense of detachment or "holy indifference" to it. As you continue saying "no" to a troublesome situation, you first cast out fear about that situation. With the release from fear, then comes release

---

2. See Chapters 2, 3 and 4 of *The Dynamic Laws of Healing,* by the author, for further descriptions of the various phases of the prayer of cleansing, and the results it can bring.

from the problem which you no longer are clutching mentally or emotionally, and so it is free to adjust itself. You also feel a new freedom as the "no" power cuts away negative beliefs which were the cause of your problems in the first place. Through saying "no" to those situations that have harassed you, you not only clear up emotional blocks but you also open the way for divine intelligence to circulate freely and produce a solution.

A businessman who was healed of arthritis through using prayers of denial later explained:

"From the day I began to say 'no' to the pain, declaring, 'NO, I WILL NOT ACCEPT THIS CONDITION AS PERMANENT. WITH GOD'S HELP I AM GOING TO BE HEALED'— from that day forward, I never allowed my attention to dwell on anything else. When the old doubts and fears tried to creep in, I quickly shut the door on them with a 'no, no, no.' The arthritic pains disappeared and I never knew exactly when they left me. They tried to return often, but I constantly dwelled upon God's love and God's healing power, saying 'no' to the pain. Since that experience I have enjoyed over twenty-five years of splendid health, because I refused to accept anything else."

A man in the real estate business was told that he had an incurable disease. While awaiting further clinical tests, he began to cleanse his mind of fear by using "no" prayers: "NO, I DO NOT ACCEPT THIS DIAGNOSIS. THERE IS NO ABSENCE OF LIFE, SUBSTANCE, OR INTELLIGENCE IN ME. I PRAISE MY BODY AS THE PERFECT CREATION OF DIVINE LIFE, SUBSTANCE AND INTELLIGENCE. I AM THE PERFECT CHILD OF GOD AND I MANIFEST HIS PERFECTION NOW!"

As he continued to invoke the "no" power of prayer,

various situations arose that delayed further immediate
clinical tests. Several weeks later, when the tests were
finally made, the X-rays were clear. The incurable
appearance had faded away. This man has continued
in good health.

THE "NO" POWER CAN DISSOLVE YOUR HARDEST TRAILS

All improved conditions in the world, with every
step of progress from the beginning of time to the
present, have resulted because someone said "no" to
limiting appearances along the way and then worked
to improve conditions. *If you want your prayers answered, you must often turn from evil appearances
and cleanse your mind of any fear about them by
saying "no" to them.*

A district sales manager was assigned a new territory. She said to her superior, "No, I do not accept
this limited territory as all I am to have. I do not
accept this area as my final assignment." A few days
later she received word from the home office in another state informing her that her new territory was
being enlarged!

Evil conditions of mind, body or affairs are built
up by someone feeling bad about them. This bad
feeling not only builds up but sustains the unhappy
condition. When the bad feeling is pulled out from
under the negative appearance, that evil has nothing
to sustain it and has to fade away.

This is true because evil conditions have no life, substance or intelligence of themselves. They are created

by the fears, resentments and other negative beliefs of man. Saying "no" to those evil conditions and then refusing to be fearful, impressed, or even to give them further attention is the greatest way you can begin to dissolve them.

When you say to any apparent limitation of mind, body or affairs, "NO, I DO NOT ACCEPT THIS APPEARANCE. MY LIFE (HEALTH, WEALTH, HAPPINESS) CANNOT BE LIMITED!" *you are dissolving fear.* You are saying "no" to negative appearances. You are *not accepting them,* or giving them power, and so they have to fade away. The omnipresent good, which has been in your midst all the time, is then free to manifest as a happy result.

Thus, saying "no" to evil appearances can help you dissolve your hardest trials! A simple praying "no, no, no" to apparent limitation, or quietly saying "no, no, no" to yourself when others about you speak of evil, is a marvelous way to invoke the prayer of cleansing.

HOW HE GOT OVERSEAS HOUSING
WHEN NO ONE ELSE COULD

A young executive had just been transferred abroad by his company. His family was to join him there, just as soon as housing was available. However, the area to which he had been transferred was very crowded and housing facilities were scarce.

After several months without his family, this young executive became homesick and threatened to give up his fine job and return home to the United States unless his family was able to join him shortly.

His wife realized this job was the opportunity of a lifetime and that he might regret his impatience later if he gave up and came home at this point.

Several other executives' wives for the same company, were also awaiting overseas housing. They kept saying, "It is just an impossible situation. Things are so crowded that we will never get housing." This young wife learned of the "no" power of prayer and she began to say to herself, "No, I do not accept that for us." Then to prove her faith, she began packing and making ready for their journey abroad. She and her children received their overseas shots. As she kept getting unfavorable reports about crowded housing conditions, she kept saying "no" to them.

Suddenly her husband wrote, "This week there will be a meeting about housing. There is only one house now available in this area and there is a long list of people trying to get it, including several of my superiors. Our chances for getting this house seem dim. If we don't get this house, it may be months before another is available. Please pray for the right outcome of this situation. I will telephone or cable you as soon as the meeting is over."

The night of the meeting, her husband did not call or cable and she assumed they had not gotten the house. However, one of the other executives' wives, who had been saying so many negative things about the situation, *did* receive a call from her husband saying they had *not* gotten the house. (In fact, they never did get housing and, as his wife decreed, her husband finally was sent back to the United States to work at a much lower rate of pay).

Two nights later a telephone call came to the first executive's wife, who had been mentally denying the crowded housing conditions. Her husband said, "I don't understand it. Of all the people trying to get this one house, including some of my superiors who supposedly have seniority and influence, *I* was assigned the house! I will be flying home in just three days, and you and the children will be flying back here with me within a week."

The "no" power of prayer can dissolve apparently impossible blocks to your good because it cleanses your mind of fear and negative beliefs that block your good. You can stop evil "dead in its tracks" with the "no" power of prayer, because you cleanse your mind of the belief in evil, which is actually the cause of all your problems. As this is done, then there is nothing to stop your good!

HEALINGS INVOKED THROUGH THE POWER OF THE CROSS

The cross has long been considered a symbol of healing. There are many stories about the transforming power of the cross. The Emperor Constantine's conversion to Christianity three hundred years after Christ is attributed to his vision of the cross in the sky. In this vision of the cross he saw the words, "In this conquer," on the eve of a battle. As he dwelled upon that vision of the cross and its message, he won the battle.

We win our battles in life the same way: By keeping our vision on the cross, as we cross out any fear about those battling appearances. We, too, then conquer.

There is a legend about Emperor Constantine's mother visiting Palestine in the year A.D. 326. On this visit she was guided to the site of Jesus' crucifixion by an aged

Jew, who had inherited knowledge of the site of the cross.

The mother of Emperor Constantine, on this visit, had the ground dug to a considerable depth, trying to find the cross of Jesus. Legend states that three crosses were found. The cross of Jesus was identified when the miraculous cure of a sick woman occurred, after she stretched out upon the cross of Jesus. This was supposed to have occurred 362 years after Jesus' crucifixion. There is another legend that one of the nails from Jesus' cross, which was found by Constantine's mother, was cast into the sea during a storm and subdued it.

The symbology of these stories is significant: We, too, subdue the storms of life through crossing out our beliefs in their power to hurt or harm us. We subdue and cross out the storms of life when we say to them, "THIS TOO SHALL PASS. THIS HAS NO POWER. MY LIFE CANNOT BE LIMITED. MY GOOD CANNOT BE LIMITED." Or "I NOW CROSS OUT ALL LIMITATION FROM MY LIFE IN THE NAME OF JESUS CHRIST."

Through saying "no" to limitation in your life, your cross can become a crown.

The early Christians constantly used the sign of the cross. That was one of the secrets of their spiritual power for performing miracles. Historians say that on each journey, at each coming in and going out, at the putting on of shoes, at the bath, at meals, at the kindling of fire, at the sitting down, and at whatever occupation they were engaged, they marked their brow with the sign of the cross.

St. Francis of Assisi once healed a paralyzed man by making the sign of the cross over him from head to feet. That there is still literal healing power in the cross has been proven in modern times. One mother healed her son of acute indigestion and later of whooping cough by making the sign of the cross over him and declaring, "By this sign we conquer." Another woman came through a period of severe depression and ill health after she began to use the sign of the cross and affirmed often, "By this sign I conquer."

A Canadian was puzzled by apparently psychic visitations in her home which resulted in mystifying noises and strange happenings the moment the lights were out at night. In the morning she would find furniture overturned and articles missing or misplaced. Friends advised moving, but this lady loved her home and did not wish to leave for such strange reasons.

Finally a spiritual counselor advised her to use the "no" power of prayer, denying the mysterious noises any power. It was also suggested that the troubled one spiritually raise the cross of Christ in every room. This advice was taken literally as she cut out paper crosses, placing many of them in each room. The noises quickly disappeared and never returned.

RELEASE HEALS HUMAN RELATIONS PROBLEMS

The prayer of cleansing takes several forms: (1) Following the "no" power of denial, there is (2) the prayer of release that "lets go and lets God."

In order to become cleansed and freed from many of life's problems, it is necessary to practice renunciation or release, especially in the human relations department. This proves a pleasant process, since it frees you from people whose burdens you should not be bearing anyway!

Most human relations problems would melt away if the people involved would pray prayers of release, instead of trying to make people over to conform to *their* will and *their* way.

The prayer of cleansing includes cleansing one's thoughts and world of possessiveness. You must cleanse yourself of possessively clinging to other people in your life, telling them what to do in the name of "love," if you want your own prayers to be answered. Through possessive emotional ties, you direct the substance of your thoughts and feelings into someone else's life, which you should be using in your own; thus you deplete yourself so that you are not a fit channel for answered prayer.

After hearing a recent lecture on the prayer of release, almost everyone attending had interesting experiences in answered prayer:

A businesswoman mentally released her troublesome daughter, declaring for her: "I FULLY AND FREELY RELEASE YOU. I LOOSE YOU AND LET YOU GO. I LET GO AND LET GOD HAVE HIS WAY IN YOUR LIFE." The daughter soon married and went abroad to live.

An overly protective mother released her married daughter in the same manner, then moved out of her daughter's home to a distant city and went back to work, though she was beyond the usual retirement age. The daughter and son-in-law were then able to adopt children, which they had tried to do many times previously without success. As both mother and daughter continued praying the prayer of release, the daughter and her husband inherited money with which they bought a larger home, another car, and happily prepared for a comfortable life with their adopted children.

One couple's troublesome son settled down emotionally, went back to college and finally happily married, after his parents mentally released him. As two concerned mothers spoke words of release for their teenage daughters, these daughters enrolled in colleges away from home and became honor students. *Peace was restored in all these households through the spoken word of release.*

RELEASE DISSOLVES POSSESSIVENESS AND BRINGS PEACE

Strong possessiveness sets up a block in your consciousness, so that you are not open to the guidance and illumination of answered prayer. The prayer of release frees you from trying to outline, dominate, or force another's good. Not only does the prayer of release free your mind and your world to become a channel for answered prayer, but it also frees those you love to follow the guidance of their own indwelling Lord, and to unfold the divine plan of their lives in their own God-appointed ways.

For everything and everybody that concerns you, instead of clutching them to you, trying to force them into your will and your way, let them go to their good by declaring: "I NOW PLACE YOU LOVINGLY IN THE HANDS OF THE FATHER. THAT WHICH IS FOR YOUR HIGHEST GOOD NOW COMES TO YOU IN YOUR OWN TIME AND IN YOUR OWN WAY."

Thereafter, when that person or situation tries to get your attention, keep releasing him or it by affirming, "I HAVE RELEASED YOU LOVINGLY INTO THE HANDS OF THE

FATHER, AND I HAVE FAITH THAT THAT WHICH IS FOR YOUR HIGHEST GOOD MANIFESTS."

A troubled mother, who had tried everything from psychiatric to ministerial counseling as a means of straightening out her delinquent daughter, found that nothing worked until she emotionally released her. Thereafter, when she thought of the daughter she would say, "I HAVE PLACED MY DAUGHTER IN GOD'S HANDS. WHAT BETTER HANDS CAN SHE BE IN? NOT MY WILL BUT GOD'S WILL IS BEING DONE IN HER LIFE." Shortly the daughter began to mature and later married and became a fine wife and mother.

A father had a visit with his son for the last time before his son was returning to Vietnam for further duty with the Marine Corps. This father cleansed his mind of fear about his son's destiny and released any sense of possessiveness about him by praying, "I RELEASE YOU TO THE FATHER." Many months later his handsome son returned safely from war.

In praying the prayer of release for your loved ones, remember that nothing relinquished is ever lost. Everything finds its true balance, its equilibrium, when freed to do so. Give each soul in your life freedom to swing into his own accepted place in the scheme of life; give him freedom to do so in his own time and way, whether his methods please you or not. As you fully let go, each one will find his true place. As you give all people absolute freedom in your thoughts about them, your act of release will cause them to do whatever is best for them at their present level of understanding. They must learn life's lessons for themselves. You cannot grow or overcome for another. Through the act of releasing them to their own indwelling Lord, you not only free them to their good, but you also free yourself to become an open, receptive, peaceful channel for answered prayer.

Emerson might have been describing the sheer necessity of releasing our loved ones when he wrote: "If you put a chain around the neck of a slave, the other end fastens itself around your own."

PRAYER OF RELEASE BRINGS MARRIAGE

When you let go of strain, of pushing and shoving, of self-assertion and the determination to have things go your own way; when you cease fighting, struggling, and grasping for your good; when you relax, release, let go, leaving everything to the perfect outworking of the Power Within after having done all you know to do to make things right; when you give up your human efforts and accept what comes, you find that what comes is fulfillment of the very desires of which you had let go!

A businesswoman, for many years widowed, had tried every physical and mental trick she knew to re-marry. But in her zealousness to marry, she had sub-consciously repelled every man who crossed her path. Finally she began to speak prayers of release saying, "FATHER, I FULLY AND FREELY RELEASE MY DESIRE TO MARRY. I LOOSE AND LET GO. I LET GO AND LET THY PER-FECT WILL BE DONE IN MY LIFE. I WOULD LOVE TO HAVE A HAPPY HOME, BUT I RELEASE THE MATTER TO YOU. I AM YOUR DAUGHTER AND YOU LOVE ME. YOU KNOW WHAT IS BEST, SO DO WITH MY LIFE WHATEVER YOU WISH." With that, she gave a sigh of relief and released the matter completely.

Within a matter of weeks she was introduced by

friends to a fine widower, whom she happily married within a matter of months. When later asked by astonished friends the secret of her sudden success she explained: "It's simple. Nothing worked out until I practiced the prayer of release. I had to let go completely and trust God to make my life right. That was the key to results."

HOW CONFESSION HAS BROUGHT HEALINGS

Along with speaking words of release for and to those people in your world; along with speaking words that you are released, another healthy form of release is the act of confessing to a priest, minister or trusted friend. The Bible spoke of this act as "repentance."

An unhappily married man had had a series of affairs with "other women" and in the mounting frustration finally was hospitalized. Neither his health nor his state of mind improved until he confessed his severe unhappiness to a minister, who had the wisdom to release him from his mistakes by saying to him: "Do not condemn yourself for your unhappy marriage, for the affairs you entered into with other women, or for your present illness. You did the best you knew at your level of understanding. Release it all, let it go and let God show you the way out of your dilemma." They then prayed together prayers of release for everyone involved in the marital mix-ups of past and present, and asked for forgiveness of the sins of all involved. With that act of prayer, the unhappy man cried tears of relief, and his healing began.

Later he and his wife were reconciled, their marriage became happier than ever before, and he went on to business success such as he had never known. But only after confession in which a wise spiritual counselor did not condemn his sins but prayed with him for release from them.

It is an established fact that people who go regularly to a church confessional rarely end up on a psychiatrist's couch or in a mental hospital, so potent is confession as a form of relief and release from life's problems.

If no priest, minister or trusted friend is available to hear your confession (and many ministers have neither the training nor the spiritual or emotional understanding for it, so be careful to whom you confess), then go directly to God with your confession. Talk directly to Him as a loving Father who cares. You may wish to do this: (1) on your knees in the formal act of prayer.

The wife of a brilliant corporation lawyer became an alcoholic and no amount of treatment or therapy seemed to help. After three years of searching for healing in countless ways, one night this troubled woman realized that not once in those three years had she prayed directly to God, asking His help. Getting down on her knees in formal prayer, she confessed: "Oh God, what can I do? Help me to conquer this habit. I have tried but nothing has helped. I am laying this burden at Your feet, Father. Only You can save me. Only You know what is best."

Suddenly she felt God's presence enfolding her as an indescribable warmth and love. A feeling of peace then came and the desire for drink was gone by the time she arose from her knees. She never needed it again. Simple confession direct to God in prayer had done for her quickly what no amount of expensive treatment or therapy had been able to do for her in three years of searching. She proved what statistics show: *That far more people are still healed through prayer and spiritual methods than through all other methods of healing combined!* You do not always hear about these spiritual healings because people wisely keep quiet about them, knowing that what is sacred should often remain secret.

Another simple, satisfying method for confessing your sins directly to God is: (2) to write them out honestly and fully, leaving out nothing. Then, placing your hands on your written confession, pray asking God's help and forgiveness. Finally, give thanks for cleansing of those mistakes: "THE FORGIVING LOVE OF JESUS CHRIST NOW SETS ME FREE FROM MISTAKES OF THE PAST, AND FROM THE RESULTS OF MISTAKES OF THE PAST. I FACE THE FUTURE WISE, FREE, AND UNAFRAID." A real soul cleansing will take place and you will be freed of the previous guilt and condemnation that had kept you emotionally bound to past sins. Your *last* act should be to: (3) destroy your confession and rejoice in your freedom.

Through his famous book of *Confessions*, St. Augustine revealed himself as the last of the great metaphysicians of the Patristic period, and also the first of all modern psychologists. In his *Confessions*, St. Augustine gave consolation to the frustrated and neurotic that no psychologist since has ever been able to top. He proved that true peace of soul is found not so much on the psychological couch as on the bended knee, and that help comes as soon as man realizes he cannot lift himself by his own bootstraps, and then confesses his need to God. It is little wonder that his book, *The Confessions of St. Augustine*, has been a best-seller since A.D. 400.

GETTING RELEASE FROM OTHERS

Sometimes the problem is to get others to release you emotionally from their possessiveness and domination. This can come secretly as you speak words of release that cause them subconsciously to free you. Simply declare "JOHN BROWN, YOU NOW FULLY AND FREELY RELEASE ME. YOU LOOSE ME AND LET ME GO. YOU LET GO AND LET GOD." If there is a need for freedom both ways, you might declare: "CHRIST IN US IS OUR RELEASING POWER." For situations that need freedom from a number of personalities declare: "CHRIST IN THIS SITUATION IS ITS RELEASING POWER." As you daily declare prayers of release, the freedom will come, sometimes suddenly, sometimes more slowly; often severe unpleasantness cuts clean the release. But that severe unpleasantness is like the pain connected with physical healing. It is necessary and thus a blessing in disguise.

FORGIVENESS CAN CAUSE YOUR DREAMS
TO COME TRUE

Forgiveness is the *third* type of prayers of cleansing.

One of the major causes of unanswered prayer is unforgiveness. Jesus repeatedly emphasized that you cannot pray aright if you are bound to grudges, prejudices, bitterness, and an unforgiving attitude toward God, man, yourself, or the world in general. (And almost all of us are holding unforgiving thoughts in one or more of these areas of life.)

If you want to develop your prayer powers and get your prayers answered, you must pray the prayer of forgiveness often. *Forgiveness can dissolve whatever stands between you and your good as it cleanses your*

*mind, body and relationships, opening the way for
your dreams to come true.*

*You can solve more problems through prayers of
forgiveness than in any other way: health, financial
and human relations problems all quickly respond to
forgiveness. When there is a problem of any kind there
is a need for forgiveness. One person speaking prayers
of forgiveness for a situation can dissolve the emotional
blocks and clear up the problem, regardless of what
others are saying or doing. That is the potency of
forgiveness, which simply means "to give up."*

When I have problems on any level of life—health,
financial or human relations—I give myself a "universal forgiveness treatment." I simply speak the word of
"universal forgiveness" for the situation declaring that
everything and everybody connected subconsciously
joins me in forgiving whatever needs to be forgiven,
thus dissolving the invisible cause of the problem:
"CHRIST IN THIS SITUATION IS ITS FORGIVING POWER. THE
CHRIST IN ME FORGIVES THE CHRIST IN YOU. THE CHRIST
IN YOU FORGIVES THE CHRIST IN ME. WE ARE ALL FOR-
GIVEN AND GOVERNED BY THE DIVINITY WITHIN US, AND
THE PERFECT RESULTS NOW MANIFEST." Invariably they
do!

FORGIVENESS HEALS, PROSPERS, HARMONIZES

A fine couple was faced with problems of every kind.
They both suddenly found themselves without jobs.
Their debts mounted and their creditors harassed
them. Furthermore, the wife had a painful lump in
one breast, and her husband's former wife was causing
them legal and financial difficulties.

Learning that all problems can be resolved through forgiveness, this couple decided to prove it. While the husband continued looking for work, the wife remained at home daily declaring prayers of forgiveness, writing out statements of forgiveness to both friends and foes alike: "I FULLY AND FREELY FORGIVE YOU. I LOOSE YOU AND LET YOU GO. I LET GO AND LET GOD. THE FORGIVING LOVE OF JESUS CHRIST HAS SET US FREE FROM ALL MISTAKES OF THE PAST OR PRESENT."

These acts of forgiveness first brought great peace of mind. After a week of daily practice of forgiveness in this way, this previously sick woman realized that the painful lump in her breast was gone. (It is estimated that 70 percent of all disease is caused by suppressed emotion. Forgiveness releases that suppressed emotion.)

Meanwhile, her husband had been promised several jobs but none had materialized. After her healing, she went out to look for work, too. On the street one day she saw a former business associate. Meeting him brought to memory a period several years previously when she had been in business with a man who bankrupted her. Facing their mutual friend on the street she said, "Do you ever see my former business partner?"

"Yes," he replied.

"Will you please deliver a message to him for me? Will you please tell him that I have forgiven him for bankrupting me. It was a blessing in disguise. I did not need that job with all the responsibility, worry and problems it presented."

Relieved, the mutual friend went on his way. Whether he ever delivered her message of forgiveness, she never knew. But the next day, she obtained the best job of her life! Speaking words of forgiveness had turned the tide for her.

On still another day, she saw a man across the street who had promised a good job to her husband but had not come through with it. Her first reaction was silently to resent and criticize him. Her second reaction was: "He has come to my attention to be forgiven." Mentally, she said to him, "I forgive you for not giving my husband that job you promised him. I release the matter completely."

The next day that man telephoned her husband, again offering him the job that had been previously promised! He took it on a part-time basis while seeking a better-paying job. As the prayers of forgiveness were continued, suddenly he was offered not one or two, but six fine jobs! He took the best of the lot and has since enjoyed the greatest success of his life.

As for the former wife who had caused this couple so much trouble, their prayers of forgiveness for her began to bring peace. Often they had prayed: "YOU FULLY AND FREELY FORGIVE US. YOU LOOSE US AND LET US GO. YOU LET GO AND LET GOD. CHRIST IN YOU IS YOUR FORGIVING POWER. THE FORGIVING LOVE OF JESUS CHRIST HAS SET US ALL FREE FROM MISTAKES OF THE PAST OR PRESENT. WE ALL GO FREE TO BE HAPPY."

Finally harmony was established to such a point that this couple was able to give the former wife my book, *The Dynamic Laws of Healing,* even suggesting the chapter on forgiveness in it to her. She later confessed to them that she was "living with that book."

Thus health, good jobs, and harmony were re-established for this couple through the prayer of forgiveness.

If you will sit for half an hour every day and forgive yourself, the people of the past and present in your world, and also forgive your wrong ideas about God (knowing that instead of being a hostile faraway Entity,

He is a loving Father who is near and dear), you will soon be describing forgiveness as "the miracle prayer." Declare often, "I AM FORGIVEN AND GOVERNED BY GOD'S LOVE ALONE. GOD LOVES ME, GOD IS GUIDING ME, GOD IS SHOWING ME THE WAY."

FORMING A VACUUM BROUGHT ANSWERED PRAYERS

Along with: (1) the "no" prayer, (2) the prayer of release, (3) and the prayer of forgiveness, there is also a *last* type of cleansing prayer: (4) the vacuum prayer.

In effect, the other three prayers of cleansing are for the purpose of forming a vacuum in one's mind and emotions, cleansing them of negative emotions which have blocked one's prayer powers. After invoking the prayer of cleansing in *inner* ways through saying "no" to fearful appearances, releasing one's loved ones and forgiving one's enemies, it is then time to cleanse one's world in *outer* ways through forming a vacuum.

There is psychological value in cleansing one's world by forming a vacuum in *outer* as well as *inner* ways: the subconscious mind becomes more quickly convinced that you mean business about all the praying you have done when you follow through by taking some *outer* action as well.

Through saying "no" to fearful appearances, thereby cleansing yourself of fear; through emotionally releasing your loved ones; and by forgiving the unloving people in your life—you have already begun forming an *inner* vacuum. It is good to complete the cycle by forming a vacuum in an *outer* way too.

I once lectured to a group of insurance executives

who got very excited about this vacuum law and rushed home afterward to form a vacuum. A number of them later reported to me the satisfying results that followed.

The vacuum prayer of cleansing is this: Nature abhors a vacuum. If you want your prayers answered, form a vacuum to receive that answer! Get rid of what you do not want to make room for what you do want.

A doctor of chiropractic related how his little daughter learned of this vacuum method and immediately used it with gratifying consequences: She wanted some new clothes, so she secretly formed a vacuum by giving away some she had in the faith that the vacant places in her closet would cause new substance to rush in and fill it with new clothes. That very afternoon her mother came in with some new dresses explaining: "I didn't expect to buy these for you now, but they were on sale." When her daughter did not seem surprised the mother asked why. "I formed a vacuum only this morning to receive them," was her quiet reply.

A businessman had been praying for some time for the healing of a relative who was suffering from a chronic heart condition. In studying my book *The Dynamic Laws of Prosperity,* this businessman realized his relative needed to invoke the vacuum law as a phase of cleansing, so he gave her a copy of my book and asked her to study the law of vacuum.

In the book she read: "You can form a physical vacuum for new peace, health and plenty by releasing, giving away, selling or otherwise getting rid of what you no longer want or need. Do not retain items of clothing, furniture, letters, files, books, or any other personal possessions that you no longer need or use. Get them out of the way to make room for what you do want. As long as you retain them, they take up space in your world that is needed for your new good. Declare

to yourself as you go through your personal effects: 'I
FULLY AND FREELY RELEASE. I LOOSE AND LET GO. I JOY-
OUSLY MAKE WAY FOR NEW GOOD, WHICH NOW APPEARS
QUICKLY IN SATISFYING, APPROPRIATE FORM.'"

This ailing relative immediately went up into the
attic (forgetting that because of her heart condition
she was not supposed to climb stairs). Among the clutter she found there was some antique furniture that
she had previously offered as a gift to a charitable
institution.

Since there had been no response to the offer, she
now contacted an antique dealer, who arrived, in-
spected the antiques, purchased them, and immediately
gave her a check for a substantial sum of money. As
she continued to dwell on the various inner and outer
ways she could release, loose, let go, and get out of her
old negative state of mind, it occurred to her that she
needed to forgive a daughter with whom she was out
of harmony. As she daily spoke words of forgiveness
for the daughter who lived away from home, this
daughter subconsciously responded by paying an unexpected visit. Furthermore, she offered as a gift to
her mother and father round-trip tickets to Europe.
This, with the money acquired from the sale of antiques, made the trip possible.

As this previously sick woman continued speaking
prayers of forgiveness and release, and then followed
through by forming a vacuum in outer ways, she realized that her former heart condition had faded away.
That a complete healing had occurred became obvious
on her trip. She suffered no ill effects from it, and she
enjoyed Europe immensely.

Pray the prayer of vacuum by declaring: "I NOW GET
RID OF WHAT I DO NOT WANT IN MY LIFE TO MAKE WAY
FOR WHAT I DO WANT. DIVINE INTELLIGENCE NOW SHOWS

ME IN WHAT AREAS OF MY LIFE TO FORM A VACUUM. I
NOW LET GO THE LESSER TO MAKE ROOM FOR THE GREATER
GOOD TO RUSH INTO MY LIFE. I LET GO AND TRUST."

Another marvelous prayer of vacuum for freedom
from possessions and possessiveness is this: "CHRIST IN
ME NOW FREES ME FROM EVERY ATTACHMENT *TO* PEOPLE,
PLACES OR THINGS OF THE PAST OR PRESENT. CHRIST IN ME
NOW FREES ME FROM EVERY ATTACHMENT *FROM* PEOPLE,
PLACES OR THINGS OF THE PAST OR PRESENT. I MANIFEST
MY TRUE PLACE WITH THE TRUE PEOPLE AND WITH THE
TRUE POSSESSIONS NOW."

The mystics of old formed a vacuum by taking vows
of poverty, not so much because they wished to be poor
but because they wished to be free. Their vows included freedom from negative emotions and freedom
from being possessed by things. Through the prayers
of cleansing described in this chapter you form a vacuum and get rid of outer possessions as well as inner
negative emotions. This frees you from the chains of
possessiveness and possessions that bind so many and
keep them from developing their prayer powers and
the deeper, more satisfying qualities that truly make
life worth living.

Freedom is one of the first requirements for answered
prayer. The prayer of vacuum and the other types of
cleansing described herein give you that inner and
outer freedom. So take it!

FASTING: A PRAYER METHOD FOR
OVERCOMING PROBLEMS

The act of fasting is another method of invoking a
vacuum in mind and body, thus cleansing them of both
mental and physical poisons. Indeed, fasting can be

an act of cleansing prayer. Mohammed said, "Prayer leads halfway to God, fasting brings one to the doors of heaven."

I was first introduced to the power of fasting by a doctor who pointed out that the body can easily go without food for many days, taking only water; that instead of starving the body, fasting rejuvenates it and cleanses it; that the fast is not an ordeal, but a rest of mind and body; that after the first twenty-four hours of fasting all desire for food gradually leaves one until the body has been cleansed and is ready to again receive food, at which time hunger will return normally.

This doctor suggested plenty of fresh air and sunshine while fasting, though it is not necessary to abstain from one's regular activities. He felt that prayer and spiritual study should be a "steady diet" during the fasting period.

This doctor often used fasting as a method for overcoming personal problems. I know of one instance in which he went on a fast because of some troublesome personality conflicts that had arisen in his private life. After he quietly went on a diet of prayer and fasting, the troublesome personalities suddenly left town, moving out of the state!

Fasting existed in prehistoric cultures, and was an accompaniment of prayer common to the people of both the Old and New Testaments alike. As Gibbon's famous book, *The Decline and Fall of the Roman Empire,* pointed out, the healing success of the early Christians even into the end of the second century was extraordinary. They were able literally to raise the dead, who often lived for many years afterward. Their secret seemed to lie in their practice of prayer and "great fasting."

Jesus pointed out the power of fasting as a means of

overcoming severe problems, as in the case of healing the epileptic boy: "This kind cometh out by nothing save prayer and fasting" (Mark 9:29). Jesus' definite advice on fasting was: "But thou, when thou fastest, anoint thy head, and wash thy face; that thou be not seen of men to fast, but of thy Father who is in secret; and thy Father, who seeth in secret, shall recompense thee" (Matthew 6:17, 18).

Hippocrates, the father of medicine, suggested fasts up to seven days. Fasting in modern times has returned as a method prescribed by some doctors for losing weight. Dr. Herbert M. Shelton, who conducted over thirty thousand fasts, found, as the title of his book points out, that *Fasting Can Save Your Life.* It is also a fine method for loosing and releasing one's problems and letting them go to solution. Those who do not wish to abstain from both food and liquids and go on a severe fast of distilled water only often find it helpful to go on a fast consisting of liquids such as vegetable juices.

This seems to cleanse the mind and body and raise the one fasting to a higher level of consciousness where his prayer powers are heightened and illumination comes more quickly. *Fasting is especially powerful for overcoming severe problems, because fasting intensifies your prayer consciousness.*

A friend of mine had a puzzling problem which she did not know how to resolve and decided to go on a fast, consuming only liquids, until the problem was solved. The prayers she used with her fast were these: "JESUS CHRIST IS IN ABSOLUTE CONTROL OF THIS SITUA- TION, AND JESUS CHRIST IS PRODUCING PERFECT RESULTS IN THIS MATTER NOW." Amazingly, a man she had never seen called her "out of the blue," informing her just how to resolve her problem.

It was as though the act of prayer and fasting had set up a high-powered vibration that went forth into the ethers and worked through a total stranger, who then went to the trouble to seek her out and supply the answer to her prayer. Thus, within a week from the time she secretly went on the fast and began using special prayers to clarify the problem, it was solved by an individual she was yet to meet!

And so I repeat: Fasting is especially powerful for overcoming severe problems, because fasting intensifies your prayer consciousness.

There is a saying: "First the fast. Then the feast."

The dramatic accomplishments of Paul and the apostles, both in their healing ministries and in their strenuous missionary travels for establishing the early Christian church all over the ancient world, seemed to be accompanied by strenuous fasting. The severities of the ancient fasts, particularly as they were practiced in the 3rd and 4th centuries, were abandoned by later Christians, since they in some instances caused bodily damage to the fasters. However, in many religious groups down through the centuries, fasting has continued as a spiritual practice strongly suggested as an accompaniment of prayer in time of stress, strain or spiritual overcoming.

CLEANSING: A CONSTANT, SELF-RENEWING PROCESS

The prayer of cleansing includes (1) the "no" power of prayer, often known as denial; (2) prayers of release from possessiveness, particularly in one's human relationships; (3) prayers of forgiveness for one's self, one's fellow man, one's experiences of unhappiness of past or present, and even of one's false ideas about God; and (4) the vacuum prayer, which includes both *inner* and *outer* methods of letting go that which is no longer of value in one's life, to make way for the good one is praying for.

Purification and cleansing of one's thoughts and life is a constant process. You will never get through invoking these various prayers of cleansing. But you will pleasantly discover that each time you use them anew, they unblock the good in your life, and open fresh, new ways to answered prayer!

THE PRAYER OF PROTECTION

— Chapter 5 —

One of the most powerful, yet least known, forms of prayer is the prayer of protection. Through the prayer of protection, you can mentally say "no" to negative experiences and even stop them completely for yourself or others. Though the act of prayer itself protects, definite prayers of protection are even more powerful.

Through prayers of protection, you can dissolve unhappy experiences in which you have gotten involved. You can also help dissolve the negative experiences of others.

The 91st Psalm is one of the most powerful prayers of protection in the Bible. The Psalmist knew how important it was to pray prayers of protection as he guarded his helpless sheep against wild animals, inclement weather and a thousand and one ills. Thus he filled his psalms with protective prayers.

F. L. Rawson, who was a noted engineer and one of England's great scientists, got interested in spiritual healing and became a fine metaphysician soon after the turn of the century. He was a firm believer in prayers of protection for those in war.

He related the story of a British regiment under the command of a Colonel Whittlesey, which served in World War I for more than four years without losing a man. When asked how his regiment was able to serve four years in the thick of battle without a single casualty, Colonel Whittlesey said it was because the officers and men in that regiment memorized and repeated regularly the 91st Psalm, which they called their "Psalm of Protection."

A man once lived through a shipwreck that took the lives of many. When asked how he survived when death came to all those around him, this wise man replied he had prayed over and over the 91st Psalm.

As a spiritual being, made a little lower than the angels (8th Psalm), you can gain dominion of your world, and completely cast out or dissolve negative experiences from your life! The word "protect" means to shield from injury, danger or loss. The prayer of protection helps you do just that, as it shields you against loss, injury, danger, unhappiness and all the unnecessary experiences of life.

A very successful businesswoman has often stated that one of her success secrets is that she sends forth prayers of protection before her into her business world each day. At a time when almost everyone in her com-

pany was being fired by the new owner and was suffering the loss of thousands of dollars in income, this
woman retained her job and went on to work in peace
and harmony with her new boss as she daily used this
protective prayer: "I CLOTHE MYSELF SAFELY ROUND
WITH INFINITE LOVE AND WISDOM."

*If you are already in the midst of unhappy experi-
ences, prayers of protection can get you out of them!*
Immediately after the great fire in San Francisco in
1906, a businessman rose one hour earlier than usual
each morning through those first chaotic months, in
order to meditate upon divine protection, wisdom and
peace. The results were astonishing to his friends and
business acquaintances. Many of them asked him how
he was able to reestablish his office in an orderly working manner when people all around him were still so
unsettled.

As he daily affirmed divine protection, wisdom and
peace, he was able to locate workers easily, systematize
his work, and harmonize his records. All this was done
without experiencing the weariness, confusion, exhaustion and depression that other people thought a necessary part of those hectic days.

In these challenging times, when one hears so much
about war, crime, disease, poverty and a thousand
inharmonies of mind and body, you should constantly
use prayers of protection so that "it will not come nigh
thee." *If some of these inharmonies are already in
your life, prayers of protection can help you to victoriously dissolve them.*

HOW TO BE PROTECTED FROM ROBBERY

A little girl was disappointed when she realized that one of her playmates had taken a doll and cradle from her room. At first she got angry and blamed various friends, planning to complain to her teacher at school about the theft.

But her mother reminded her of the power of speaking a prayer of protection and together they declared, "LOVE ENVIETH NOT," and stated that no one wanted her doll and cradle or anything else that was hers by divine right. That very night the doll and cradle were returned to their usual place in her room.

A woman once saved her house from being robbed, at a time when burglaries were being committed on all sides, as she declared these same words, "LOVE ENVIETH NOT."

There once was a woman in San Francisco who was suddenly approached by two masked men as she descended from a streetcar one dark night. They said to her, "We are short of cash and we want the money in your handbag."

She replied with an affirmation of protection: "GOD IS MY PROTECTION. THERE IS NOTHING IN THE SEEN OR THE UNSEEN THAT CAN HARM ME OR MAKE ME FEARFUL. I AM OVERSHADOWED BY DIVINE LOVE."

One masked man said to the other one, "Take her pocketbook. We've got to have it." As the other man snatched it the robbed woman kindly said, "I hope it will do you some good." Then she added, "We are all God's children. We are all brothers and sisters in the one human family. If one has a need, the other should be glad to divide with him. I hope that money will be a blessing to you."

The two robbers looked at each other helplessly, shook their heads, and returned the pocketbook to the victim, whereupon she bade them, "Good night, boys." As she went on her way, she realized they had never even opened her bag!

At a time when nearly every house in the neighborhood was being robbed, a housewife spent time in nightly meditation, mentally building a wall of protection around her home and that of her next-door neighbor's. She would picture the wall of protection as a brilliant white light about a foot thick, and she would affirm: "WE ARE SURROUNDED BY THE PURE WHITE LIGHT OF THE CHRIST, INTO WHICH NOTHING NEGATIVE CAN PENETRATE AND OUT OF WHICH ONLY GOOD SHALL COME." Her property and that of her next-door neighbor were never touched.

Paul might have been pointing out this protective method to the Romans when he advised: "Let us therefore cast off the works of darkness, and let us put on the armor of light" (Romans 13:12).

PRAYERS OF PROTECTION BRING PEACE, HEALTH AND PLENTY

Prayers of protection work in all departments of life, for health, wealth and happiness. A businessman was very worried about his wife, who fretted over everything. She got very upset at night if he did not arrive home on the dot. They were heavily in debt because of his wife's illness, and this man worked at a distasteful job as a bill collector in an effort to make ends meet. It was very unpleasant work, and life seemed just a series of unhappy experiences for this couple.

One day when his wife was in town shopping, she noticed a sign that read "Silence hour. Come in. You are welcome." The word "silence" interested her, because she was trying to get free from fear and gain peace of mind. Hopefully she attended this noon prayer meeting. The speaker on the platform, with his eyes closed, kept affirming over and over these words of protection: "THERE IS AN INFINITE POWER WITHIN US THAT PROTECTS US FROM ALL HARM."

For an hour, over and over, this speaker declared these words and the audience joined him. Following the use of this prayer, there would be long periods of silence in which the people meditated upon these words of protection.

At the end of this quiet hour, the formerly nervous, high-strung woman felt like a completely reborn person. She realized that most of her fears were groundless; she determined to go home, clean house, prepare a good meal for her husband, and just relax and enjoy life. She vowed to stop worrying about so many little things.

When her husband arrived home for dinner after a trying day of bill-collecting, he could hardly believe the change he saw in his wife. Instead of being distraught that he was late, she was calmly sitting by the fire sewing, while the evening meal remained warm in the oven.

When he asked what had brought about this change, she related the day's events and the great impact that the prayer of protection had made upon her: "THERE IS AN INFINITE POWER WITHIN US THAT PROTECTS US FROM ALL HARM." Amazed, he told her that that very afternoon, one of his customers who had not been able to pay his bill for some time had told him that he, too, had attended that same noon prayer meeting and was using that prayer of protection in faith that he would soon be able to pay up. This couple found as they continued using this protective prayer that it opened the way to a whole new life of peace, health and plenty.

YOUR PROTECTIVE PRAYERS CAN HELP OTHERS

You also have the ability to do protective mental and spiritual work for others, as well as for yourself. *In fact, some of the greatest prayers you can ever pray for other people are prayers of protection.*

A worried widow was concerned about her headstrong teenage son who insisted upon racing his new car. He had met with several accidents in driving and his mother feared for his life, but had been unable to persuade him to stop racing. At a weekly prayer group, the members joined her in using the well-known Unity Prayer of Protection for him: "THE LIGHT OF GOD SURROUNDS YOU. THE LOVE OF GOD ENFOLDS YOU. THE POWER OF GOD PROTECTS YOU. THE PRESENCE OF GOD WATCHES OVER YOU. WHEREVER YOU ARE, GOD IS, AND ALL IS WELL."

The mother then said no more about the forthcoming races but trusted to divine protection. The results were interesting: When her son's car was tested at the "time trials," it was found defective and he was not allowed to race it. Continued prayers of protection helped this energetic teenager begin to mature and develop other interests.

A young businessman was driving across the country to Southern California on a business trip. His mother read in the morning paper of a flood and she immediately spoke words that her son was divinely protected. Later she heard from him saying some local business had interfered with his leaving home when originally planned. By being detained, he had avoided the flooded areas entirely.

One of the humorous stories that Florence Shinn relates in her book *The Power of the Spoken Word*[1] is that of a lady who had seven children. Instead of worrying about them all the time, she casually spoke words of protection for them, and they all grew up safe and sound.

One day a neighbor had rushed in and said, "You had better call your children. They are all climbing up and down trees. They are going to kill themselves." This mother calmly replied, "Oh, they are only playing tree tag. Don't look at them and nothing will happen." She refused to worry about them, and nothing did happen.

If worried mothers of teenage daughters and sons, and worried wives of philandering husbands would fret less and surround their loved ones more with prayers of protection, there would be fewer unwanted pregnancies, less illegitimacy, drug use, and adulterous behavior in their family circles. Through prayers of protection by even one member of the family, true family happiness can be restored for its members. *Replace nagging and name-calling with prayers of protection. The results will astound you!*

People in public life should be surrounded by prayers of protection so that they will not become the subconscious victims of the jealousies and criticisms of others. As pointed out in my book *The Healing Secrets of the Ages,* ill health and even death can result for a person from someone else's "ill" thoughts about him, if he is not protecting himself mentally. Cold, critical, envi-

1. Florence Shinn, *The Power of the Spoken Word* (Marina del Rey, Calif.: DeVorss & Co., 1945).

ous, jealous thoughts directed toward the sufferer can cause everything from overweight to cancer and emotional disturbances.

Pray protectively for yourself: "I AM SURROUNDED BY THE PURE WHITE LIGHT OF THE CHRIST. I AM FREE FROM THE NEGATIVE THOUGHTS OF OTHERS." Declare for other people: "YOU ARE SURROUNDED BY THE PURE WHITE LIGHT OF THE CHRIST. I PRONOUNCE YOU FREE FROM THE NEGATIVE THOUGHTS OF OTHERS."

It is a good practice to begin the day with prayers of protection, both for yourself and others. Upon rising in the morning, entrust the day to God's keeping. Place yourself and your loved ones in His loving care. This attitude will give calmness and strength. If there is any special challenge or troublesome situation that has to be met that day, declare for it, "I RELEASE YOU TO DIVINE PROTECTION. GOD IS IN CHARGE AND ONLY GOOD SHALL COME FROM THIS EXPERIENCE. EVERYONE INVOLVED SHALL BE DIVINELY SATISFIED AND BLESSED."

Remind yourself that God is truly taking care of that which you have given into His charge. This will give you the assurance, conviction and realization that you, your life, and all whom you hold dear are safe and secure in God's loving presence, and you will go forth into your day relaxed and happy.

If you have been harboring thoughts of fear for yourself or for your loved ones or if you have feared storms, accidents, disease, epidemics, war, then prayers of protection will help you release such negative fears. As you go forth to meet your day, you will find yourself denying fear as you continue affirming God's protective presence in each experience. Slippery roads, speeding cars, and all the seeming hazards of modern living will cause you no uneasiness. As you meet each experience you will find yourself releasing it to divine protection.

Through this prayerful, protective outlook on life, you will find yourself guided and blessed with wisdom and good judgment day by day, and you will be brought safely through every experience. *Daily use of prayers of protection can be the secret to successful living in this challenging age!*

PRAYERS OF PROTECTION CAN AFFECT CROPS AND WEATHER

There was a farmer who believed that a "praying man" comes under divine protection in his fields. This man's father had been a successful potato farmer in England. Once his father had united with a number of neighbors in leasing a long strip of land, which was divided so that every farmer had two rows of potato hills. The men bought seed together and plowed and planted at the same time. However, the father was a strong believer in the power of divine protection in the affairs of man. So while planting his seed, he made it a habit to invoke the blessing of the Almighty upon them, for he believed that all his prosperity came through remembering God in his financial affairs.

When the time came to gather the potatoes, the farmers found that a potato disease called "dry rot" had attacked every tuber, causing almost a total loss to each farmer — except this one man. When he turned over the soil in his two long rows of hills, he found that not one potato had been touched. This made a very deep impression upon all the country round, especially since this farmer ascribed his protection to the goodness of God in answering his direct and believing prayer for the perfect yield of his crop.

A protective prayer that has been used by many to

produce good crops is this: "DIVINE ORDER IS ESTABLISHED IN THE ATMOSPHERIC CONDITIONS PRODUCING THE KIND OF WEATHER NEEDED FOR THE EARTH TO BRING FORTH ITS BOUNTIFUL HARVEST."

A woman in Southern California lived in the midst of a large orange grove, which was then in full bearing and promised a fine crop and income that year.

This woman had a neighbor who also owned orange groves and was expecting a good crop, but this neighbor scoffed at the idea of divine protection.

One night freezing temperatures were predicted for early morning. At that time "smudge pots" were used in the groves when there was a danger of frost: smoking pots that warmed the air.

The husbands of both these women were away on business, and there was no one on hand to do the smudging. The woman who did not believe in divine protection spent that night walking the floor wringing her hands. But the woman who believed in divine protection was quiet and calm, and spoke these words of protection: "GOD CAN PROTECT MY GROVE. THE PRESENCE OF GOD IS THERE, AND EVEN NOW FOLDS IT ROUND AND KEEPS IT FROM EVERY HARMFUL THING." She remembered the 91st Psalm and affirmed it over and over. Suddenly she felt that her grove was covered over with a great invisible canvas of protection. With this realization came a sense of peace, so she retired for the night and slept peacefully.

That night the frost came, and every orange grove that had not been smudged was lost — except this woman's. The grove of her unbelieving neighbor was a total loss. Yet this woman who had spoken words of protection for her grove found not one orange damaged! Through prayers of protection her grove had been saved, and an income of thousands of dollars salvaged. Needless to say, her previously scoffing friend never again criticized her belief in divine protection.

A powerful prayer of protection regarding weather conditions for good crops, safe travel, etc., is this: "DIVINE ORDER NOW BLESSES THE EARTH WITH PERFECT WEATHER, AND THE PROPER AMOUNT OF MOISTURE. ORDER, HARMONY AND SAFE CONDITIONS ARE ESTABLISHED AND MAINTAINED."

PROTECTION PRAYERS PUT OUT FIRE

There once was a fierce fire raging out of control in the northern part of the province of Ontario, Canada. The flames had been spreading rapidly for three days, destroying hundreds of homes in their wake, when a homeowner decided to telephone a spiritual counselor in Toronto for prayers of protection.

Within fifteen minutes from the time the spiritual counselor and members of her prayer ministry started speaking words of protection, that fire of three days was completely wiped out as the wind stopped and the whole area was flooded with rain. What was their method that so quickly put out a three-day fire?

The spiritual counselor had spoken directly to the wind: "IN THE NAME OF JESUS CHRIST, I SAY TO YOU: PEACE, BE STILL."

Then to the flames of the fire she had said: "YOU HAVE NO POWER IN YOU TO HURT OR DESTROY ANY GOOD THING. IN THE NAME OF JESUS CHRIST YOU ARE NOW FIN-ISHED. YOU ARE WIPED OUT."

In conclusion she had said, "THE WET BLANKET OF JESUS CHRIST NOW LOWERS AND SPREADS OVER THE WHOLE LAND AND THE FIRE IS OUT. FATHER, I THANK YOU THAT IT IS NOW DONE."

As for the spiritual validity of praying about crops, weather, and atmospheric conditions, the prophet Zechariah advised: "Ask ye of Jehovah rain in the time of the latter rain . . . and He will give them showers of rain, to every one grass in the field" (Zechariah 10:1).

PRAYER CAN PROTECT IN WAR

There is an interesting World War I story that came out of France about the power of protective prayers: A young lieutenant and his eighteen men were cut off from both communications and supplies. The enemy was closing in on them and there seemed no way of escape. This young officer suddenly remembered a letter from his sister, which he had not had time to read. Upon impulse he opened it. She wrote that her prayers were surrounding him and his men with divine protection, and that she had a number of other people praying for their safekeeping.

The lieutenant and his soldiers were haggard and scared, as well as hungry and tired. In his sister's letter she quoted from the Psalms:

> I will say of the Lord, He is my refuge and my fortress. My God in whom I trust. . . . His truth is a shield and buckler. Thou shalt not be afraid for the terror by night, nor for the arrow that flieth by day. Or the pestilence that walketh in the darkness, nor for the destruction that wasteth at noonday. A thousand shall fall at thy side and ten thousands at thy right hand, but it shall not come nigh thee (Psalm 91:2, 4-7).

The young officer read these words, then folded the letter, placing it inside his shirt. No longer fearful, he said to his men, "Keep your chin up. Nothing is going to harm us, because we're being prayed for. If you guys have a prayer in you, I suggest you pitch in and help."

One soldier replied, "The Lord be with us." The others chorused "Amen" solemnly. They had barely finished when the big guns of the enemy tore loose and for five hours there was terrific gunfire. These soldiers were completely helpless. Annihilation seemed inevitable, to all human appearances. In spite of this, none of these soldiers were hit, nor were their quarters in an old house disturbed in any way. It was as though a circle had been drawn around the house and barn that they occupied, though the rest of the village was wiped out.

The young lieutenant later concluded: "Nobody ever again has had to convince me of the power of prayers of protection. It's a potent and dynamic prayer method that works."

YOUR ANGEL-PROTECTORS

The ancients believed that the Angel of God's Presence is a miracle-working presence that is available to every man; that there are angel-protectors all around us who are only too glad to guide and protect us, when called upon to do so. They felt that every person has an angel or higher self.[2]

When challenges arise, say to yourself, "I HAVE NOTHING TO FEAR. MY GUARDIAN ANGEL GOES BEFORE ME,

---

2. The angel-writing method is further described in the author's books *The Dynamic Laws of Healing,* Chapter 11, and *The Prospering Power of Love* (Rev. ed. 1983), Chapters 5 and 6.

MAKING RIGHT MY WAY." Decree this often for others, too. A businesswoman was concerned about having to make an out-of-town buying trip, since she would have to drive two hundred miles in rain and fog accompanied by her sick husband, whom she could not leave at home alone. A friend said, "You have nothing to fear, because I prayed that your guardian angel will be with you."

Upon returning from the buying trip, this businesswoman reported, "I did seem to be accompanied by an angel. As I drove out of town, the sky cleared of fog, the rain stopped, and the sun shone through. There was no more bad weather on the entire trip. The drive lifted my husband's spirits and he suffered no ill effects from it. Financially, this proved to be the most profitable buying trip I have made in a long time."

Two missionaries were passing through a dangerous jungle region where robbers were waiting to attack them. But as the missionaries prayerfully approached, the robbers saw a "third person," much larger than life-size, traveling with them and apparently hovering over them protectively. The presence of this third party, or Angel of Protection, both puzzled and frightened the robbers, so that the missionaries were saved from harm.

ANGELS OF PROSPERITY AND HEALING

The Hebrews of old felt that Raphael was the angel of healing. At times you may wish to decree: "ANGEL OF HEALING, COME FORTH HERE AND NOW." Or you may wish to call on the Angel of Prosperity, or the Angel of Love, Harmony and Marriage in the same way.

Before traveling or going forth into any challenging situation, it is well to affirm: "THE ANGEL OF CALM GOES BEFORE ME, PROTECTING ME FROM ANY NEGATIVE EXPERIENCES" or "THE ANGEL OF GOD'S PRESENCE GOES BEFORE ME AND PREPARES MY WAY." The prophet Malachi might have been speaking of his angel-protector when he said, "Behold, I send my messenger, and he shall prepare the way before me" (Malachi 3:1).

Once when I was going on a six-week lecture trip, I decided to test the angel idea by affirming that the Angel of Prosperity went before me making prosperous and successful my way. When lecturing for business, professional or convention groups, a professional lecture fee is in order, whereas the offerings received when lecturing in churches are often so small they do not pay one's expenses—and this was to be a lecture trip for churches.

However, on this trip, after sending the Prosperity Angel before me, something happened that had never happened before: Along the way people kept privately saying, "I have read your books and have been helped by them. I want to show my appreciation by sharing a special tithe offering with you." The result was that I came home carrying a number of tithe checks as special gifts to me individually, which helped defray costs I had so often had to meet personally. That experience convinced me that there is an Angel of Prosperity.

As for the Angel of Healing, a story came out of England many years ago, appearing in the *London Daily Mirror* and *The Central News Agency,* about a woman who had been ill for five years and was dying from advanced tuberculosis. Doctors had long despaired of saving her, and relatives had gathered round as she stopped breathing and appeared to be gone. Eight minutes later, she suddenly took a deep breath and roused as she said conversationally, "Yes, I am listening. Who is it?" At that moment she saw an angel bending over her who said, "Your sufferings are over. Get up and walk."

When she asked for her robe so that she could walk, it caused a great commotion among her relatives, because she had not walked for months. She then walked into another room and asked for food, though she had not had a solid meal for six months.

As she quickly regained her health, medical tests revealed there was not a trace of the disease left in her body, after five years of intense suffering. Thereafter, she ate well, slept well, and was quite calm and peaceful. Nothing seemed to tire or excite her. The angel had told her that her life was being spared in order that she might help to heal others, so she spent a great deal of time in intercessory prayer for the sick in her village, asking the Angel of Healing to make them whole. Many healings occurred and her life took on new meaning and new satisfaction.

DIVINE PROTECTION IS PROMISED MANKIND

Perhaps of the many promises for divine protection given to mankind, one of the most famous and satisfying was that given in the "Psalm of Protection":

"There shall no evil befall thee. Neither shall any plague come nigh thy dwelling. For he will give his angels charge over thee, to keep thee in *all* thy ways" (91st Psalm).

THE PRAYER OF DECREE

— Chapter 6 —

A businessman quipped, "Of course, I believe in the power of prayer. I pray—every morning—for the stock market to go up!"

Whether he realized it or not, that man was invoking the prayer of decree, though in a rather casual way.

Prayers of decree have been described as "handles of power" and I agree. When you know how to pray affirmatively without fear through prayers of decree, you know how to take hold of "handles of power" which can guide you victoriously through life's experiences.

Many of the blessings of life have not been obtained simply because you have not asked for them affirmatively. Affirmation, or the prayer of decree, releases power into the subconscious mind, where it is freed to go to work and produce positive results. Prayers of decree, especially the type described in Chapter 7, reach the deepest level of the mind, which is the super-conscious, and often release miracle power that is dormant there.

Knowing about the simplicity and power of affirmative prayer gives you a sense of spiritual and emotional security that nothing else does because, once you know how to use prayers of decree, you will never again feel alone or defenseless. You will be armed with spiritual ammunition with which to meet life's challenges and come out "the winner."

Though I had been reared in a church-going family, I never really knew how to pray until I learned about the prayer of decree. Suddenly it was as though I had discovered the greatest treasure on earth, because at last I had something to hold to, to steer me through life's good times and bad. For several decades now, I have been using affirmative prayers for myself and others. I have found that you can literally "blast your way" out of limitation, if you will but speak the word of truth and decree your good regardless of appearances. Prayers of decree can be your "spiritual dynamite" to remove troublesome barriers to your good in all areas of life.

Once after I had served as guest minister at the Unity Temple on the Country Club Plaza in Kansas City, Missouri, the main comment about my lectures was, "Why, she's nothing but a bundle of affirmations!"

If the belief you have previously given to evil were consistently turned to the belief in good for even one hour, it would be sufficient to revolutionize your life! You can begin to revolutionize your life through prayers of affirmative decree, which help you to dwell upon the good in life and call it into expression. Your words

*can dissolve obstacles and remove barriers. Affirmation
seems to be the form of prayer that sets in motion the
whole power of God.*

The word "affirm" means to "make firm," and prayers of affirmation help you to make firm the good in
life. The prayer of affirmation is so simple that it takes
away the feeling of mystery and complexity generally
associated with prayer. Its simplicity dissolves the usual
psychological blocks about prayer being difficult.

The prayer of affirmation has been described as
"scientific prayer," or "spiritual treatment," in modern
times. The Bible is filled with affirmative prayers
which were known then as "decrees." Job described the
simplicity and power of affirmation when he promised:
"Thou shalt decree a thing and it shall be established
unto thee and light shall shine upon thy ways" (Job
22:28). Jesus used the power of decree often to heal and
prosper his followers. The Lord's Prayer, in some trans-
lations such as the Fenton, is a series of affirmations.
The Psalmist loved affirmative prayers and filled his
psalms with them. A good example is the beloved 23rd
Psalm. The creation story of Genesis emphasized the
creative power of decree over and over with the phrase:
"God said 'Let there be . . .' and there was."

*Owing to the vibratory power of words, whatever you
decree—that you release within yourself and your world.
The word "utter" and the word "outer" have the same
root meaning. What you "utter" literally becomes an
"outer" part of your world!*

AFFIRMATIONS PRODUCED THE AUTHOR'S
FIRST BOOK

Study shows that nearly all Bible prayers were spoken in a loud voice. Historians assume this was true because they were usually prayed before a large assembly. However, Biblical prayers were also spoken in a loud voice because the ancients knew about the dynamics of sound: That every spoken word has tremendous power; and that by certain arrangements of words, such as in an affirmative decree, a tremendous vibratory force could be set up in the invisible which profoundly affected substance and produced the specific results decreed.

The power of the spoken word was used for healing long before Bible times. Chanting of affirmative decrees was used in the healing temples of Atlantis, Egypt, Persia, India and Greece to bring again into harmony the vibratory forces in man. In the East, mantra yoga, or salvation through affirmation, has long been practiced.

My first book, *The Dynamic Laws of Prosperity,* got into print as a result of affirmations. During the recession of 1958, by request I taught a class on the spiritual and mental laws of prosperity. The people in my ministry were helped so much by it that they asked me to put the material from that class into a book. Having never written a book, I felt I had neither the time nor talent for such a project and plainly said so.

However, one fine businessman in that prosperity class felt so strongly that I should write such a book that he offered to meet with me for an hour every morning in the prayer room at the church to pray affirmatively about it. At the time we started saying affirmations together, I had neither a book, a title, a publisher, nor any experience for such a task, so it seemed a fantastic prayer project.

Nevertheless, as we began daily to use decrees, the whole format for the book unfolded to me in prayer, even to the chapter headings. As we next prayed for a name for the book, a stockbroker in that prosperity class suggested the appropriate title, *The Dynamic Laws of Prosperity.* Then we needed a publisher. Under the circumstances, it seemed preposterous that I could just "break into print" successfully as an unknown writer. But as we prayed affirmatively, decreeing the God-appointed publisher, an amazing thing happened: A man in the public relations business who had been helped by the class instruction walked into my office one day and said, "Your prosperity class has helped me and my business so much that I want to do something for you. What can I do?"

When I explained my writing project he exclaimed, "I have a friend in New York who is a well-known literary agent. Ordinarily she does not take on unknown writers, but I will ask her about representing you." The result was that I soon had an agent and publisher.

Thus the book, its title and publisher all came after the power of decree was employed. Then, as we affirmed that I would have the time to write the book amid a heavy schedule of church work, somehow the book got written in the middle of the night and at odd moments.

Affirmative prayer did a very thorough job of providing me with all that was needed to launch my books into print. The only "contact" or "influence" I had as an unknown writer was the "contact" or "influence" of affirmative prayer.

The prayer of decree is the only contact or influence you need to get your prayers answered, too!

PRAYER BEGINS WITH WORDS

Perhaps you are asking, "But why does just speaking forth words have spiritual power? Isn't prayer more than just words?" Yes, prayer is more than words, but *prayer begins and ends with words.* As the great religions of the world have always known, the word is God in action. "In the beginning was the Word . . . and the Word was God . . . and without him [the word] was not anything made," explained the mystical John (John 1: 1,3).

The word is dynamic because it creates. Speech is the very breath of God because it creates. Nothing is more alive with power, nothing has more creative power than affirmative words. This is true because words of truth have life, intelligence and substance within them, which are released through decree.

The reason the prayer of affirmation has been used by all civilizations and cultures from the beginning of time until the present is because the great minds down through the ages have known that the word has creative power. Words of truth are sharp as a two-edged sword (Hebrews 4:12) and quickly cut through negation and dissolve it, thereby releasing the omnipresent good.

The Hindu scriptures pointed this out: "If a man speaks or acts with an evil thought, pain follows him. If a man speaks or acts with a pure, affirmative thought, happiness follows him." The Egyptian creation story emphasized the power of affirmative words for creating, just as does our own Genesis story of creation: "It was the Egyptian god who made the world, speaking it into existence. That which flows from his mouth happens, and that which he speaks comes into being." The Greeks said the word is filled with cosmic power. In India, the spoken word of affirmation is considered the greatest power in the world. The Chinese have long believed that words are so powerful that no piece of paper containing written words should ever be destroyed, even when it is no longer of value.

THE POWERFUL RESULTS OF AFFIRMATION

One of the Popes of the early Christian church decided, when he was just a little boy working out in the fields, that he would become Pope of Rome. As he affirmed it, he released the most dynamic, creative power in existence which then shaped circumstances and events that caused this farm boy to become Pope, as he had said he would.

A little Greek boy, the son of a fruit dealer, affirmed as a child that he would make his life worth something, and he rose from the son of that fruit dealer to the friend of Socrates.

One of the early Roman poets had been a baker's son. Then he lifted his thoughts so high in affirming the good that he became a great poet and playwright, and the Roman people showed him the same reverence they paid their emperors. There was also a Greek slave who was sickly and badly deformed but, through affirmation, was lifted from the bondage of slavery to a cruel master and became the honored companion of lords and princes.

The Scottish philosopher Thomas Carlyle said that if you will proclaim your freedom from bondage, that bondage will vanish, and you can lay hold of some new good each moment. He promised that through affirmation you will notice you are becoming free from sickness. As you continue affirming the good, you will see how much better you get along with people who previously seemed difficult. As you persist in affirmation, you will notice that your disposition improves. You will soon be more prosperous. Many things that previously hurt you will change in your favor. *Affirmative prayer is among the simplest, yet most powerful ways offered to mankind to change and improve life!* This is why people in all ages have known and used the prayer of decree.

WHY VERBAL PRAYER IS NECESSARY

Many people become frustrated in prayer because they try to pray silently, through meditation and the silence (as described in Part II), when they have not first relaxed, dissolved their fears through prayers of cleansing, and then spoken affirmative decrees. If you do not learn how to pray the prayer of relaxation, the prayer of cleansing, and the prayer of affirmation first, you cannot possibly skip these and learn how to pray the deeper, more spiritual types of prayer such as meditation, silence and realization.

Sincere seekers on the pathway of prayer sometimes become discouraged because they try to master the deeper phases of prayer when they have not yet learned the first basic types of prayer, which include the spoken word of decree. They are trying to get their master's decree in prayer when they have not even learned the kindergarten phases of prayer!

Do not underestimate the prayer of relaxation, the prayer of cleansing, and the prayer of decree. These verbal phases of prayer must come *first* in your prayer development. Verbal prayers (such as prayers of cleansing and decree) break up all kinds of negative thought patterns in your conscious and subconscious mind. It is these old, negative thought patterns of inharmony, unforgiveness, resentment, fear, jealousy, envy and condemnation, that have kept your good from you, and that have kept you from being able to pray in a deeper way.

Spoken words clear away these old negative thought patterns that have crowded your mind and emotions. When these are cleared away, and your mind and emotions have been cleansed, then you can pray in deeper ways through meditation, the silence and realization.

But there are layers and layers of thought in your mind and emotions that have got to be cleansed first, before you can pray more deeply. The ancients believed that man had seven thicknesses or layers of the mind that constantly needed to be cleansed of negative thought in order for his prayers to be answered.

Verbal words, verbal prayers, which often seem more mental than spiritual, are the one thing that can clear these layers and layers of negative thought out of man's mental and emotional strata. It is only after such a mental and emotional cleansing that man's prayers get answered.

THE PSYCHOLOGICAL VALUE OF VERBAL PRAYER

Psychology, as well as religion, agrees that you should use a lot of verbal prayer. Psychology insists that the spoken word has more suggestive power, is more likely to reach and improve the deeper psychic levels of the mind, than mere inarticulate thought. Psychology insists that verbal prayer is very powerful for cleansing and improving the mind and emotions, *because psychology has found that your centers of speech are closely connected with your mental life. Thus, when you speak forth good words, you improve your mental life.*

The early Christians, as well as the Christian mystics of the Middle Ages who were such experts in prayer, insisted that some vocal prayer should enter into the daily life of even the most contemplative, silent souls. They said that the use of higher degrees of prayer did not and should not ever mean giving up or totally abandoning the lower phases of prayer such as verbal prayer.

The early Christian mystics pointed out again and again in their writings, from their own profound prayer experiences, that health in your spiritual life, like that in your mental life, depends to a great extent on variety in your prayer life.

Therefore, you should never be afraid of variety in prayer. You should never feel that you are losing ground spiritually if you again find yourself using verbal prayers after having learned how to practice meditation and the silence.

St. Teresa, St. John of the Cross, and others insisted that for your own spiritual balance you must constantly go back to affirmative prayer. There are "prayer neurotics" who insist they have "outgrown" verbal prayer; they feel that the prayer of decree is too "simple" for them. Invariably such warped individuals become confused, upset, unbalanced as they try to be "advanced," practicing only meditation and the silence. Often they end up having psychic obsessions and other psychological problems, because they did not balance their prayer life.

Through variety in prayer, you open your soul to

fresh new areas of spiritual development. The great
Christian specialists in prayer always began with vocal
prayer, the most direct and powerful instrument of sug-
gestion, which tuned up the psychic levels of the soul.
They then proceeded to meditation, the silence and
the deeper levels of prayer. Verbal prayer is all powerful in the beginning of your prayer development, and
later on, too! You never outgrow the verbal prayer of
decree.

*There is one theory that for every fifteen minutes of
spiritual study, there should be five minutes of affirmation to balance it.* Study helps you know *about* the
truth. Affirmation helps you to release it.

VERBAL PRAYER BRINGS QUICK FINANCIAL HELP

*Anyone can pray, anyone can get results, who dares
to pray the prayer of decree! This is true because prayer
power is centralized at the root of the tongue.* "Death
and life are in the power of the tongue," explained
Solomon in the Proverbs (Proverbs 18:21).

Because prayer power is centralized at the root of the
tongue, the ancients believed that the word must be
tried and tasted before it became powerful, that it is
not enough just to say an affirmation, but that you
should "eat" your decrees. Take a bite—a few words—
then chew, assimilate, think about them. Swallow,
digest, meditate upon them. The word then becomes
flesh and dwells among you as results (John 1:14).

To speak forth words of life, health, prosperity, success, happiness and peace over and over releases an
atomic vibration. Those words then move in the ethers
to form the conditions described right out of the omnipresent intelligence of the universe! Affirmation is a

simple, easy method of prayer. It is a handle of power which anyone can take hold of and then produce satisfying results.

A shopkeeper in England suddenly found herself in dire financial circumstances. She owed a considerable amount of money on her business property. The mortgagor of this property had passed away and his heirs wanted to settle the estate. They notified her that she must pay off her indebtedness or be sold out. She wished to retain her property, but did not have the money to meet their demands.

Realizing that prayers of affirmation "make firm" one's good, she began affirming: "ALL FINANCIAL DOORS ARE NOW OPEN TO ME. ALL FINANCIAL CHANNELS ARE NOW FREE TO ME. DIVINE SUBSTANCE NOW APPROPRIATELY MANIFESTS FOR ME."

As she continued in affirmative prayer, "at the eleventh hour" a stranger walked into her shop. While he browsed through the merchandise, they chatted. Their conversation revealed that he was a bank manager. Although her own bank had refused her a loan, this bank manager offered the services of his bank to cover her financial needs. Thus the right financial door opened, but only after she decreed it—verbally and definitely.

Speak forth your prayers of decree verbally into the ethers at regular daily intervals. As you do, your spoken affirmative words move on the substance of the universe, set up an atomic vibration, form your good into definite results and manifest it visibly for you. *You literally release atomic energy through spoken decrees of good.*

Phillips Brooks once said, "Prayer is not the beseeching of a reluctant God, but the opening of ourselves to God's willingness." Affirmative prayer helps you to do just that: Open your mind and heart to God's willingness to shower you with infinite blessings!

Emerson described God as a "vast affirmation," and he described prayer as "God in man pronouncing His works good." A powerful prayer technique is to affirm for *every* experience in life—positive or negative—"I PRONOUNCE THIS GOOD."

POWERFUL TYPES OF AFFIRMATION

Though all my books are filled with prayers of decree, see *The Dynamic Laws of Prosperity* for specific prosperity decrees; *The Dynamic Laws of Healing* for specific healing decrees; and *The Prospering Power of Love* for human relations decrees. Over the years I have observed that there are certain types of affirmative prayers that seem the most powerful for getting results:

FIRST: THE PRAYER OF TALKING DIRECTLY TO GOD

You may be amazed how quickly your prayers will be answered when you treat God as a loving Father and speak directly to Him. For instance, talk to God about the good things you want in life. Robert Collier has described this simple process in his book, *Riches within Your Reach.*

> Start with what you have, and suggest to Him each day that you are getting stronger, healthier, richer, happier. Talk to Him as a rich and loving Father, describing the improvements you would like to see in

your affairs, the finer body you have in your mind's eye, the more important work you should be doing, the lovelier home, the richer rewards. Talk them over for ten minutes each day when you are alone with Him. You will be amazed at how readily He will help you to carry out your suggestions. Don't worry about *how* He is to bring about the conditions you desire. Just talk to Him confidently, serenely, happily—and then leave the rest to Him.[1]

The person who faithfully prays in this way is certain to succeed, because he is attuning himself to the most successful force in the universe. This method of prayer is a simple way of fulfilling the promise of Jesus: "All things whatsoever ye shall ask in prayer, believing, ye shall receive" (Matthew 21:22).

Many people have not employed the power of prayer because they have the erroneous idea that it is wrong to pray for *things*. Jesus did not mean that praying for things was the only form of prayer, or even the highest form of prayer, when He made this promise. But He knew that if you first pray for things, you will learn the power of prayer as a means of communing with God and His goodness.

It is right and just that you should pray for things if you need them. You are living in a rich God-created universe that desires to fulfill all your needs. Among Biblical figures who prayed for definite things and got them were Abraham, Asa, Daniel, David, Elijah, Joshua, Moses, Nehemiah, Samson, and Solomon. On a number of occasions Jesus prayed for things and they manifested.

When you are in doubt about whether you should

---

1. Robert Collier, *Riches within Your Reach* (Tarrytown, N.Y.: Robert Collier Publications, Inc., 1947).

pray for a certain thing or not, ask yourself three questions:

First, is it spiritually legal? Would getting it hurt anyone else? Would getting it be good for all concerned? There is a saying, "The good of one is the good of all."

Second, do you really want what you are asking for —to the extent that you are willing to accept the responsibility that having it will bring? New good always brings new responsibilities and challenges.

Third, are you willing, if necessary, to give up something you now have to make way for the good you want which would replace it? Emerson said that for everything you gain, you lose something.

You never go wrong, when praying for things, to pray for "divine results."

SECOND: THE PRAYER OF ASKING

At times man is inclined to decide personally what he wants, then formulate an affirmation to get it, and through use of that decree, try to force God to give him his desires. Struggle and strife often result. Delay, disappointment, barriers and obstacles may stop the answer.

However, the "prayer of asking" simply asks God for what you want, knowing you do not have to try to force Him to give it to you, because it was God in you wanting it for you that gave you the desire in the first place! You cannot ask for anything that has not already been given you on the invisible plane. The simple prayer of asking wipes out time and space between you and the receiving. Often just saying, "THIS OR SOMETHING

BETTER, FATHER. LET THINE UNLIMITED GOOD APPEAR,"
is all that is needed to get results—either the result you
had in mind or a far better one.

Remind yourself often that if it were not God's good
will for you to experience fulfillment of the deep desires
of your heart, you would not desire them in the first
place. Selfish, human, limited, surface desires do not
last. They soon pass away, whereas the deep desires of
the soul quietly persist, seeking fulfillment.

The word "desire" means "from the Father." If God
did not want you to be happy and successful, you could
not possibly achieve happiness and success no matter
what you did, no matter how hard you tried. Regardless of how much you might strain and press toward
success, you would fail if God did not want you to
succeed!

A housewife once related how just by asking God for
what she wanted, her needs were met in an incredible
way:

> One summer day I had to drive from Graham to
> Tyler, Texas, and I had only $15 in cash, which was
> enough for the trip since I planned to return the same
> day. I started at 4 A.M. in order to be there at 9 A.M.
> My husband had been in Tyler for several days and
> planned to return home with me, but he, too, was out
> of funds. We had a fairly new car with which we had
> had no trouble, but on the return trip from Tyler back
> to Graham before we had eaten lunch, the car stopped
> running. We gave a man $1 to get it started. He then
> pushed us to a station, worked on it some more, and
> after finally getting it running, charged us $2.50 more.
> At this point, we were left with only $9 (having used
> a portion on the earlier trip that morning) to buy gas
> to drive two hundred and twenty miles home.
>
> After we drove about ten miles the car stopped

again. This time we were near a garage, so the mechanic there got it started. By then it was 6 P.M. and we were only thirty miles from where we had started four hours previously. We were tired and hungry, but felt we should drive a while and stop for coffee, since we did not have enough money to spare for a meal.

About 5 miles from the garage, the car stopped again in a desolate area. Since we had done all we knew to do, we pushed the car off the road and decided to spend the night there. My husband walked up the road looking for water for us before we retired for the night.

I had been praying all day but things looked hopeless. Worse still, my son was ill in Graham and I was concerned about him. The sky turned black, became stormy and it looked like rain. During the long wait, I kept wondering why my prayers had not been answered that day. Then suddenly I remembered having read an incredible story about two ladies who had a flat tire and no spare. *So they closed their eyes and asked God for a tire and kept affirming that God had a tire for their car.* All of a sudden they heard a lot of noise and opened their eyes to see a tire rolling down the street, until it hit their car. It was the right size and they used it! Its origin remained a mystery. They were never able to discover just where it came from.

I decided if God could do that for them, He could fix our car. *So I got busy praying, asking God to repair our car and get us home safely,* when a lady and her husband stopped their car and asked, "Lady, can we help you?" Before I could answer, her husband raised the hood and with the use of a flashlight in the dark, looked at the engine. She said to me, "Don't worry, honey, my husband is a good mechanic and he will know what to do." By the time my own husband returned with some water, this man had our car running again. He and his wife invited us home with them, where he had parts and equipment to make further repairs.

On the way to their house, my husband and I wondered how we would pay for the parts, but I told my husband how I had been asking for help when they arrived and that we should just go in faith, knowing somehow our prayer was being answered. Upon arriving at their home, the wife fixed sandwiches and coffee and asked me to telephone my son in Graham. The phone call revealed that other relatives had come in and were caring for him, so everything was fine.

After our car had been repaired that night, we had a good night's rest and a nice visit the next day with these people. They explained there was no charge for the car's parts and repairs because they made it a habit to help people in trouble. It seems they always prayed and asked God to guide them to those who needed help, and this mechanic had repaired many a car for a stranded traveler. Often this mechanic had prayed, "Now, God, You know everything. Should I help these people?" He felt this was one way he could tithe his time and talent. No wonder that couple was so happy and prosperous. *This experience proved to me the power of asking God directly for what you need and want. When I finally got around to that, my prayer was immediately answered!*

THIRD: THE PRAYER OF ASKING
FOR DIRECT GUIDANCE

If you don't know what to ask for directly, pray for guidance. Say, "Father, what is the truth about this? Make the truth about this situation so plain and clear that I cannot mistake it." The people of the Bible called it "asking for a sign." They often asked God to give them a sign of answered prayer. You can, too!

Decades ago, while driving from Missouri to my home state of North Carolina, I had stopped at a little rustic restaurant in the mountains of Tennessee. As I sat there tired and travel-worn, awaiting my meal, I kept wondering whether I should accept the offer of a job in Birmingham, Alabama.

For some time I quietly pondered all aspects of the situation. There was a time element involved that made it necessary for me to make a quick decision. There were grave financial considerations involved that would affect both myself and my small son. Logically it didn't seem the thing to do, but intuitively I felt strongly that it could be a great step in the right direction.

Finally the thought came, "You do not have to try to figure this out or reason it through on the human level. Just ask for direct guidance, ask for a sign, and then release the matter. You will be shown what to do." And so I quietly thought, "Father, what is the truth about this job? Am I to take it or not? Make your guidance so clear that I cannot mistake it." As I then relaxed and again became aware of my immediate surroundings, I suddenly realized that background music was playing in the distance and the tune being played was "Stars Fell on Alabama." That song led me into the ministry and to my first church—in Alabama.

Many times a day I pray aloud, "Father, help me," or "Father, what is the truth about this?" or "Father, let there be light," or "Father, what do you want me to do about this?" or "Father, what is the answer, what is Your guidance, what is your good in this situation?" or "Father, if you love me, show me!" How often these direct prayers for guidance produce quick results.

You should make it a practice to ask God about anything that concerns you—from finding a parking place on a crowded street to obtaining an appointment with a busy person whom you suddenly need to see. The

17th-century French mystic Brother Lawrence called this prayer method "practicing the presence of God." It certainly makes for a delightful, easier way of life.

When Solomon asked for wisdom to discern between the true and the false, he was asking for guidance, and that guidance brought him all the blessings of life, plus. Paul pointed out the power of simply asking for guidance and wisdom to meet life victoriously when he promised, "If any of you lacks wisdom, let him ask for God . . . and it shall be given him" (James 1:5).

In her book, *The Healing Gifts of the Spirit,*[2] Agnes Sanford emphasized the importance of praying for guidance or wisdom. She relates how she was once unable to be a channel of healing to someone, because she did not first ask for the wisdom to know what to do. The decree for guidance or wisdom will always lead you to answered prayer, if you but follow that guidance when it comes. George Fox, founder of the Quakers, wrote in his *Journal* about becoming blind when he did not follow definite guidance that came to him. Later, when he realized his mistake and made the effort to carry through on that guidance, his sight returned.

FOURTH: THE DECREE OF DIVINE INTELLIGENCE

Along with asking for guidance and wisdom from a universal Father, it is sometimes wise to call on the "divine intelligence" within you. Psychologist William James has written that, along with a conscious mind and subconscious mind, man also has a deeper level of

---

2. Agnes Sanford, *The Healing Gifts of the Spirit* (Philadelphia: J. B. Lippincott Co., 1966).

the mind in which resides infinite intelligence that longs to work for and through man. By recognizing it, giving it your attention, and decreeing it, you release this superwisdom within. Decrees of "divine intelligence" tap it.

If you will invite this divine intelligence to solve any problem that concerns you, it will. "THERE IS AN AN-SWER. DIVINE INTELLIGENCE NOW SHOWS ME THE PERFECT ANSWER TO THIS PROBLEM. I RELAX, LET GO, AND LET IT."

A schoolteacher decreed that divine intelligence was showing her what to write in a contest, so that she might win a trip to Europe. The ideas came in a rush and she quickly submitted her entry, which won her the trip. Later she could not remember what she had written—only that it came quickly after she asked. Infinite intelligence is just teeming with right answers and solutions and awaits your attention. Your act of asking opens the channel for receiving that intelligence, as it did for this schoolteacher.

When things in your life seem to be going wrong, affirm that "divine intelligence" is showing you the way. When business or other conditions appear to have reached a deadlock, affirm that divine intelligence is producing a solution. When you seem up against a stone wall and there is apparently no way out, affirm that divine intelligence is producing perfect results. For health, financial or human relations problems affirm, "I RELEASE YOU TO THE PERFECT OUTWORKING OF DIVINE INTELLIGENCE NOW." Set aside a little time every day and meditate upon divine intelligence at work in every phase of your life. This is the way to bring vast improvement quickly![3]

3. Also see Chapter 8 on "The Wisdom Concept" in the author's book *Open Your Mind to Prosperity*.

FIFTH: THE DECREE OF DIVINE LOVE

After the more contemplative phases of decree, such as asking for guidance and then being flexible to receive it, you now come to actual affirmation or decree, a positive method of assertion Walt Whitman described when he said, "I no longer ask for good fortune; I *am* good fortune."

One of the most powerful prayers of decree is that one which decrees divine love. To affirm "divine love" releases the all-powerful "love vibration" which then moves among people and events, producing harmonious results.

Why are decrees of divine love so powerful? Certain words used persistently release mind power to mold and transform conditions in the mind, body and affairs of man. The words "divine love" dissolve hate, resistance, opposition, anger, and other mental and physical frictions that cause pain in mind, body and relationships. *Through decrees on "divine love," you can free yourself from all kinds of problems!*

I have often heard a housewife say, "Divine love always has and always will work any miracle that needs working!" And "work it" she has. For every problem — physical, emotional, financial, and in family relationships — she uses decrees of divine love. The result is that she has put a son through college on "divine love." She obtains part-time jobs when she needs extra money by affirming divine love. She even came into a sizable inheritance after affirming divine love. And she has healed a number of physical ailments, her own and others', after affirming divine love. Some of her favorite decrees are these: "DIVINE LOVE IS DOING ITS PERFECT WORK IN THIS SITUATION NOW FOR THE GOOD OF ALL CONCERNED." "DIVINE LOVE GOES BEFORE ME AND PREPARES

THE WAY." "I CALL ON DIVINE LOVE TO WORK ANY MIRA-
CLE THAT NEEDS WORKING IN THIS EXPERIENCE."

A businessman had become bored with his job,
having gone to the top in it, and wanted a change into
something better, but did now know which way to
turn to find it since he was "at the top" professionally.
Remembering the power of love to work any miracle
that needs working, he began affirming, "I INVITE THE
POWERFUL, LOVING ACTION OF GOD INTO MY LIFE NOW.
I INVITE THE POWERFUL, LOVING ACTION OF GOD TO PRO-
VIDE ME WITH MY OWN TRUE PLACE IN LIFE NOW."

Shortly, the president of the board of trustees of a
large, successful corporation "got the idea" to fly across
country and invite this man to head up the corporation, whose previous director had retired. The change
of scene, pace and work proved to be the perfect
answer to this previously bored executive's prayer.
Love *had* worked its miracle!

A widower with six children was assured by all his
relatives and friends that he would never find a woman
who would love him enough to marry him *and* his six
"live wires." It seemed for several years that they were
right, until he remembered to call on divine love. The
affirmation he used was, "THE IRRESISTIBLE LOVE OF
JESUS CHRIST NOW DRAWS MY OWN TRUE WIFE TO ME."
He soon met a beautiful lonely widow, who was only
too glad to have a new family to care for. They were
married and it proved a happy union.[4]

----

4. Also see chapters on Divine Love in the author's books
*Open Your Mind to Prosperity, The Dynamic Laws of Prosperity,
The Dynamic Laws of Healing, The Healing Secrets of the Ages,*
and *The Prospering Power of Love.*

SIXTH: THE DECREE THAT GOD'S WILL
IS BEING DONE

Contrary to what most people think, to declare that God's will is being done in a situation is the highest form of prayer and always brings the perfect, happy, satisfying answer for all involved. This is true because God is a God of love, so His will for His children is always the highest and best. A heavenly Father would hardly want less for His children than would an earthly father.

Among the most powerful prayers of decree you can ever pray, ones which often bring almost instantaneously happy surprises are: "NOT MY WILL BUT THINE BE DONE, FATHER." "I WILLINGLY DO THE GOOD WILL OF GOD IN THIS SITUATION." "GOD WORKS IN ME TO WILL AND TO DO WHATSOEVER HE WISHES DONE, AND GOD'S GOOD WILL CANNOT FAIL!" "GOD WORKS IN THIS SITUATION TO WILL AND TO DO WHATSOEVER HE WISHES DONE AND GOD CANNOT FAIL!" "I CALL ON GOD'S WILL TO DO ITS PERFECT WORK IN THIS SITUATION NOW FOR THE GOOD OF ALL CONCERNED."

Jesus said, "My Father worketh . . . and I work" (John 5:17). When you affirm "God's will" you unconsciously cast the burden of the problem on the Highest Power of the universe, which is then free to resolve it in the highest and best way. Miracles happen when people dare to affirm God's will in their lives.

I once visited in Hollywood with television and movie actress Mala Powers, whose mother was a minister friend of mine. Beautiful Miss Powers related how in 1951, after returning from a USO Christmas show in Korea, she came down with flu in Hawaii. There she was given an antibiotic to which her system proved allergic. After she returned to California, it was discovered that this drug had destroyed the bone marrow, and her system stopped making new blood cells. It also dissolved the blood cells that fight off disease. Her condition developed into complete anemia which, at that time, medical science could not cure. Most people with this malady died from hemorrhaging.

Finally, in a Los Angeles hospital with her mother, Silent Unity and her minister, Dr. Ernest Wilson, all praying with her, she realized a death sentence was hanging over her, so she prayed, "Father, if You want me to live, tell me what to do. If You want me to die, tell me what You want me to do before I go. Not my will, but Thine be done." With that prayer came an instant inner feeling that she would live, but that she had to contribute to her own recovery in terms of cheerfulness and inner peace, and by patiently believing she would be healed whether it seemed so or not.

In the weeks and months of slow recovery that followed, she often used an affirmation that Dr. Wilson had given her: "WITHOUT HASTE, WITHOUT DELAY, IN PERFECT WAYS AND UNDER DIVINE GRACE, MY HEALING MANIFESTS." Though she was in and out of bed for nine months, the day came when her doctors assured her she would get well. Though she continued medication and treatment for some time, and tired easily for a couple of years after going back into movie-making, she now leads a normal life. The turning point from death to life came after she had prayed, "NOT MY WILL BUT THINE BE DONE." God's will is always supreme good for His beloved children. When you invoke His will, you also invoke His miracle goodness for you![5]

5. Also see the chapter on Will in the author's book *The Healing Secrets of the Ages.*

SEVENTH: DECREES OF THE DIVINE PLAN

There is a divine plan for your life. The divine plan is the sublime plan and includes health, wealth, happiness and perfect self-expression. As you affirm "the divine plan," you begin to draw to yourself the ideas, opportunities, events and people that are meant to be a part of your divine plan.[6]

I know a man who was suffering the agony of an unhappy marriage and of divorce problems, indebtedness, confusion, and a limited income; but who went from that to a brand-new job filled with self-expression at double his previous income, a happy second marriage, peace of mind, increased health, and a whole new lease on life, after he began affirming the divine plan at an apparently hopeless period in his life. This transformation came within just six short months! Some of the prayers he used were these:

"I NOW RELEASE EVERYTHING AND EVERYBODY THAT IS NO LONGER A PART OF THE DIVINE PLAN OF MY LIFE. EVERYTHING AND EVERYBODY THAT IS NOT A PART OF THE DIVINE PLAN OF MY LIFE NOW RELEASES ME. I NOW LET GO AND LET GOD UNFOLD THE DIVINE PLAN OF MY LIFE. I AM NOW ATTUNED TO THE DIVINE PLAN OF MY LIFE. I NOW COOPERATE WITH THE DIVINE PLAN OF MY LIFE. CHRIST IN ME NOW MANIFESTS THE DIVINE PLAN OF MY LIFE IN LOVE AND IN PEACE. I NOW RECOGNIZE, ACCEPT AND FOLLOW THE DIVINE PLAN OF MY LIFE AS IT IS REVEALED TO ME STEP BY STEP. I REJOICE IN THE DIVINE PLAN WHICH IS THE SUBLIME PLAN AND INCLUDES HEALTH, WEALTH, HAPPINESS AND PERFECT SELF-EXPRESSION FOR ME NOW."

6. See chapter on the Divine Plan in the author's book *Open Your Mind to Prosperity*.

EIGHTH: THE DECREE OF DIVINE ORDER

Order is heaven's first law, and by affirming "divine order" you somehow release a heavenly form of order to manifest in your mind, body and affairs. *Answered prayer inevitably manifests when things get into divine order.*[7]

One of the most powerful and popular affirmations which thousands have used to produce health, increased prosperity and personal happiness is: "DIVINE ORDER IS NOW ESTABLISHED IN MY MIND, BODY AND AFFAIRS BY THE POWER OF THE INDWELLING CHRIST. DIVINE ORDER IS NOW ESTABLISHED AND MAINTAINED." I have found that by placing this affirmation near my telephone, only necessary calls come through. My telephone becomes courteously silent.

Recently a housewife wrote of needing to leave her home to shop but the gas company had notified her the gas would be turned off that day for certain repairs to be made in that neighborhood. She was required to be at home when the gas man arrived and departed. Instead of fuming about the timing in the situation, she sat down quietly in her living room and affirmed "divine order" for the situation. At that moment the gas worker arrived and promptly completed his task and reconnected the gas service. Thus, no time and energy were wasted in needless fretting.

Another housewife often gets through a long waiting line at the check-out counter at the military commissary where she shops by affirming "divine order," while housewives all around her gripe and complain about

---

7. See chapter on Order in the author's book *The Healing Secrets of the Ages.*

the long wait in their lines. In another instance, this housewife literally stopped a freight train with the affirmation of "divine order" when she was late to an appointment and needed to get around the shifting train cars quickly.

In situations where time elements are involved, it is also good to affirm "divine timing," or "perfect timing."

NINTH: THE DECREE OF BLESSING

The people of the Bible felt that the act of blessing carried great power to accomplish good. To bless means "to make holy or whole by spoken words," "to ask divine favor for some situation or person," "to wish a person or situation well," "to make happy or prosperous," "to gladden, glorify, praise." When you bless a troublesome person, financial situation, or bodily ailment, you are praising the good in it. You are invoking divine favor, which is then released to produce happy results for you.

Bless a thing and it will bless you. Curse it and it will curse you. To bless means to bring forth good in a situation or personality, whether there seems any good to be brought forth or not! How often you have condemned, criticized, or cursed a situation and only brought forth more problems and unhappy experiences from it, whereas if you had dared to take the opposite view and had blessed the situation, something good would have come from it.[8]

A doctor's wife recently wrote me the sad story of

_____

8. Also see Chapter 2 of the author's book *The Prosperity Secrets of the Ages.*

her life: How she had worked hard to help her husband through medical school; then more hard work to help get him established in his practice. Finally overwork and anxiety brought on her own bad health, after which her husband began having an affair with one of his patients.

Later he had a series of serious health problems and finally had to give up his practice, after which his wife went back to work, though she was not well physically. But she closed her letter by saying, "In spite of all our problems and a lifetime filled with hurt, disappointment and pain, I have begun using the practice of blessing, instead of cursing, our situation. As I have begun blessing my husband, these experiences, and our life together for the good that is in it, new blessings have begun to appear. The prayer of blessing is starting to work! For the first time in years, I have hope of a better life unfolding for us."

TENTH: THE PRAYER OF FAITH

One of the most powerful forms of affirmative prayer is the decree of faith. Jesus promised, "All things, whatsoever ye shall ask in prayer, believing, ye shall receive" (Matthew 21:22). "According to your faith be it done unto you" (Matthew 9:29).

The psychologist William James emphasized the power of faith to make things right: "Our belief at the beginning of a doubtful undertaking is the *one thing* that assures the successful outcome of our venture." Dr. Smiley Blanton, the noted psychiatrist, found that in dealing with people and helping them resolve their

problems, *everything hinged on their faith.* Those people who did not have faith in anything — God, themselves, their business, family, the world — never got very
far until they changed their beliefs and began to declare they did have faith.[9]

If you have had a life of disappointment, how do
you begin to believe in the goodness of God, man, the
world? By decreeing it anyway! *Faith can be developed
as the result of many affirmations.* Charles Fillmore
has scientifically explained the potency of faith to produce practical results in your life: "Just as the electric
current precipitates certain metals in an acid solution,
so faith stirs into action the electrons of man's brain
and, acting concurrently with the spiritual ethers, these
electrons hasten nature and produce quickly what
ordinarily requires months of seedtime and harvest."

Thus, instead of complaining that you do not have
enough faith to improve your life, begin decreeing
that you do have faith; this act will hasten the power
of faith in people and events and will produce quickly
for you what ordinarily would require months or years!

A little old lady who ran a boarding house had
always had trouble trying to collect the rent from her
boarders. Then she learned of the amazing power of
decrees of faith and began to affirm: "I HAVE FAITH IN
GOD. I HAVE FAITH IN PEOPLE. I HAVE FAITH IN THINGS."
Quickly her boarders responded by paying their rent
on time or even ahead of time, as good things began to
happen to them. Not only did their attitudes and
financial situations improve, but the word of faith

---

9. See chapter on Faith in the author's book *The Healing
Secrets of the Ages.*

seemed to affect the cook, maid, janitor and everyone else connected with this boarding house. All were prospered and blessed as the landlady continued privately decreeing her faith in God, man, things. She proved that by affirming for another what you desire for yourself, both of you are blessed!

You can invoke the miracle prayer of faith by affirming often: "I DARE TO BELIEVE THAT ALL THINGS HAVE WORKED TOGETHER FOR GOOD IN MY LIFE. I DARE TO BELIEVE THAT ALL THINGS ARE NOW WORKING TOGETHER FOR GOOD IN MY LIFE. I DARE TO BELIEVE THAT ALL THINGS SHALL WORK TOGETHER FOR GOOD IN MY LIFE (or in this situation or person)."

ELEVENTH: THE PRAYER OF
DIVINE RESTORATION

One of the least-known prayers of decree, yet one of the most important for getting your prayers answered, is the decree of divine restoration. If you could trace back in memory the cause of the unhappy experiences in your life, you would doubtless discover that most of those experiences in ill health, financial difficulties, and human relations problems were related to a belief in "loss." The thought of "loss" lodged in the conscious and subconscious phases of the mind causes many—perhaps most—of life's difficulties. The word "loss" literally means "destruction," and the thought of loss held in the mind is a destructive one.

However, a belief in present and future fulfillment blots out previous beliefs in loss as promised by the prophet Joel: "I will restore to you the years the locust hath eaten" (Joel 2:25). You can establish such a belief in present and future fulfillment by affirming "divine restoration." The word "restore" means "to make beautiful again." As you affirm "divine restoration" of your good, so much can be added to the present that it seems even to fill the emptiness of the past. In the process, whatever has been taken from you is then divinely restored. Always there is a balancing, restoring power for good at work in every person and in every experience of apparent loss. Instead of trying to force your good, affirm that it is now divinely restored in God's own time and way and it will still appear. Affirm often: "I CALL ON THE POWER OF DIVINE RESTORATION. MY GOOD OF PAST AND PRESENT IS DIVINELY RESTORED TO ME NOW. THIS IS A TIME OF DIVINE FULFILLMENT. I GIVE THANKS FOR DIVINE RESTORATION IN MIND, BODY, FINANCIAL AFFAIRS AND IN ALL MY RELATIONSHIPS NOW."[10]

WRITE OUT YOUR DECREES

Along with speaking forth your prayers of decree into the ethers every day from at least five to fifteen minutes, another dynamic method for getting your prayers answered is *to write* out your decrees. I have a prayer notebook in which I daily write out affirmations about all that concerns me or that I wish to accomplish that day. It is amazing in checking back later to see how often my prayers are answered, after I write out my affirmations.

By writing down your decrees and reading them over

10. See also Chapter 5 of the author's book *The Prosperity Secrets of the Ages,* and Chapter 10 of her book *Open Your Mind to Prosperity.*

at intervals, both aloud and silently, you help fasten your mind on what you want. As one woman recently wrote me, "When I begin to feel depression coming on, I write down affirmations until I feel a sense of peace. This seems to be the turning point from negative feelings into a time of hope and renewed faith that good will come."

Another prayerful person who has gotten fine results from affirmations writes out her decrees in the form of a letter to God, saying "Dear God, grant this or endow that." An age-old prayer method is to write your affirmation of healing, prosperity, happiness and then to wear it secretly on some part of your body, or to carry it with you in your personal effects until it has manifested the answer you seek. Also, quietly putting your affirmative decrees in your Bible is a literal method of releasing them to their perfect outworking in your life.

PRAYERS OF DECREE IN SUMMARY

Use often the various types of decree herein described: (1) talking directly to God; (2) the decree of asking; (3) the decree of guidance; (4) the decree of divine intelligence; (5) the decree of divine love; (6) the decree that God's will is being done; (7) the decree of the divine plan; (8) the decree of divine order; (9) the decree of blessing; (10) the decree of faith, and (11) the decree of divine restoration.

Now proceed quickly to Chapter 7 and learn of the advanced prayer of decree that can produce miracles for you!

PART II

ADVANCED METHODS OF PRAYER
That Can Bring Dynamic Results
to You!

Introduction . . . .

LIFE'S GREATEST SUCCESS SECRET

An interviewer asked me, "From your perspective of spending several decades, first in the workplace, then as a minister, what is the most important thing you have learned? What is life's greatest success secret?"

More recently my sister, who lives three thousand miles away, paid me a rare visit in my desert home. She is now a retired schoolteacher with her children educated and settled and her husband nearing retirement. It was the first time in several decades that we had had the time to span the miles and years, and get caught up on all the things sisters talk about.

After visiting in my home, learning something of my global work, and enjoying some of the mystic glamour of this tropical desert area, my sister seemed genuinely puzzled. She finally asked, "How has all this happened to you? How have you managed to become a minister, found churches, write books, and lecture far and wide? How have you managed to overcome the trauma of death of loved ones, raise your son alone, even take care of family members in their twilight years—all in the midst of a heavy work schedule, and while leading the semblance of a normal life? After all, we grew up together, knowing the same people and attending the same schools."

To both that interviewer and to my sister the answer was the same: "The dynamics of prayer is life's greatest success power. Without it I could not have survived, much less later thrived."

A simplistic answer? Hardly! The contents of this entire book is contained in that answer.

Although I have written books on prosperity, healing, love and other inspirational subjects, when those books are closely studied, one quickly discovers that what I was writing most about in all of them was prayer: ways to pray so as to experience love, prosperity, healing, guidance and inspiration. A book reviewer once commented on one of my healing books, "It's nothing but a book on prayer." He meant that comment as a criticism, but I took it as a compliment. In the final analysis, the practice of prayer *is* the ultimate secret to success on all levels of life.

NOT JUST FOR MINISTERS

People sometimes regard prayer as a dull subject. Yet just the opposite is true: It's the people who do *not* pray who lead dull, colorless, problem-filled, failure-prone lives.

So often when people have tried to tell me their problems, I have asked, "And what prayers are you using for that situation?"

"*Prayer?*" they would often respond blankly, even incredulously.

You may be thinking, "Well, what can one expect from ministers? Naturally they're going to equate everything in life to prayer. That's their job."

Not necessarily. I don't like to admit it, but some of the most problem-prone people I've met—though they were in the minority—were ministers who had not slowed down long enough to learn about and use the power of prayer effectively. One said, "I don't have time to pray." I replied, "You don't have time *not* to!"

Prayer is not just something to be used by desperate old people and innocent little children. Prayer is the only assured method I've found to get your problems solved and to help your dreams come true. To by-pass daily prayer is to by-pass life's greatest blessings—needlessly.

Furthermore, I stumbled upon the power of prayer —not in a seminary or church—but while still working in the business world long before I became a minister. Then and there in the marketplace, I discovered that prayer is the "hot line" to successful living, no matter what your station in life.

FROM THE SUBLIME TO THE RIDICULOUS

I had an experience while serving in my first ministry several decades ago that proved to me the result-getting power of prayer—even when one finds oneself in a ridiculous situation. I had just had lunch at a downtown

restaurant with a friend, when we both suddenly realized how late it was, and that we had other appointments. This friend, whom I had picked up in my car
on the way to lunch, suggested that I take a shortcut
back to our destinations. This proposed shortcut led
us down a back street with which I was unfamiliar.

As I turned a narrow corner into this street, the rear
fender of my car became lodged against the high
cement side of the alley into which I had attempted
to turn. Not only did my car now block off any passage-
way through the alley for other drivers, but I could not
move my car backward or forward without tearing
off the rear fender.

Of course I felt foolish, finding myself in such a
predicament. Without a word to my passenger who had
suggested this "shortcut," I leaned against the steering
wheel, closed my eyes and said aloud, "Dear God, if
I ever needed You, I need you now." I then tried to
dwell upon the goodness of God and His ever-present
help, even in a back alley, and I found myself affirming
weakly, "WHEREVER I AM, GOOD THINGS HAPPEN."

A sense of relief swept over me, and I somehow felt
my prayer would be answered. I opened my eyes just
in time to see a workman appear from across the alley
and view with great interest the close proximity of my
car's rear fender to that high cement curbing.

Alighting from the car I tried to sound positive:
"You *can* help me, can't you?"

The workman quietly replied, "I think so," and then
quickly disappeared across the alley into a large warehouse, from which he soon re-emerged followed by
several husky laborers.

Without a word about "women drivers" and trying
not to look amused, these men simply placed their

weight against the car fender, while one of them backed the car away from that high cement curb. They did so quickly and easily, without so much as scratching the fender!

One by one the men then quickly disappeared back into the warehouse across the street. To the one who had master-minded this rescue operation I said, "I want to thank you for being the answer to my prayers."

"Prayer?" he replied, perplexed.

Then looking past me to my beautiful passenger, who was a well-known model and television personality, he commented dryly, "Prayer had nothing to do with it. If you ladies had been big, fat, baldheaded old men, you would still be sitting on that curb!"

With that firing shot he walked away convinced that looks, and not prayer, had been the attraction. But I knew better.

Not only in the sublime, but also in the ridiculous experiences of life, the dynamics of prayer can work.

HOW PRAYERS FOR THIS BOOK WERE ANSWERED

When I first developed this manuscript a couple of decades ago, I wanted it to be a "prayer classic" — the kind of book I had searched the bookshelves for. Yet my New York editors considered it necessary to cut out several chapters on the advanced methods of prayer. I felt those cuts made the book incomplete, so I "lost my cool" on the last subject anyone should get upset about: prayer. Then I remembered to pray and release the matter to a loving Father.

Now, at last, I am free to add those chapters in Part II and to retitle the book as originally planned: *The*

Dynamic Laws of Prayer. Even though the title my original publisher insisted upon, *Pray and Grow Rich,* reached and helped many people, I felt my own suggested title more completely described what this book is all about. I trust that this expanded, updated, retitled version will have an even greater impact on those who read it.

One reader wrote, "Of all the books you've written, your prayer book is my favorite. I think everything you've ever learned is in that book!"

FROM NOTHING TO EVERYTHING

Compared to where I was when I took up the practice of prayer—and what my life is now—prayer has taken me from nothing to everything. Yet readers of this book have "topped" my own improved life experiences many times over:

A businessman studied this book and inherited a fortune. A California housewife's marriage was miraculously saved as she studied the original edition of this book. Her husband, who had deserted her a year earlier, suddenly reappeared, asked for a reconciliation and they now begin their day studying this book together, using some of its prayer methods. A medical doctor in Texas gives a copy of this book to each of his patients. A psychiatrist in Florida has used this book with mental patients in group therapy with good results. My files are bulging with success-testimonials.

INCREASED GOOD FOR YOU

It is with pleasure that I now share with you in Part II those deleted chapters on the advanced methods of prayer not previously included in the earlier edition of this book (Chapters 9 and 12). They were developed, placed in my files, and moved through a series of apartments and several homes, from the great Southwest to the "desert empire" of Southern California. Their inclusion in this updated edition is evidence to me of how prayer can work to surmount thousands of miles and several decades. It's but further proof that the dynamics of prayer is life's greatest success secret.

As you proceed now to study these advanced methods described in Part II, may you find prayer to be life's greatest success power for you too!

THE AUTHOR

THE PRAYER FOR MIRACLES

— Chapter 7 —

Miracles can happen to you when you learn how to use miracle decrees, because all things are possible to the Christ consciousness!

In *Part I,* you learned about the prayer of relaxation, the prayer of cleansing, and various forms of the prayer of decree. In most instances, these forms of prayer will work through the conscious and subconscious phases of your mind, clearing the way for answered prayer.

But at times none of the foregoing prayer methods will seem sufficient to meet your need, perhaps because you are ready to go more deeply into your prayer consciousness and tap another level of prayer power; or perhaps it may be because the situation about which you pray simply needs a miracle! It needs a release of power and energy more dynamic than the usual prayer methods seem to activate. You may be in desperate need of prayers that can break through the negative thought stratum that has bound you, raising you to higher levels of consciousness quickly, where you automatically are in tune with divine energy that floods you with power. Nothing less will suffice.

There *is* such a prayer of decree to help you do this! It is the miracle decree—the prayer that releases the Christ consciousness. The ancient people who in their aloneness with nature knew the great secrets of the universe felt there was such a miracle consciousness, which when discovered and tapped, could perform miracles in an instant. I believe it!

In fact, I know there *is* such a miracle consciousness which you can tap and release. The first time I discovered it, I did so almost by chance and did not realize at the time what I had tapped. After I had prayed for guidance about an impossible situation over which I had struggled for some time, helplessly trying to extricate myself, the answer came in the mail from a stranger who seemed to have tuned in on my cry for help through the ethers, and responded by sending me an affirmation that literally released miracle power, as I faithfully decreed it. Had I not gotten that prayer when I did and used it to break out of a negative thought stratum in which I seemed helplessly bound by the limited thinking of others, I could not have remained on this earth plane much longer. The prayer of decree that literally saved my life was: "THE MIRACLE-WORKING POWER OF JESUS CHRIST IS RELEASED IN THIS SITUATION NOW FOR THE GOOD OF ALL CONCERNED."

At still another low level in my life when I was again bound by the negations of others from which I seemed helpless to free myself, I kept praying for the right thoughts and decrees that would loose me. The prayer that came that time through inner realizations, and which I then wrote down and decreed over and over in a loud voice as I walked the floor, was: "OF MYSELF I CANNOT DO IT, BUT JESUS CHRIST CAN AND IS PERFORMING MIRACLES IN MY MIND, BODY AND AFFAIRS HERE AND NOW!" I literally heard the ethers crack as I said that miracle-decree, and I could feel my whole consciousness lifted out of an inharmonious thought stratum that had previously almost smothered me. My outer life quickly changed and I found myself hundreds of miles away among new people in new congenial circumstances amid fulfilling work. I had had my miracle!

Sometimes in prayer we try to improve or change the people or situations for which we pray, and we become quite frustrated when they do not seem to respond to our prayers. God gave spiritual man the power of choice to improve or not improve as he wishes. In using the miracle prayer, instead of trying to change and improve others, you cast the burden of your prayers on that higher power of the Christ consciousness. *If the people and situations for whom you pray do not wish to respond to your prayers, their lack of cooperation does not stop your prayers from being answered!* The Christ consciousness simply helps you overcome or, literally, "come up over" those troublesome people and situations and be freed from them as you rise into higher levels of understanding, which invariably lift you into higher levels of living as well.

PSYCHOLOGISTS KNOW ABOUT MIRACLE
CONSCIOUSNESS

Two noted psychologists were the Swiss doctor Carl Jung and the father of American psychology, William James. Both of these great men felt that man has not only a conscious mind with which he daily thinks, and a subconscious mind which contains his memory and emotions, but that man also has a deeper third level of the mind — a superconscious level — in which resides an infinite intelligence that longs to work for and through both the conscious and subconscious phases of the mind to produce fantastic good in man's life quickly.

What these psychologists referred to as superconsciousness, divine intelligence, or Divine Mind in man, is referred to by some as "the Christ Mind" or "the Christ consciousness." The reason some people refer to this deeper superconscious level of the mind as the Christ Mind or Christ consciousness is because Jesus Christ seemed to know about and to have developed this miracle level of the mind, as is reflected in His life, ministry and teachings.

He knew that all men had the same Christ Mind within them, too, which, when activated, could produce apparent miracles for them in an instant. He promised His followers (and His promise applies to His modern-day followers as well): "He that believeth on me, the works that I do shall he do also; and greater works than these shall he do; because I go unto the Father" (John 14:12).

Jesus Christ broke through the negative thought stratum into which the race had fallen. By breaking through this mental negation, He opened the way for all who

become attuned to His power to do likewise. Through
the consciousness Jesus generated through His life,
crucifixion and resurrection, He aimed to arouse this
superconscious miracle power in man and reconnect
mankind with it, to get man back into an Eden state
of mind where all things are possible, when man was
given dominion over the earth and himself.

That Jesus did reestablish this miracle consciousness
which man can tune in on is evident in the miracle
power that the early Christians had. They knew how
to tune in on the Christ consciousness Jesus had activated, and for several centuries they were able to do the
works Jesus had done. This miracle consciousness was
finally suppressed by human personality that took over
the church and ruled it for many centuries. Even so,
there are many isolated instances of great souls down
through the centuries who became aware of and quietly
developed and used the miracle consciousness that
Jesus had aroused.

ANCIENTS KNEW HOW TO ACTIVATE
SPIRITUAL CONSCIOUSNESS

People of all ages have searched for the superconsciousness within them and a method by which to
activate it. Long before the time of Jesus, the ancient
people had various secret names they intoned for activating this superconsciousness—this third deeper level
of the mind—that is filled with miracle power in man.
They felt that if you would hold to that secret word,
motto or text in time of trial, it would rearrange your
affairs, bringing you through to victory.

The priests of the Old Testament aroused this superconscious level of divine power in man by affirming

and meditating, over and over, upon the words "I AM" or "I AM THAT I AM." Moses had learned this secret text from the Egyptians who had written it upon the walls of every Egyptian Temple.[1]

The Hebrews of the Old Testament released the superconscious power within them by meditating upon the name "JEHOVAH," which they considered so powerful that they did not speak it. They meditated upon variations of this name for producing specific results: "JEHOVAH-JIREH" for prosperity; "JEHOVAH-RAPHA" for healing; "JEHOVAH-SHALOM" for peace of mind; "JEHOVAH-NISSI" for protection; "JEHOVAH-TSIDKENU" for claiming God's goodness; and "JEHOVAH-RA-AH" for guidance and love.

The word "Jehovah" is the Old Testament Hebrew word which corresponds to the New Testament Greek word "Christ." *By taking the word "Jehovah," meditating upon it, affirming it, you can feel its quickening power through and through. The word "Jehovah" (Christ) is charged with spiritual power far above and beyond any other word in the human language.*

The people of Asia have long intoned "AUM" or "OM" as the name for God and the release of His goodness. An Eastern mystic releases the superconscious power within him by drawing in his breath and decreeing aloud the word "AUM" or "OM" twelve times. He then holds his breath and repeats the name twenty-four times, until he finally feels the God power which he has released within and around him. The Brahmins attained to great power and wisdom by meditating much on the word "OM."

---

1. See Chapter 9 of the author's book *The Dynamic Laws of Healing*.

HOW TO ACTIVATE YOUR MIRACLE
CONSCIOUSNESS

Scientists tell us there are no miracles—only the working of higher laws not commonly understood. Actually there seems to be one set of natural laws for the physical world and another set for the invisible world of mind and spirit. The laws of mind and spirit are so much stronger that they can be used to neutralize, accentuate or even reverse the laws of the physical world, when necessary. Jesus knew the higher laws of mind and spirit and used them to perform apparent miracles. By developing the Christ consciousness you also have access to that same miracle power!

The Christ consciousness is the miracle state of mind that contains within it the power to resurrect a miracle where previously there had seemed only crucifying problems. The Christ consciousness or superconsciousness within you is filled with peace, power, plenty. To bring it alive within you is to bring alive your spiritual nature, your divinity, the divine level of the mind, through which all things are possible. If people the world over knew about this indwelling Christ consciousness and would bother to develop it, mankind's problems could all be solved effortlessly, through the peaceful, powerful, efficient Christ Mind within mankind.

When you invoke the Christ consciousness, you step up your prayer power. You speed up results!

How do you develop your miracle Christ consciousness, the divine intelligence, the Divine Mind within you? By first realizing that you have this third superconscious level of the mind within. You then develop it by recognizing this Christ consciousness, meditating upon it, and decreeing its presence and power at work in and through you. Decrees about "the Christ Mind," "the Christ within," "Jesus Christ," and "Christ Jesus" help you do this. Writing and picturing it also helps. The following simple techniques will help you develop and invoke the Christ consciousness and release its miracle power in your life!

THE CHRIST MIND

You can develop the third level of the mind, the superconsciousness, by dwelling upon the Christ Mind within you. Psychologists tell us that we develop whatever we concentrate our attention upon. If you turn your attention upon your innate divinity, the Christ Mind within you, you will begin to arouse it, in the same way as did Paul and the apostles.

Paul knew about the Christ Mind which had spoken to him out of the ethers as he trod the road to Damascus, and which converted him from a tireless persecutor of the Christians to a tireless advocate of Christianity. Paul developed the Christ Mind to such an extent that he became known as the "versatile genius" of the early Christian church, teaching, preaching, traveling, writing and organizing churches throughout the ancient world. In his writings, he talked constantly to the early Christians about the Christ Mind, once explaining: "It is no longer I that live, but Christ liveth in me" (Galatians 2:20).

In my book *The Healing Secrets of the Ages,* I have explained the ancient secret teaching which shows the Christ Mind in man as located at the crown of the head, while the conscious mind functions, metaphysically, from the front forehead, and the subconscious functions from the heart and abdominal region. The interesting thing about the Christ Mind being located in the crown of the head is that it not only activates the superconscious wisdom found in that area but, when activated, it "opens up" — or has access to — the universal wisdom, universal good, which flows into the mind and body of man through the crown of the head.

You can greatly accelerate the awakening of the Christ Mind within you by using affirmations that identify you with the Christ, such as Paul's "CHRIST LIVETH IN ME."

Recognizing and calling on the Christ Mind through repeated affirmations seems especially powerful in the face of "it can't be done" or "impossible" situations. Calling on the Christ Mind seems to release a super-wisdom, a tremendous executive power, that sweeps through people and situations to do what "can't be done," to make the "impossible" possible.

The once popular motion picture made from Lloyd C. Douglas's book, *The Robe,* was based on the seamless robe that Jesus Christ wore. For this movie, a woman and her daughter were given the task of weaving a robe that would be an authentic reproduction of the one worn by Jesus. They spent several months gathering special yarns, dyes, and other special materials and then began to weave the robe. It took them thirty-six hours. When the robe was completed, the woman and her daughter were to deliver it to the studio within sixteen hours, in order to meet the producer's deadline. But suddenly they discovered that the daughter's three-year-old son had snipped a piece of cloth from the beautiful seamless robe.

It seemed impossible that they could weave another

seamless robe in just sixteen hours when it had taken thirty-six to weave the original one, but when these women got quiet and prayed, affirming that the Christ Mind was showing them what to do, their guidance was to do just that: weave another robe. As they affirmed that the Christ Mind was expressing perfectly through them, they finished their second seamless robe in only nine hours, or one-third the time taken on the original robe!

One might first reason that these women were able to cut their time on the second robe by as much as 75 percent because they had had practice in weaving the first one. But later these women tried twice to weave another seamless robe. Each time the task took them the full thirty-six hours! Thus, the Christ Mind, in their hour of need, had helped them do the impossible: weave in nine hours a robe that ordinarily took thirty-six!

When faced with "impossible" situations, call on the Christ Mind to help you by affirming: "THE CHRIST MIND IS PRODUCING PERFECT RESULTS HERE AND NOW," or "I AM LETTING THE CHRIST MIND THINK THROUGH ME NOW. I KNOW. I REMEMBER. I UNDERSTAND. I EXPRESS THE TRUTH PERFECTLY IN THIS SITUATION NOW." The tide will turn.

Early in my writing career I spent time daily affirming, "I AM THE CHRIST MIND. I AM. I AM. I AM. I AM LETTING THE CHRIST MIND EXPRESS PERFECTLY THROUGH ME NOW. I AM. I AM. I AM." It was as though a superwisdom was turned on within me, and I have been writing prolifically ever since! Thus, for increased knowledge, wisdom, understanding and for proficient results call on the Christ Mind.

Consciously centering your mind with repeated affirmations of the Christ Mind opens a channel of intelligent communication within the silent forces at the depths of your being, where new thoughts, words, wisdom, flow forth, and where entirely new sources of power are developed in you.

THE POWER IN THE NAME "JESUS CHRIST"

The early Christians felt that the phrase, "JESUS CHRIST," was the lost word of power for which the priests had been searching for centuries, and that this "lost word of power" could produce miracles in an instant.

One has only to experiment in prayer with the name "JESUS CHRIST" to discover that speaking that name over and over sets up a mighty vibration, which sets into activity forces that bring results! *No person's name ever stood for such colossal achievement as the name "JESUS CHRIST."* There is power for colossal achievement along all lines—healing, prosperity, human relations—for those who call upon that name today.

Decree over and over that "JESUS CHRIST IS PRODUCING PERFECT RESULTS IN EVERY PHASE OF MY LIFE NOW," and you will be amazed at the good things that will happen to you! The words "JESUS CHRIST" are among the most powerful upon which you can ever concentrate! To meditate and affirm often the words "JESUS CHRIST" can transform your mind, body, affairs, relationships —any situation that confronts or troubles you.

If you desire to demonstrate over problems that no amount of prayer, spiritual study, medical treatment, psychiatric therapy or just plain hard work have been

*able to overcome—then begin dwelling upon the name
"JESUS CHRIST," asking His help. As you daily affirm His
name and call on His power, you will make a "major
breakthrough" out of the negative thought stratum
that had bound you, into higher levels of consciousness. There you will be free to claim your good.*

Jesus taught his followers to pray "in His name" since
He was their mighty intercessor with God. The early
Christians performed mighty works by praying "in His
name." "Whatsoever ye shall ask in my name, that
will I do" (John 14:13), was the promise and it still
applies today.

You can ask "in His name" in several ways.

CALL ON THE NAME "JESUS CHRIST"

Calling on the name "JESUS CHRIST" invokes a miracle
consciousness.

A schoolteacher climbed a high ladder to take down
holiday decorations in her schoolroom. Suddenly she
lost her balance and fell head first onto a hard cement
floor. On the way down she decreed, "JESUS CHRIST,
JESUS CHRIST," and then blacked out. Her doctors were
puzzled because, from the position in which her head
hit that hard cement floor, she should have had permanent brain injuries, but she only had temporary bruises
and imbalance in her equilibrium, which cleared up
quickly as she continued daily decreeing that Jesus
Christ was healing her. She proved that there is miracle
healing power in this name.

Though we have often felt that the name "JESUS
CHRIST" had spiritual and mystical meaning, we have
usually doubted that it had practical, result-getting

meaning in our daily affairs; and through this false assumption, we have missed many of life's daily blessings.

One of the most powerful decrees you can ever pray amid daily situations of inharmony, friction, tension, or troublesome people is the decree: "JESUS CHRIST IS HERE PRODUCING PERFECT RESULTS." In fact, it is better to prove the Christ presence in little ways in your mundane work-a-day world first, and then "graduate" into proving the power of this name in more profound ways later.

WRITE OUT JESUS CHRIST PRAYERS

I recall once sitting in my church study in the early morning hours, planning my work for that day and realizing there were not enough people to help with it. I needed a fast typist to do some special work that suddenly had to be done. I wrote out on a card this decree: "JESUS CHRIST NOW MANIFESTS THE PERFECT TYPIST TO PRODUCE THIS WORK QUICKLY."

Within an hour a lady came—not walking but running—into the church. Breathlessly she said, "Here I am. While having breakfast I suddenly had the feeling you needed me. What shall I do?"

"Can you type?" I asked, trying to sound casual.

"Can I! Before marrying my husband, I was his secretary and I am one of the fastest typists in this town." Within a few hours she had done—as a gift, free of charge—what would have taken the average typist several days to accomplish.

In another instance, I had tried for weeks to get a repairman to my apartment to make repairs. He had promised to come, but had not. In prayer about it again one night, I found myself decreeing, "JESUS CHRIST IS HERE, MAKING THE PERFECT REPAIRS NOW." Later I wrote down these words in my book of affirmations. A great sense of peace descended over me and I released the matter. The next morning quite early there was a knock at the door, and the repairman quickly did what he had promised to do weeks before!

PICTURE JESUS CHRIST

Along with calling on the name "JESUS CHRIST" verbally, and also writing out the name "JESUS CHRIST," you can invoke a miracle consciousness by picturing Him at work in any situation that bothers you, producing perfect results. There is tremendous power in picturing Jesus Christ working for you and with you.

A successful businessman was once asked the secret of his success after his business suddenly boomed. He explained that when he had a business engagement, he would always spend a few minutes beforehand quietly thinking about that appointment, declaring that Jesus Christ was in charge, producing the perfect results for all concerned. He would then behold the Christ in the people with whom he was to do business. He said he would try literally to see the Christ in the faces of the people involved.

This man said that by picturing the Christ at work in the situation and people, his success had been so marked that he had noticed that always a splendid congeniality was felt between himself and his clients. By picturing the Christ at work among them, deep friendships developed, and even with new clients it seemed they had always known each other, even at their first business meeting.

If you will spend ten minutes a day picturing the Christ at work in your business affairs, family affairs, in other situations, or in personalities that concern you for whom you are praying, the results will amaze, delight and surprise you!

In my book *The Dynamic Laws of Prosperity* is the story of a housewife who restored her marriage by picturing Jesus Christ in the midst of it:

> For twenty years I had as my husband a man whom I had grown to hate. I am married now to the same husband, a man who is daily more companionable and loving. Strive as I did, I could not bring myself to love the first man. He seemed dead spiritually, was very selfish, crude, hard, careless, and unloving. It seemed like a hopeless situation, and how I longed for freedom. I had little ones to care for and was unable to work to keep them, so of course, I had to stay with my husband. Then I began to think of the presence and power of Jesus Christ, and decided to prayerfully picture Jesus Christ at work in the situation.
>
> Daily I began to think of Jesus Christ going to work with my husband. I saw the Christ working in and through him, working with him, even having lunch with him. I visualized my husband and the Christ with him coming home to his wife and family to well-cooked meals, happy and contented.
>
> Now, as a result of this, although I am still married to the same man, he is truly a different man, one who is kind, thoughtful, happy, and loving. At this very moment, he is sitting out on the back veranda happily whistling 'Rock of Ages' as he mends his leather jacket in preparation for work tomorrow. *Through prayerfully bringing Jesus Christ into the situation, I have found the companionship I longed for.* Truly I love

my husband. I feel like telling other wives who continually quarrel with and condemn their husbands just to try my prescription.

If it is hard for you mentally to behold the Christ at work in a situation, then get a literal picture of Jesus Christ and look at it. Anytime you feel upset, confused, disturbed, look at a picture of Jesus Christ, and you will begin to feel peaceful and powerful again.

Genevieve Parkhurst, the wife of a minister, once described in her book, *Healing and Wholeness Are Yours,*[2] how she was healed of cancer of the breast by doing this. One afternoon she was propped up in bed reading a book by Dr. Frank Laubach, which contained beautiful pictures of the Christ. She was studying these pictures carefully when suddenly the physical presence of Jesus Christ appeared in the room before her. He was standing in profile with His face lifted—just as in the picture she had been studying. She held her breath while the visible form of Jesus Christ turned slowly and looked straight at her. As she studied this visible form of Jesus Christ, suddenly a sharp stab of pain went through her diseased, painful breast. The pain ran down her arm and out at the elbow. She quickly discovered that the lump was gone.

BEHOLD THE CHRIST IN OTHERS

This is a marvelous way to pray for other people. Instead of dwelling upon their problems and failures, behold the Christ at work in them and within their

---

2. Genevieve Parkhurst, *Healing and Wholeness Are Yours* (St. Paul: Macalester Park Publishing Company, 1957).

problems. A retired businessman found himself in a deep state of depression. His wife had passed on, leaving him very lonely, as well as sick in mind and body. He had a small house in Florida and a grove of mango trees, which were his only means of livelihood. In his depression he had let them deteriorate, so he was suffering from financial problems, too.

Feeling he could no longer go on, one day he went out to the end of the pier and jumped in the bay, expecting to "end it all." But instead of being the end, this experience opened the way to a wonderful new beginning. This man was rescued by an early-morning swimmer, who then went on to breathe new life and hope into him. The neighbor fixed up this depressed man's house and run-down grove, teaching him how to love, praise and bless his house, fruit, health and life.

Later when the man was leading a prosperous, healthy, contented life again he explained, "My neighbor is responsible for all this because he knew how to behold the Christ in me when I was at my lowest ebb, and by seeing the Christ in me, he wrought a miracle."

You may expect and look for wonderful things to happen whenever you behold Jesus Christ at work in a situation or person. You may even expect the "impossible"!

I like to take little pictures of the Christ and place them around the picture of anyone for whom I am praying. I like to write out any situation that I am concerned about, then around the written words describing that situation, paste pictures of the Christ. This helps me literally to behold the Christ in people and situations that I am concerned about, and it works.

When anyone gives you a "hard time," take his picture or his name, and place it on a sheet of paper. Around the name or picture place pictures of Jesus Christ. You will be amazed at the results that come, sometimes slowly but other times quickly. Sallman's famous picture of the Christ has been reproduced in small pictures and is ideal for placing on your prayer list.

HOW TO BEHOLD THE CHRIST IN YOURSELF

Also, don't forget to behold the Christ in yourself! Once when I had prayed and prayed about a difficult situation, apparently to no avail, the "still, small voice" within me whispered quietly, "Why don't you behold the Christ in yourself, as well as in this situation? Pray for yourself for a change!" I did so by calling my name often and affirming, "CATHERINE PONDER, I BEHOLD THE CHRIST IN YOU. I BEHOLD THE CHRIST AT WORK IN YOUR LIFE, PRODUCING PERFECT RESULTS." I also placed a picture of Jesus Christ near my own picture and viewed the two together often. These acts proved to be the turning point toward answered prayer in that particular situation.

It is also good when you have prayed for yourself, apparently to no avail, to just release yourself to the "Christ within," to cast the whole burden of answered prayer on the Christ within you. This often brings the right results quickly. A series of affirmations such as the following can help you to do this:

"MY LIFE CANNOT BE LIMITED! CHRIST IN ME IS MY FREEING POWER."

"CHRIST IN ME IS MY FORGIVING POWER. CHRIST IN ME IS MY RELEASING POWER."

"CHRIST IN ME NOW FREES ME FROM ALL ATTACH-
MENTS TO PEOPLE, PLACES OR THINGS OF THE PAST
OR PRESENT."

"CHRIST IN ME IS MY HEALING POWER. CHRIST IN
ME NOW RAISES ME UP TO PERFECT HEALTH."

"CHRIST IN ME IS MY PROSPERING POWER. CHRIST
IN ME IS ALWAYS WORTHY."

"THROUGH THE CHRIST WITHIN, I GIVE OF MY
BEST AND I RECEIVE ONLY THE BEST IN RETURN."

"CHRIST IN ME NOW REVEALS ANY BLOCK TO BE
REMOVED MENTALLY OR EMOTIONALLY, SO THAT I
AM RECEPTIVE TO ALL HEALTH, WEALTH AND HAP-
PINESS."

"CHRIST IN ME NOW GUIDES ME INTO MY TRUE
PLACE IN LIFE WITH THE TRUE PEOPLE, AND I RE-
JOICE!"

"CHRIST IN ME IS PRODUCING PERFECT RESULTS IN
EVERY PHASE OF MY LIFE NOW AND ALL IS WELL.
I RELAX, LET GO AND LET HIM!"

"I RELEASE MY LIFE (THIS SITUATION, THIS PER-
SON) TO THE PERFECT OUT-WORKING OF THE CHRIST
CONSCIOUSNESS NOW."

HOW INVITING THE CHRIST WITHIN
HEALS ONE

Paul pointed out that this "Christ in you" is your
hope of glory (Colossians 1:27). He said this is the mystery that has been hidden for generations. The word
"Christ" means "anointed one." It describes your spiritual nature. When you use words or affirmations that
identify you with the Christ, you awaken, arouse, bring
back to life the Christ child, the Christ within you.

Sometimes it is good to talk directly to this Christ nature within yourself. It is wise to invite the Christ within you to heal, harmonize, guide, prosper or bless you. *The Christ within you awaits your attention and recognition. The Christ within you is very polite. It waits to be asked, invited or noticed. But when it is, how quickly it responds! Just as you awaken a child by calling his name, you awaken the Christ child within you by calling His name.*

During World War I, an American soldier was badly gassed on the battlefields of Europe and was expected to die. For months he lay in an Army hospital, near death, and was finally given three months to live.

As he lay near death in that hospital, he began to remember that at the age of twelve he had met a spiritual healer who had been an Essene. (Jesus may have studied with the mystical Essenes.) For one year this man had received instruction from the Essene healer, after which he had studied many other phases of Truth.

Now, with death hovering over him, he remembered a great healing secret he had learned at the age of twelve, about the Christ being within him. He said to himself, "Within me lives One who has overcome death, so what have I fear?"

Then he began to talk to this living presence and power within himself: "Forgive me, Friend and Lover of my soul, for being so long unaware of Your presence within me. I cast the whole burden of this body upon Your love and I go free to perfect health now." Not only did the man recover, but he lived to become an outstanding spiritual healer of the 1920's and '30's.

This man later said, "Regarding the effect upon your practical business life, this technique of inviting

the Christ within to participate in it is as potent and
effective as it is in healing the body. There is a great
adventure awaiting you—the greatest adventure any
human being can have! It is in seeking, finding, arous-
ing, and activating the previously hidden Christ within!"

HOW TO INVOKE THE PEACE OF JESUS CHRIST

One of the most powerful ways to invoke the miracle
consciousness is to affirm "the peace of Jesus Christ."

A prayerless person usually repels his good by his
repelling vibrations. He scares away his good with a
sense of rush, worry, force or agitation, whereas a prayerful person attracts his good by his quiet, peaceful,
powerful vibrations. A prayerful person is magnetic to
his good and unconsciously draws it to him. A tranquillity of bearing, a facial and bodily repose, are usually observed in those whose inner lives are enriched
through prayer. Prayer quiets your mind, body, emotions, vibrations. In that peaceful, prayerful state of
mind, you unconsciously draw your good to you.

If prayer has not had this effect on you, perhaps it
is because you should deliberately invite it by affirming
"the peace of Jesus Christ."

When you battle life, people and circumstances,
your soul gets twisted out of shape. Decrees of "peace"
take away your spirit of fuss and give you a gentleness
of pace. If there is one experience which marks true
prayer, it is the deep peace which it brings to the soul.
Decrees of peace slow you down to your good and give
you a gentleness of pace that really gets the job done.
Decrees of peace help you to pray things through
rather than trying to force them through. Peace is the

forerunner of victory, and prayers decreeing the "peace of Jesus Christ" give you that peace and that victory.

You will soon notice that the first thing that happens when you begin to think about Jesus Christ is that a great calm descends upon you. You immediately begin to feel better about everything in your life. I know someone who healed insomnia after many sleepless nights by affirming, "THE PEACE OF JESUS CHRIST IS POURED OUT UPON ME NOW AND ALL IS WELL."

I know of a human relations problem filled with confusion, inharmony and conflict that was resolved after someone affirmed for it, "THE PEACE OF JESUS CHRIST IS POURED OUT UPON THIS SITUATION NOW, PRODUCING PERFECT RESULTS."

A fine black schoolteacher was placed in an integrated school for the first time. At first there were grave behavior problems. This was the first time most of the children had had a black teacher, and the Hispanic students seemed especially resentful. This teacher was rather frightened and upset over this challenge until she began to affirm, "JESUS CHRIST IS TEACHING THIS CLASS. THE PEACE OF JESUS CHRIST REIGNS SUPREME IN THIS CLASS. I BLESS EACH STUDENT WITH THE PEACE OF JESUS CHRIST AND ALL IS WELL." Everything quickly calmed down and harmony was restored. A happy teacher with a class of happy students was the ultimate result.

It has been estimated that 80 percent of all illness results from suppressed emotion. We see it happen all the time: headaches, colds and many common ailments appear after an emotional conflict. The Christ consciousness is very powerful in healing because the first thing it does is give peace of mind. In that peace of mind comes healing from the hurts, fears, resentments, jealousies and other emotional conflicts, which just fade away in that peaceful Christ consciousness.

Thus, affirming "the peace of Jesus Christ" is a marvelous prayer decree for bringing fulfillment to all phases of your life—and the lives of others. The marvelous thing about affirming "the peace of Jesus Christ" is that everyone around you responds to that prayer unconsciously, slows his tempo, becomes happier and more efficient. Tension, stress and strain just fade away in this prayer consciousness of peace. One person decreeing "the peace of Jesus Christ" in a situation can quiet the whole atmosphere and produce harmony.

HOW TO AFFIRM THE FINISHED WORKS OF JESUS CHRIST

Something often transpires in the way of a miracle when you affirm "the finished works of Jesus Christ," or that "the finished results of Jesus Christ" now manifest in some situation or condition. When I have more to do than it seems I can, often it gets done in half the time as I affirm "the finished results of Jesus Christ now manifest." Ideas flow, helpers appear volunteering their services. Events occur unexpectedly. The job gets done.

Often you will pray and things will begin to unfold which point the way to answered prayer, but never quite materialize and you wonder why. This is the time to affirm, "THE FINISHED RESULTS OF JESUS CHRIST NOW MANIFEST IN THIS SITUATION FOR THE GOOD OF ALL CONCERNED. THIS IS A TIME OF DIVINE COMPLETION."

Often, prayers are *almost* answered that never quite

get answered, simply because no one spoke the word of completion. Don't miss your good by praying a situation almost all the way through and then become discouraged when it doesn't quite materialize. It is simply waiting for you to seal the results by affirming "the finished works of Jesus Christ." This is the miracle prayer that can quickly "wrap up" situations that have lingered on the brink of results. *Often the decree of completion is all that has stood between you and answered prayer!*[3]

WAYS TO INVITE THE UNIVERSAL CHRIST PRESENCE

Along with the innate Christ Mind, Christ consciousness, or Christ nature within you, there is also the resurrected universal Christ presence that is available to you!

After the disciples of Jesus saw this resurrected Christ Jesus presence in their midst, these previously downtrodden, defeated, helpless men were transformed into the fearless, undaunted, inspired apostles who then uplifted and converted thousands of people to the Christ message in a way that no one has ever been able to equal since. Because of their sudden transformation, this previously confused, discouraged, insignificant group converted three thousand people at their first public meeting! They also caused Christianity to spread quickly throughout the ancient world and to continue to spread for twenty centuries.

---

3. See chapter on Completion in the author's book *The Millionaire Moses.*

The same resurrected Christ presence that was seen by Jesus' followers after His crucifixion, and which transformed them and their followers so thoroughly, is still in the ethers of this planet and longs to help you transform your problems into solutions in this modern age as well! "Lo, I am with you always," was the promise (Matthew 28:20). Many have seen the radiant resurrected Christ presence in their midst in modern times, as it lovingly ministered to them. Jesus Christ is still Lord of this planet!

Like the Christ within, this universal Christ does not press upon you, but awaits your attention and recognition. The Christ presence is polite. It longs to be invited into your life to help you and quickly responds when it is. After the time of Jesus, His followers often invited His resurrected presence into their midst by calling, "Come, Jesus Christ!" They knew that spiritual man had been given power of choice and dominion over his world, so that it was up to him to invite the Christ presence into His midst if he wished the benefits of its spiritual power.

Once, when lecturing in a hotel ballroom, I mentioned that I would soon be giving a series of lectures on the Christ consciousness. At the close of that lecture, as I gave the benediction, a lady attending felt a presence near her right shoulder, looked up and saw the literal figure of Jesus Christ standing in the midst of the ballroom.

In another instance, I had a health problem which I had not been able to overcome through prayer. One afternoon I sat quietly while another minister prayed with me about my health, and in her prayer she invited the healing presence of Jesus Christ to make me whole again. After her prayer for me, I felt relaxed and peaceful, and took a nap. As I was awakening I was aware that the filmy figure of Jesus Christ had been standing over me with outstretched hands, as though in blessing. It was only for a fleeting moment that I saw Him, but I knew then our prayer had been answered. In due time my health problem resolved itself.

Inviting the living presence of Jesus Christ into your mind, body or affairs brings it! Your invitation also invites its quiet, peaceful, miracle power.

A woman who was suffering from shingles was unable to attend church one Sunday morning and was listening to the radio broadcast of a Sunday morning church service. Her minister was speaking of the healing power of Jesus Christ. Suddenly, as he described one of Jesus' healings in his sermon, the literal presence of Jesus Christ appeared to this woman in her home!

As she looked at the Christ, with His eyes filled with love for her, she noticed that He wore an exquisite robe, too beautiful to describe. Then He spoke saying, "Thank you for loving me. Go, tell John" (her minister). The next day when she described her experience to the minister, he explained that he had been praying for an appearance of the living Christ, feeling it would strengthen his faith and that of his congregation. Her experience was the answer to his prayers. As she sat describing her experience to him, she realized for the first time that the painful case of shingles from which she had suffered was gone, having been healed by the resurrected Christ Himself!

Whoever you are, wherever you are, Jesus in His spiritual consciousness is waiting for your mental recognition. Whatever your objective, He will show you how

*to attain it, if you will only invite His help and presence
into your life.*

The early Christians proved this. As you read the
Book of Acts of the Apostles, you discover that that
book is not so much a record of the acts of some of the
apostles as it is a record of the acts of the Holy Spirit
through the apostles. Thus, historians have described
the Acts as "The Gospel of the Resurrected Christ"
acting *through* the apostles.

It is very interesting that the physician Luke wrote
both the Gospel of Luke and The Book of Acts. His
first book (Luke's Gospel) related the results of Jesus
Christ's spiritual power while on earth. His second book
(Luke's Acts) related the resurrected Christ's spiritual
power as this Christ presence poured forth His power
from the ethers *through* the early apostles.

Is it any wonder those early apostles seemed filled
with an indescribable electrifying, intoxicating power
which quickly ran the gamut of the entire ancient
world?

Isn't it exciting to realize that that same indescribable, electrifying, intoxicating power is available to
you and to me today? That it only awaits our mental
recognition in order to pour forth through us as healing power, harmonizing us and our world?

HOW A SOPHISTICATED WOMAN
WAS HEALED

A very sophisticated woman—hardly the type one
would expect to be in communion with the resurrected
Christ—recently told me how she was healed: As she
lay in pain she cried out, "Oh Christ, You promised

that if we asked anything in Your Name, you would help us. Please heal me now of this pain."

A sense of peace first descended upon her troubled spirit. Then she saw the hand of Christ as it was extended to her from the ethers. She unhesitatingly placed her hand in His and an electric shock went through her body, carrying with it all former pain. Just that quickly and simply, she had been healed.

HOW THE FORGIVING POWER
OF JESUS CHRIST WORKS

If decrees of "the peace of Jesus Christ" and "the finished results of Jesus Christ" do not give you the peace and completion in your life you think they should, it may be that you have unfinished business in the department of forgiveness.

Often just affirming, "THE FORGIVING LOVE OF JESUS CHRIST NOW SETS ME FREE IN MIND, BODY AND RELATIONSHIPS FROM ALL MISTAKES OF THE PAST OR PRESENT" will cleanse and free you. Or "THE FORGIVING LOVE OF JESUS CHRIST NOW SETS ME FREE FROM ALL FINANCIAL MISTAKES OF THE PAST OR PRESENT" will clear up financial problems. Or a cover-all forgiveness decree such as "CHRIST IN ME IS MY FORGIVING POWER. THE CHRIST IN ME FORGIVES THE CHRIST IN YOU. THE CHRIST IN YOU FORGIVES THE CHRIST IN ME. THE CHRIST IN THIS RELATIONSHIP (SITUATION, CONDITION) IS ITS FREEING, FORGIVING POWER" will bring peace and relief.

If this does not get the job done, it may be because you should invite the living presence of Jesus Christ to help you forgive. Agnes Sanford, the widow of an Episcopalian minister, has explained in her books, *The*

Healing Gifts of the Spirit,[4] and *Behold Your God,*[5] how she helped a number of people find healing by inviting the living presence of Jesus Christ into the memories of the past. As they did, Jesus Christ healed the unhappy memories of hurts, disappointments and frustrations that had filled their past, but He did so in the present. They actually felt His healing power as it went to work in their subconscious minds, clearing out those hurts—often with a rush of emotion—then producing peace. Thereafter, when they later remembered those old hurtful experiences, they realized the bitterness was now gone.

I agree with Mrs. Sanford that Jesus Christ came to heal not only the conscious but also the subconscious mind, which contains all the memories and emotional blocks that stop our prayers from being answered. Since there is no human time element on the spiritual plane, you can invite Jesus Christ into your childhood, into your prenatal life even, into your teens, young adult years, etc., to heal and comfort whatever unhappy or bitter memories linger there: "COME INTO MY LIFE, JESUS CHRIST. I INVITE YOU, JESUS CHRIST, INTO MY SUBCONSCIOUS MEMORY TO HEAL WHATEVER NEEDS TO BE FORGIVEN, RELEASED, REDEEMED. CLEANSE ME AND FREE ME FROM IT NOW!"

Then picture the living presence of Jesus Christ going back into your childhood, taking your hand, comforting, loving, forgiving, healing you and those bitter experiences. Thereafter, whenever you think of the process that is taking place, just say, "THANK YOU,

---

4. Agnes Sanford, *The Healing Gifts of the Spirit* (New York: J. B. Lippincott Co., 1966).

5. Agnes Sanford, *Behold Your God* (St. Paul: Macalester Park Publishing Company, 1958).

JESUS CHRIST. THE FORGIVING LOVE OF JESUS CHRIST HAS NOW SET ME FREE FROM THE UNHAPPY EXPERIENCES OF THE PAST OR PRESENT (or get specific, "THAT UNHAPPY MARRIAGE, THAT HEALTH PROBLEM, FINANCIAL LOSS," etc.) AND I NOW GO FREE TO BE HAPPY."

You will be amazed at the mental, emotional and physical blocks that will be removed, at how happy, cleansed and relieved you will feel. Your prayers will probably then be answered in a rush of happy events!

THE MIRACULOUS POWER IN THE NAME "CHRIST JESUS"

The early Christians invoked the miracle consciousness by intoning the name "Christ Jesus." In reading the Acts and the writings of Paul and his co-workers, you find that they described the living presence of the resurrected Christ not so much as "Jesus Christ," who was the man of Nazareth, but as "Christ Jesus," who was the universal resurrected Christ presence (who had been the man of Nazareth while on earth) but who had become Lord of this planet when making His ascension.

When the early Christians realized that Jesus was not dead but had ascended into a powerful universal presence that could appear and disappear to help them as needed, they gathered in an upper room in Jerusalem and remained there for many days, calling on His presence and intoning His name over and over. It was after tuning into His miracle presence and power that they then went forth to establish Christianity in the entire ancient world—a magnificent feat by any standard, even today.

These early Christians produced miracles by calling on the name "Christ Jesus." Thus, along with affirming the name "Jesus Christ"—which awakens within you the same healing, prospering miracle power that Jesus the man of Nazareth had—you can invite into your midst the universal Christ presence that fills and surrounds this planet by affirming the name "Christ Jesus" as did Paul and the early Christians. You will find a far different vibration is aroused by intoning these two names.

When you affirm over and over "Jesus Christ, Jesus Christ, Jesus Christ," a vibrant, alive, warm, electric feeling comes alive within you and within your circumstances, producing almost instantaneous results of good. Whereas when you affirm over and over the name "Christ Jesus," you will find it invokes a far more impersonal vibration, which seems to work more quietly, more slowly, and more universally. At some levels of your spiritual growth you will find soul satisfaction in decreeing one name; in other phases of your growth, you will be spiritually fed and satisfied only by decreeing the other name. Either has miracle power, contains great soul satisfaction, and opens the way for great soul growth.

Emma Curtis Hopkins described the power released in decreeing the name "Christ Jesus" in her book *Resume:*[6] "The Christ Jesus name is an embodying name, causing one to see embodying of beauty, wealth, strength, fresh life." The word "embody," which Mrs. Hopkins made a significant point of using twice in this one short sentence, means "to give bodily form," "to give definite, tangible, or visible form," "to give definite, tangible, or visible form," "to collect." By affirming over and over the name "Christ Jesus," you can

---

6. *Resume* (Chicago: Ministry of Truth International, 1985).

give definite, tangible, visible form to your prayers. You can collect your good!

I know of a small prayer group whose members had spent years dwelling upon the name "Jesus Christ" and felt the time had come to begin meditating upon the name "Christ Jesus." As they did so, they literally saw the embodying of beauty, wealth, fresh life. Many changes came in their affairs and relationships: changes of jobs, places of residence, the acquisition of new cars, clothes, homes. A much deeper spiritual insight seemed theirs in facing the challenges of life and how to meet them victoriously through intoning the Christ Jesus name. Their prayer consciousness noticeably deepened and strengthened. It can prove so for you, too!

THE WHITE LIGHT OF THE CHRIST

Along with intoning the various names for the Christ consciousness, another way to invoke its miracle consciousness is by meditating upon and picturing the "white light" of the Christ. The mystical followers of the Christ, down through the centuries, saw and wrote about the "white light" of the Christ. As Dr. Bucke pointed out in his book *Cosmic Consciousness,*[7] Moses, Jesus and Paul, as well as many of the great saints and mystics of the early church, knew about this light within. George Fox, of the Quakers, constantly spoke of the inner light. Among modern mystics, Dr. Albert Schweitzer was prominent in writing about the light within.

Whether there seems to be a light within or not, you

7. Richard M. Bucke, *Cosmic Consciousness* (New York: E. P. Dutton & Co., Inc., 1901).

can invoke the pure, white light of the Christ and its
protecting, miracle-working power, by deliberately picturing it around people and situations for whom you
pray. Decree that it is there whether you can visibly see
it or not.

In his book *You Try It,* Dr. Robert Russell wrote of
this light:

> This is an age of light. Electric light, violet light,
> neon light, black light, X-rays, Beta rays and light in
> countless other forms serve man. But there is another
> light that transcends in power every form of material
> light. It is the beneficent and protecting power of the
> luminous energy flowing directly from God that illum-
> ines the lives of those who accept the promise, "Christ
> shall give thee light."
>
> "Ye are the light of the world," said Jesus. The
> mystical light is in you; it is at the very center of your
> being now. It is the same light that led Moses and his
> people through the wilderness, that blinded St. Paul
> on the highway to Damascus . . . God brought order
> out of chaos with the creative phrase, "Let there be
> light." The "children of light" referred to in the Bible
> are those who have surrendered personal consciousness
> for Christ consciousness. Christ consciousness repre-
> sents spirit in action. If one dwells in spiritual con-
> sciousness (walks with the indwelling presence), he is
> secure. The spiritual man, then, is distinguished from
> other men by a certain light that shines through him.
>
> When you look to the source of light, you find a
> great change coming about in your life and affairs.
> You feel more alive than ever before. Commonplace
> things are glorified. Difficult tasks become easy. Every-
> thing in your world is transformed for the better. One
> of the amazing things about living in the light is that
> we are so often guided into the things we have sub-
> consciously wanted to do all our lives.

Are you failing in the business of living? Then step into this light and it will send you forth with new life, new faith, new hope, new affections, and new ideas. How, then, do we magnify the light? By consciously recognizing it. When we identify ourselves with the light, our prayers flash forth like lightning and open the way for us. Demonstrations, demonstrations, demonstrations follow — so many we cannot count them. With such speed does the light operate in our affairs that we are astounded.[8]

I know of a tangled human relations problem, filled with conflict and confusion, that cleared up quickly when a praying onlooker quietly surrounded the situation and all the people involved with the pure, white light of the Christ. Though this was a situation that had been filled with confusion, hard feelings and conflict for several years, within a matter of weeks it had been quickly resolved as the white light of spirit was released to penetrate it.

In another instance, it seemed that a dominating personality was going to overpower a small organization and gain a willful foothold for selfish, personal reasons. But one of the members of this organization began decreeing that it was surrounded by the pure white light of the Christ, into which nothing negative could penetrate and out of which only good could come. The domineering personality soon began to lose interest in that organization and later disassociated from it completely — to the relief of everyone concerned.

Instead of thinking of yourself or others as problem-

8. Robert Russell, *You Try It* (Marina del Rey, Calif.: DeVorss & Company, 1953).

ridden, downcast, limited and bound to unhappy conditions, begin to surround yourself in your prayerful
meditation periods with the pure white light of the
Christ. Mentally saturate yourself with the light. Affirm,
"LET THERE BE LIGHT" or "I AM A CHILD OF THE LIGHT
AND I WALK IN THE LIGHT." This decree has been known
to heal those who appeared to be dying. Fill yourself
and your world with "the light" and, as Dr. Russell
promised, the miracle of answered prayer will begin
coming your way!

INVOKE THE CHRIST CONSCIOUSNESS
THROUGH THE WORDS OF JESUS

Another method of invoking the Christ consciousness is to meditate upon the words of Jesus from the
Four Gospels. When you have a healing need, meditate
upon Jesus' healings and you will tune in on that same
healing power.

Why? *Because words of truth have life in them. The
words of Jesus Christ have moved men for nearly two
thousand years to dare to demonstrate as have no other
words ever uttered on this planet!*

He who meditates upon Jesus' words, turning them
over and over in his mind, using them as his own,
studying the very essence and spirit of them, will receive new thoughts, new revelations and inspirations
each day of untold value. This method leads to a life of
infinite satisfaction. Eat and drink the words of Jesus!

I know a lady who was once healed of a chronic,
nagging malady by writing out one of the healing
promises of Jesus and wearing it next to the skin over
the diseased area of the body. Sleeping with one of

Jesus' promises under one's pillow has been known to heal others. *There is fantastic power and vitality in the words and promises of Jesus now, as in His time.*

There was formed at Jerusalem, about the year A.D. 40, a school whose whole purpose was to understand the sayings of Jesus. The early Christians, who studied in that school and who invoked the Christ consciousness by studying the sayings of Jesus, went forth repeating His words and parables with such power that they were transformed, and they also transformed the lives of those to whom they ministered. One had only to touch them to be healed.

Why did they have such power? Because, in addition to other spiritual techniques which they used, they prayed the Lord's Prayer over again and again. H. B. Jeffery in his book *Mystical Teachings* has written:

> The Lord's Prayer is all command. To speak authoritatively is to renew and strengthen one's courage. We learn to speak authoritatively by repetition of the Lord's Prayer. Repeat the whole prayer over and over. *The repetition of the Lord's Prayer has a certain energizing effect, like eating and drinking. Let it fire the whole being with energy.*[9]

Instead of taking for granted the Lord's Prayer and ripping through it in fifteen seconds, begin to speak it over and over slowly, deliberately, authoritatively (preferably in a loud voice) and you will feel its electrifying, energizing, transforming effect upon your life. Such use of the Lord's Prayer is another way to invoke the words and consciousness of the Christ. In doing so,

---

9. H. B. Jeffery, *Mystical Teachings* (Fort Worth: Christ Truth League, 1954).

the Lord's Prayer may literally shock you into greater good than you have ever known. Jesus was quite positive and determined in the big claims He made on God. The Lord's Prayer is a series of determined affirmations.

The early Christians discovered that when they affirmed over and over the most powerful prayer Jesus ever uttered—the Lord's Prayer—the hidden Christ within each one of them was called into action. They further discovered that by affirming the prayer over as many as fifteen times, hard conditions, diseases and tribulations faded away. This same prayer technique later proved powerful at the Healing Shrine of Lourdes too.

Praying the Lord's Prayer over repeatedly is a great success formula for invoking healing, peace of mind, vitality, right action in one's affairs, prosperity and guidance, as well as a great power for breaking up and dissolving hard—even "incurable"—conditions quickly. Use it often as another way of invoking the miracle Christ consciousness.[10]

RELEASE YOUR MIRACLE POWER

Regardless of which of the foregoing prayer methods you develop for invoking the miracle consciousness, call on the Christ consciousness often. When you do so, you release into your mind, body, affairs, and relationships a spiritual force, a spiritual energy, an atomic vibration, that shatters fixed states of mind. *When you*

---

10. See the chapter on the Lord's Prayer in the author's book *The Millionaire from Nazareth.*

call on the Christ consciousness to help you in any way, you release a high-powered energy to do for you what you cannot do for yourself!

If you do not at first seem to get results, after invoking the Christ consciousness, do not fret. Just keep on. Practice makes perfect and repetition is the mother of wisdom. It is through repeated affirmations of the Christ consciousness that miracle power is released. When you keep calling on the Christ consciousness to help you, the Christ power goes to work for you, helping you break out of the negative thought strata that have bound you. You can then prove to your own satisfaction that through the Christ consciousness, your life cannot be limited, and that you have tapped a miracle power!

THE PRAYER OF CONCENTRATION

— Chapter 8 —

When I think about concentration, I am always reminded of the Longhorn Band at the University of Texas. For five years I heard practically every practice session conducted, because I lived near the practice hall.

During all those years they followed the same routine: When they gathered to practice their music for the next football game, they began by playing "The Eyes of Texas Are Upon You," as though they had never played it before.

Then at the close of each practice session, they concluded the same way: by again playing "The Eyes of Texas Are Upon You"—as though they had never played it before. Day in and day out, month in and month out, football season in and out, they practiced that song over and over. Those musicians really concentrated!

It has been estimated that what usually takes six hours to do could easily be accomplished in only one hour by the person who knew how to practice concentration; that absolutely nothing is impossible to the one who knows about the power of concentration. I believe it!

Psychologists have estimated that you use only 1/10 of 1 percent of your energies and powers. The rest of your forces are lost, because they have been expressed outward through scattered thought and action, instead of inward through deliberate concentration.

Your forces have been expressed outward, instead of inward, because you have not known the fantastic power of deliberate concentration—which could help you dwell upon all the right things in life, thereby drawing your forces inward and upward so that they would produce fantastic good for you and through you.

"But," you may object, "I have neither the time nor the energy for concentration." Or perhaps you are thinking, "I do not have a strong enough mind to concentrate."

Nonsense!

There's nothing hard, complicated or forceful about concentration. You do not grit your teeth, get into a rigid body position or do some kind of mental gyrations in order to concentrate. *No force or hard mental effort is involved in true concentration.* The act of concentration is meant to be a normal, pleasant activity to the mind.

The word "concentrate" means "the act of drawing to a center." To concentrate is to rest the mind on an idea, to draw the mind back again and again to an idea. *You are concentrating all the time!*

The normal action of the mind is to concentrate as it dwells upon and feeds upon ideas. Every time you think about all that is wrong in your life and dwell upon your problems, you are concentrating. Every time you think about all that is good and right in your life, you are also concentrating.

Often you have concentrated as you have rested your mind on ideas, drawn your mind back again and again to certain subjects that interested you. But usually you have concentrated in a casual way as your mind flitted from one subject to another. Since what you concentrated upon you became one with, you simply became one with a lot of scattered, helter-skelter results; whereas, in deliberate, constructive concentration, you draw your thoughts to a common center and they then have the power to manifest deliberate, constructive results in your life.

There is a saying: "What you look to, looks to you." That's concentration.

THE HISTORY OF CONCENTRATION

There is no great world religion that does not have its method of concentration. What the Hindu calls "yoga" or the prayer of concentration, the Christian simply calls prayer.

The importance of concentration is an ancient teaching. The people of Rome, Greece, Persia, Egypt, India all knew that in order to experience anything worthwhile in life, they had to concentrate upon it.

The great teachers of the Bible emphasized the importance of prayers of concentration. Jesus referred to the prayer of concentration in healing when He said: "If thine eye be single, thy whole body shall be full of light" (Matthew 6:22). Concentration played a big part in many of His healings as well as in His prosperity miracles. Paul's powers of concentration had much to do with the successful establishment of early Christianity in a hostile world.

Among the spiritual giants of the Old Testament, the prophet Elijah was among the more obvious in his use of concentration; by the power of his thought, Elijah penetrated the atoms and precipitated an abundance of rain. By the same power he increased the widow's oil and meal.

Madame Guyon, a Christian devotee of the 17th century, was an expert at concentration and described it in her treatise as "a simple method of prayer."

The Hindus regarded concentration as being "one-pointed." They felt that concentration was the basis of all success in life. The masters of the East have long felt that the man who was truly "one-pointed" was destiny's darling and was bound to succeed.

The Hindu philosophers, who are among the deepest students of psychology, called the practice of spiritual concentration "yoga," which means "union." In Raja yoga, or the yoga of mental development, the second step is concentration. The Hindus felt that, through the prayer of concentration, man united with his indwelling spiritual nature and literally got "turned on," so that all things were then possible to him.

Hindu devotees have spent whole lifetimes in the study and practice of concentration because they felt that, through constructive concentration, every good thing would come to them in life: power, knowledge, bliss. They also felt that through the practice of concentration they would be delivered from every ill.

THE INCREDIBLE POWER OF CONCENTRATION

"One-pointed" concentration releases extraordinary powers within you as it unites the conscious, subconscious and superconscious phases of your mind, bringing heretofore undreamed-of-powers and energies into play in your behalf.

In the simple act of concentration, you draw the mind back again and again to an idea, which taps and releases deeper potent energies of the mind not ordinarily touched. Those deeper, finer, more penetrating currents have the capacity to produce extraordinary results because it is those finer, more potent currents that give the mind the power to exercise complete control over all the actions and forces of the mental world.

Furthermore, *the emotional blocks that exist in the minds of most people, keeping them from getting what they want, are eliminated in the minds of people who know how to concentrate. Thoughts of doubt, fear, fatigue, discouragement can be completely dissolved through concentration.*

Thus, *concentration is more than a mental action. It is also an emotional one as it purifies, calms and stills surging emotions.* According to the psychology of the Hindus, prayers of concentration can help you gain control of your emotions. They even felt that three distinct types of emotional personalities were especially helped through prayers of concentration:

The First Type were those suffering from ignorance, dullness, inertia, laziness. This type took no step forward toward progress.

The Second Type were those who expressed their passion in hurry, struggle, strife, worry, agitation, and in other emotional disturbance. This type is easily upset and overreacts.

The Third Type were the over-proud, self-assertive, self-righteous, often feeling they have been wronged, misunderstood, filled with thoughts of their personal rights, egotistical, egocentric. This type is inclined to battle and fight life.

A HOUSEWIFE'S DELIVERANCE FROM TROUBLE

A housewife used the power of deliberate concentration to calm the emotions of those around her and to bring deliverance from an unhappy situation:

"My husband and I were on our way home from a Christmas trip. We had our seven-month-old baby with us. In the mountains of Pennsylvania, miles from anywhere, our car just quit running. It was getting dark, the baby was crying, and my husband was mad. He got out and looked under the hood and could find no reason for the car trouble.

"In the meantime I remembered an affirmation from one of your books and started dwelling upon it: 'DIVINE SUBSTANCE APPROPRIATELY MANIFESTS FOR US HERE AND NOW.' I did not understand what it meant, but I used it anyway.

"In a little while, the baby calmed down and so did my husband. He got back in the car, tried the ignition and the car started. After that we had no more trouble. All the way home as we drove along, he kept saying, 'I sure don't get it.'"

Through concentration, you create what you want mentally first. Then through continued concentration,

you bring into play the incredible powers of your con-
scious, subconscious and superconscious mind powers.
Next, you gain control of them and make them work
for you in a constructive, productive way. Through
this process you become master instead of slave, victor
instead of victim.

Until deliberate, constructive concentration is prac-
ticed, all your other prayer efforts are like scattered
forces that have little visible effect.

THE NECESSITY OF CONCENTRATION
IN PRAYER DEVELOPMENT

There are those misguided souls who say, "I do not
need the simpler types of prayer such as relaxation,
release, forgiveness, decree or concentration. I pray
in an 'advanced way.' My method of prayer is meditation and the silence." Those confused people then often
let it slip that their prayers are not being answered.

You have got to get ready for the deeper phases of
prayer such as the prayers of meditation and the silence
by first taking prayer's preliminary steps. The prayers
of relaxation, release, forgiveness, and decree lead
you into the prayers of concentration and meditation.

There is a great difference between the prayers of
concentration and meditation. In concentration you
are resting your mind on one basic idea of good. You
are calling your mind back again and again to that
idea of good; whereas, in meditation you let your mind
roam and you let it consider many ideas. Meditation
is a mental analysis, where you consider many ideas
mentally. But before you can practice successfully the
art of meditation where your mind can roam freely in

a constructive, productive way, *you have got to have control of it.* You gain that control only through developing the preliminary types of prayer: relaxation, release, forgiveness, decree and concentration.

There are two basic methods of concentration. The *first* simple, *outer* method prepares you for the *second,* more advanced, *inner* method; and this second or more advanced method of concentration then leads you into meditation.

Before trying to arouse your innate spiritual powers within through the formal prayer of concentration which will be described later in this chapter, it is wise to begin to develop the art of concentrating upon what you want to experience in your life through the definite physical-mental methods of list-making, picturing, and decreeing it. As you use these definite physical-mental methods of concentration, they will naturally lead you into the formal prayer of concentration.

INDUCE CONCENTRATION THROUGH
LIST-MAKING

Another name for concentration is "attention." *What gets your attention, gets you!* It is a well-known axiom that *what you concentrate upon, you bring into your life.*

Among the delightful methods that induce concentration as it "focuses" your thoughts, drawing them to a center, giving them power to produce results for you, is that of list-making.

YOUR FIRST LIST: WHAT YOU WANT
TO ELIMINATE

Your first list should be a list of the things or conditions you want to *eliminate* from your life. Often you have been so busy concentrating on these undesirable problems, conditions and things, that you have spent all your mental and emotional energy dwelling upon them, thereby unwittingly inviting them to multiply in your life. And so they have!

Sit down with a pencil and paper and write down that which you wish eliminated and removed from your life. Be definite and specific. At the bottom of your list write: "I NOW RELEASE WORN-OUT THINGS, WORN-OUT CONDITIONS, AND WORN-OUT RELATIONSHIPS. I RELEASE THEM AND BLESS THEM TO THEIR TRUE PLACE NOW. THEY RELEASE ME AND BLESS ME TO MY TRUE PLACE NOW. I LET THEM GO, AND LET GOD GUIDE ME INTO MY NEW GOOD, WHICH IS MY TRUE GOOD NOW!"

In the future, instead of concentrating on these problems, secretly fighting, resenting and sulking over them — thereby holding them to you — call your mind back again and again to the foregoing words of release and blessing.

HOW A BUSINESSMAN'S ELIMINATION LIST
BROUGHT SUCCESS

I know a businessman who had tried and tried to demonstrate greater prosperity in his life. He had affirmed and prayed and made a list of the blessings he wanted to experience. *But nothing happened until he*

*made a list of the things and conditions he wanted to
eliminate from his life.*

Within a matter of weeks, a business he no longer
cared about had been sold at a profit. Several pieces of
property had been sold. And a job in a new field of
work opened to him, though he was supposed to be
"too old" to qualify. That man is happy and successful
today because he finally made a list of what he wanted
to be rid of in his life and started declaring release from
worn-out things, conditions, and relationships, rather
than continuing to dwell upon and mentally battle
with them.

To make such an elimination list, blessing worn-out
situations and relationships to their true place, helps
you to withdraw your attention from that which you
no longer want in your life. When you pull your attention out from under that which is undesirable in your
life, it no longer has anything to feed it emotionally
and so it fades away for lack of attention.

YOUR SECOND LIST: WHAT YOU WANT

Your second list should list the things and conditions
you *wish* to manifest in your life. Remember that the
word "choice" is a magic word to the mind. Choice
produces results. Your mind constantly works through
what you choose.

If you drift along without any definite goals for better experiences in life, you become the helpless victim
of circumstances. Furthermore, if your desires are
passive and not clearly defined, you become subject
to the dominant mentalities around you and often

manifest what *they* want in your life. Haven't you bought the car, house, clothes, or taken the vacation that somebody else thought you should? You became the victim of their concentrated desires because you had none of your own.

The way to overcome difficulties in life is to get a goal. If you do not know what you want and have no set purpose, your subconscious mind just produces a conglomeration of circumstances.

By writing out your list, your definite written words dissolve all obstacles and barriers on both the visible and invisible planes of life. Your written words go out into the ethers of the universe to work through people, circumstances and events, and open the way for the items on your list to come to pass.

Psychologists tell us that all things are done by choice. Choice produces results, but it is up to you to make your choice!

A HEALER'S SUCCESS FORMULA

A successful doctor of chiropractic told me what for twenty years had been his secret formula for success. At the time this chiropractor went into practice right out of college, he had nothing. But he and his wife believed that, if they concentrated on what they wanted in life, they would get it.

At the beginning of each New Year, instead of making New Year's resolutions of what they hoped the year might bring, they made a list of what they definitely expected the year to bring. The first year they listed nice rental offices and a thriving practice. The second year they listed the purchase of business property on which they planned to build their own offices. Later they listed the purchase of a home and the birth of their first child. Another year their list included the acquisition of stocks, bonds, and other investments. Still later they listed a larger professional practice. Then their list included the purchase of a private plane, more cars, a boat.

From the very first New Year's list this couple made, this method began to work for them! Once they had written down their desires for that particular year, they placed the list in their Bible and simply gave thanks for the perfect results throughout the year. In several instances by midyear the major desires on their list had manifested. At other times it was as late as December before the list began producing results. The year they listed the desire for their first child, she was born in October. Invariably the list-making method worked!

This couple now has all the blessings they have put on their New Year's lists over the years: a fine professional practice and their own business property on which they have built beautiful offices; they now enjoy a lovely home, several cars, their own private plane, additional financial assets such as stocks and bonds, and several healthy children who had first been on their list! The result is a healthy, happy, prosperous, spiritually oriented family.

"List-making is the simplest success technique in the world, if people would just do it!" declared this doctor of chiropractic.

TOP EXECUTIVES PROVE POWER
OF LIST-MAKING

After I had written about the power of listing your desires in my books *The Dynamic Laws of Prosperity* and *The Prosperity Secrets of the Ages,* a business-man from Philadelphia wrote confirming the success power of this method. He had recently given a success course to ninety-two top corporation executives for which their company had paid him a generous fee.

In this success course, these ninety-two executives were asked to write out the things they wished to experience in life as well as to list the problems they wished to eliminate from their lives. This man reported:

"Miracles happened. Everyone was healed of health problems, even of 'incurable' diseases. Out of these ninety-two men, all but two said they had gained immeasurable good. All got raises in pay of from $2,000 to $20,000 a year from this method. One man was an atheist, another an agnostic. Their friends at work said they had been impossible to work with. After this course, the co-workers reported that these executives were much more pleasant. Problems of health, prosperity and personality were all resolved by using this list-making method. Ninety out of ninety-two reported results."

A business executive from Illinois related:

"This business of writing a list of those things you feel you need in your life works! I have done just that and success became apparent almost instantly. Since then, everything I had on my list has come to me. Some of them were tremendous things, such as retirement early so that I might become a public speaker. I also listed an adequate income, so that my life might continue normally as before retirement. I now am a lecturer for business groups, from which I get several hundred dollars per lecture.

"Even such things as an expensive travel trailer, a fine motion picture camera, and other such items have come easily. I have proved beyond all doubt that God intends us to have whatever we want that will advance His work on earth. But it's up to us to mentally claim those blessings. List-making helps us open our minds to the good things we want in life, rather than fretting and fuming about the problems we don't want."

YOUR THIRD LIST: THANKSGIVING

Your third list should include the things you are now experiencing in life for which you are *thankful:*

List your talents, skills, friends, family, possessions, health, happiness, progress, understanding . . . blessings tangible and intangible. List them all. Nothing is too trivial to give thanks for. This simple act of thanksgiving has miracle power, because *words that express thanks release certain potent energies not otherwise tapped. Thanksgiving releases dynamic forces for good.*

Along with being thankful for the good you are already enjoying, it is also good to place on your list the things that have not yet appeared. Just thank God for them anyway. Your act of thanksgiving opens the way for those blessings to appear.

A businessman had been transferred out of state and had tried for months to sell his house. He had prayed to no avail. Then a friend said, "Try giving thanks

that it is already sold." He listed this sale on his "Thank
you, God" list. Within a few days the house he had
prayed about for months sold![1]

After making your three lists—(1) what you want to
eliminate; (2) what you want to *manifest;* and (3) what
you are *thankful* for—go over your lists daily, revising
them as you are guided to.

Think about what you really want, not what somebody else wants you to have. Try to please only the
Christ within you when making your list. "The highest
is the nearest." If you try to compromise, you stop
your good and bring on confusion.

This act of concentration helps clarify your thinking
about what you want and don't want in your life. That
very act of concentration then goes to work to manifest
your desires for you.

Protect your list and your desires by declaring, "THIS
OR SOMETHING BETTER, FATHER. LET THINE UNLIMITED
GOOD WILL BE DONE." Or "I RELEASE MY DESIRES TO THE
PERFECT OUTWORKING OF THE CHRIST CONSCIOUSNESS
NOW." Or "I SURROUND MY DESIRES WITH THE PURE
WHITE LIGHT OF THE CHRIST, INTO WHICH NOTHING NEGA-
TIVE CAN PENETRATE AND OUT OF WHICH ONLY GOOD
SHALL COME."

As you give thanks for "divine results" which are
sublime results, they will manifest with perfect timing
—that which you had in mind or something more
appropriate.

---

1. Chapter 8 of the author's book *The Millionaire Moses* describes the miracle power of thanksgiving.

INDUCE CONCENTRATION THROUGH PICTURING

You can practice the art of concentration through the deliberate use of the picturing power of the mind.

There is nothing new about this simple, delightful form of concentration that often produces the desired results quickly. Prehistoric man carved pictures of the food he desired on the walls of his cave. He believed that as he looked often at those pictures, an unseen power would attract the food near him in the form of game, fish, and fowl. It happened repeatedly.

Later the ancient Egyptians, who were versed in all the occult success teachings, used the picturing power of the mind in their Egyptian tombs. As soon as a child of royalty was born, a tomb was started for him. On the walls of the tombs were painted pictures of his life up to his death, showing all the desired experiences he would have throughout his lifetime: the winning of war, the capturing of large numbers of prisoners, and the living of a happy, victorious life were depicted. The Egyptians expected these pictures to come to pass in the life of the royal child.

More than 2,400 years ago, during the Golden Age of Greece, the cultured Grecians took advantage of this mental law and surrounded their prospective mothers with beautiful pictures and statuary in order that the unborn children might receive from each mother's mind pictures of health and beauty.

The Tibetan Buddhists have combined affirmations and the picturing power of the mind and used them for centuries in the form of "prayer wheels."

They feel that prayer wheels are a spiritual device whereby man may expect miraculous benefits from his frequent recitation of religious formulas or affirmations. Cylinder-shaped boxes containing sacred texts or prayers are spun in the hands, and wheels are hung up in temples where visitors can turn them. Each revolution of the prayer wheel is believed to bestow as many benefits as would be gained by reading the texts or reciting the prayers, thus setting up the picturing power of expectancy of good.

The picturing power of the mind is one of the oldest devices known to man for concentrating upon the good, thereby manifesting it!

Concentration functions best through imagination. Through deliberate, constructive use of the imagination, you bring together the many creative energies of the mind. Imaging is an invaluable aid to imagination. Concentration can, by working through the imagination, bring together into one powerful line of mental action all the best ideas of the mind and all available creative energies. A vivid, well-trained imagination tends to "light up" your entire mental world.

How much better you can concentrate when you have a distinct picture in view! Imagination has the power to take the lead in the mental world. Whenever you image a certain thing being done in the mind, you release a majority of the energies of the mind to go and do that very thing! To help achieve this purpose, make a prayer wheel.

"PRAYER IN PICTURES" CAN BE THE
TURNING POINT TO RESULTS

In connection with the prayer of concentration, I suggest that you make a modern "prayer wheel" which not only contains words describing the good you wish to experience in life, but also contains pictures of your desired good.

Such a prayer wheel is a "prayer in pictures" and is a simple way of praying and then mentally accepting the answer to your prayer through the art of concentration.

As a spiritual being made in the image of God and containing His divinity, *man is the only creature on the face of the earth that looks up. When the forces of nature move upward, through the picturing power of prayer, they always move with great energy and power. When your doubts leave, your dreams come true. A prayer wheel wipes out your doubts!*

There is an old axiom: "If you look up, you will always be provided for." Through picturing your prayers as already answered, you are invoking the highest form of faith, because you are saying, "It is already done, and it now manifests in my life as satisfying, tangible results." *Picturing your prayers as already answered* (as is done when you make a "prayer wheel" or "wheel of fortune") *is often the turning point to answered prayer.*[2]

HOW A BUSINESSWOMAN EXPERIENCED
A HAPPIER LIFE

A businesswoman was lonely and desired a more balanced life. She made a prayer wheel, picturing the

2. For instructions on making a "wheel of fortune" see the author's books *Open Your Mind to Prosperity* (Chapter 4), *The Dynamic Laws of Prosperity* (Chapter 5) or *The Healing Secrets of the Ages* (Chapter 7).

happy, balanced life she wished. Each night before retiring she would view her prayer wheel, quietly resting her mind on the pictures of good she saw there. Over and over she drew her thoughts to a common center. As she did, they gained power to produce results for her.

One day she was suddenly called out of the city on a business trip. While away, she met her future husband and soon was established in the happy way of life pictured on her prayer wheel. But none of these happy events occurred until she practiced daily concentration, resting her mind on the pictured results; through drawing her thoughts and attention often to a common center concerning that pictured result, she then fed her mind constantly on that idea.

The law of concentration is: *picture a thing and bring it through, rather than trying to reason it through or force it through.* Often you have cut off your good by thinking in strained terms of wishing, needing, wanting. Through the imaging power of the mind, you begin to think in terms of having, being, and experiencing present fulfillment. This mental action releases to you the results you have been picturing. It is a mental law.

HOW THE AUTHOR BROUGHT ABOUT COMPLETION

Once when I had been unable to complete a writing assignment, due to lack of time and many interruptions, I was in a state of despair until I remembered the picturing power of the mind: that *generalities do not produce results because they lack substance and power. Vague hopes and indefinite goals are not convincing to the mind, whereas a clear-cut picture of the good you want to experience motivates people, places and events to cooperate with your pictured desires and unconsciously produces those results for you.*

I quickly made a prayer wheel showing the book as already completed and placing on it these words in big bold print: "Get things done! Inspired manuscript. Easy success in writing. The good work hurries on. Editors glad." It worked! Suddenly the tempo changed and within a short time my manuscript was completed and everyone was glad.

HOW A COLLEGE PROFESSOR GOT ANOTHER DEGREE

A college professor wished to change his field of teaching but needed another degree in order to do so. For three years he longed to make the change, but just worried and fretted about it. Nothing happened until he learned of the fantastic power of the imagination and made a prayer wheel picturing himself with the additional master's degree, teaching in the new field of work.

Suddenly, after he made his prayer wheel, everything and everybody seemed to tune in on his pictured prayer and cooperated to help bring it to pass. His teaching schedule on campus was light that next year; his students were more mature and less demanding of his time; less of his time was taken in campus student activities; he discovered that he already had certain college credits that would apply toward the desired degree; and the subject and research for his master's thesis unfolded easily.

Within a year, this professor had that additional master's degree that he had spent three years worrying about! It all came quickly after he stopped fretting about *how* it could happen, and just dared to picture it anyway in faith. The image made the condition, but only after he had made the image.

Solomon described the power of the imagination: "He that hath a bountiful eye shall be blessed" (Proverbs 22:9).

The picturing power of the mind turns your thinking from "I cannot have this" or "It will never happen" to the thought of hope, belief, and finally to mental acceptance.

You are using the picturing power of the mind all the time anyway, so begin deliberately to picture what you want, or you will unconsciously continue to get what you do not want.

In my book *The Dynamic Laws of Prosperity* is the story of the engineer who demonstrated great success professionally after picturing it. In my book *The Prosperity Secrets of the Ages* are stories of countless people who experienced prosperity and success after developing their master plan and picturing it. In my book *The Dynamic Laws of Healing* are numerous stories of people who overcame all kinds of health problems through picturing health.

HOW A SLUM FAMILY "GRADUATED"
FROM THEIR TENEMENT

An overworked housewife, the mother of nine children, was despondent because her husband's job as a day laborer was grossly inadequate to meet the needs of their family. They were living in a crowded tenement in a slum area of their city. Upon learning of the power of prayer wheels, this housewife made one showing her husband in a well-paying job. Other pictures on her prayer wheel showed them living in a comfortable house with adequate bedrooms for all the children, and with a nice car parked out front. Other pictures showed ample outdoor space in which the children could romp.

An impossible dream for one in her poverty-stricken circumstances? It would seem so, until the prayer wheel began to work. Then one day her husband was offered the job of overseeing a large ranch. On this job he was provided with a nice house and car, and there were hundreds of acres of ranchland on which his children played!

IMAGING CREATES, THEN CONCENTRATION
HASTENS RESULTS

After making your prayer wheel, you should spend at least 30 minutes a day quietly studying your pictured desires. Concentrate by looking at them lovingly, intently, mentally enjoying the pictured results as though you are experiencing them. The quicker your feeling nature responds, mentally accepting those pictured results, the sooner they will manifest as a reality for you!

INDUCE CONCENTRATION THROUGH DECREE

In previous chapters, you have been given numerous types of prayer decrees to use as a simple method of prayer.

Prayers of decree are also another way to induce concentration. The Tibetan Buddhist's prayer wheel included sacred texts or prayers which they chanted. By affirmation they claimed and appropriated that which was already theirs on the invisible plane. You can, too!

You can invoke concentration through listing your desires and picturing them on your prayer wheel. But *you may speed up the results of your list-making and prayer wheel as much as 80 percent just by speaking forth definite decrees about your desires.* "Thou shalt decree a thing and it shall be established, and the light shall shine upon thy way," promised Job, who went from rags back to riches through the power of decree (Job 22:28).

VERBAL PRAYERS ARE "MANTRAS OF POWER"

Knowing about the power of words, the yogis have their verbal prayers they describe as "mantras of power." These are nothing more than affirmative decrees. The people on the lost continent of Atlantis reportedly knew about the creative power of decree and used it selfishly, bringing about their own destruction. For many centuries, the power of decree was a secret teaching shared with only a select few, but in this age it has been rediscovered by the masses.

NOT TOO OLD FOR A JOB

I once talked with a man who needed prayers for work. He had been jobless for four years, was fifty-five years of age, and had been informed he was "too old" to get another job. He had studied metaphysics for thirty years but had been unsuccessful in applying it to his job situation.

When I asked what affirmative decree he was using he said, "I have been reading inspirational books, but have not used any specific prayer decrees."

We talked about the fact that for every fifteen minutes of inspirational study, he should spend at least five minutes speaking forth definite decrees for work. He began following this formula and declared aloud at least five minutes each day: "I AM A DIVINE IDEA IN THE MIND OF GOD, AND I AM NOW GUIDED INTO MY TRUE PLACE WITH THE TRUE PEOPLE AND THE TRUE PROSPERITY."

I heard no more from him until about six months later when a letter arrived from South America, saying he was now manager of the South American division of one of our fine American companies, that he was happy, prosperous, and doing well. He wrote: "I can attest to the fact that spoken decrees get your prayers answered. Affirmative decrees turned the tide from failure to success for me when I had been out of work four years, was heavily in debt, and when just reading inspirational books had not brought results."

FROM "RAGS TO RICHES"

A widow who went from rags to riches within twenty years attributed her success to the daily use of one prosperity decree: "GOD IS MY SUPPLY AND MY UNLIMITED

ABUNDANCE OF EVERYTHING NOW." After beginning to use that decree she went into business on a shoestring and for a time had to pray for her daily supply. Once when she desperately needed $100, she walked the floor and spoke her prosperity decrees aloud. As she was doing so, her secretary opened a file cabinet and found five very old $20 bills "hidden" in an order pad!

Another time when she was affirming God as her unlimited abundance in an attempt to meet the payroll for her employees, a stranger walked into her store and offered to buy a piece of property he said she owned down the street. She exclaimed that she only wished she did own that piece of property! But when the stranger explained that her father (now deceased) had bought the property for her many years previously, her attorney verified this. This businesswoman then sold the piece of property she had not even known she owned a few hours previously, met her payroll, and had an abundance left over.

During the depression years, a lady daily gathered her little daughters around the kitchen table where they said prosperity decrees for the head of the house, who was out of work: "YOU HAVE A WONDERFUL JOB WITH WONDERFUL PAY. YOU RENDER A WONDERFUL SERVICE IN A WONDERFUL WAY." It worked.

At the height of the depression this man was offered a job in the bonding business, if he could raise just $25 to get him started. He raided the sugar bowl and went into business. His wife later stated: "That $25 became a quarter of a million dollars, because I have continued to speak forth prosperity decrees every day over the years." Furthermore, the daughters that helped her with the affirmations years ago are now all married to prosperous men and are busy leading happy lives.

INDUCE CONCENTRATION THROUGH SECRECY

When you write out your list, make your prayer wheel, and speak forth your daily decrees concerning the good you want to manifest in your life, you are practicing the art of concentration, and remarkable things will happen!

However, remember that concentration has been described as being "one-pointed." Secrecy, silence, and keeping quiet about what you are concentrating upon are necessary.

Many people fail in concentration because, although they draw their thoughts to a common center, they dissipate that thought force by talking about their desired good, and thus do not get results. If you talk about your lists or show your prayer wheel to others or discuss the affirmations you are using, you can dissipate their results. "In quietness and in confidence shall be your strength," cautioned the prophet Isaiah (Isaiah 30:15).

The word "sacred" and the word "secret" have the same root meaning. The good you desire in life comes from God and is thereby sacred. It should also be dealt with in secret.

Another name for concentration might be "loving attention." So persist! *List-making, picturing, and decreeing the good draws it together on the invisible plane, but the act of quiet concentration, where you repeatedly dwell upon it, hastens the good into manifestation.*

By concentrating in a superficial manner, you may secure some slight results *temporarily*. Yet it is those deeper, finer, more penetrating currents of thought and feeling that produce permanent results, and that have the capacity to manifest extraordinary good for you!

A WOMAN HEALED HERSELF THROUGH CONCENTRATION

The use of concentration for improvement in one's life can be a delightful process. As related in my book *The Dynamic Laws of Healing,* a woman had long suffered nagging health problems which the finest of medical treatment had been unable to clear up. Finally she began to read inspirational books on self-improvement and realized that her health could be restored only after she concentrated upon the picture of health. She decided to test the validity of the quip: "To be the picture of health, one must get into a good 'frame of mind.'"

She invoked concentration in a number of ways:

First, she stopped talking about her aches and pains and began to read various books on healing. She began taking physical exercises, tried a new diet, and resumed taking the vitamins previously prescribed by her physician. She also followed carefully the instructions given by a competent nutritionist.

This lady then sought healing, even concentrated upon it, by deliberately leading a more balanced life of work, play, and rest. She started working in her flower garden daily, took sun baths, and enjoyed the fresh air.

Next, she made a prayer wheel, which pictured an active, healthy life. As she viewed her prayer wheel daily, she decreed: "I AM THE RADIANT CHILD OF GOD. MY MIND, BODY AND AFFAIRS NOW MANIFEST HIS RADIANT PERFECTION."

She began to praise her body. She also made it a point to praise other people, rather than dwelling upon their faults. She associated with friends and relatives who were healthy, who spoke in terms of health. She deliberately terminated her membership in one organization whose members spent most of their meeting periods discussing their aches and pains.

She made it a point to plan ahead for special events she could look forward to: plays, movies, concerts, art exhibits, dinner parties, church events. This helped her to picture herself as healthy enough to attend those anticipated events.

She constantly blessed her body with health and her life with "divine activity." She daily gave thanks that she was whole and well, through and through.

As she worked in all these ways to deliberately set up the mental picture of health, life, and activity to replace the former beliefs in fatigue, ill health, old age, and inactivity, her mental pictures began to take control of her thoughts, emotions, body and life. She became "pregnant with the image of health."

In only a matter of weeks, her life began to reflect the beautiful images of health and happiness pictured on her prayer wheel. Later she went on to a new career. Though this lady was more than seventy years "young" when she began concentrating upon a healthy way of life, she proved that you can produce wonderful changes in your body through the act of concentration.

INNER CONCENTRATION

The foregoing methods of concentration are ways of inducing it informally amid daily living, combining mental and physical power.

However, there is the definite formal prayer of concentration that releases inner spiritual power. And it is worthwhile in your prayer development to unfold this *inner* method, because the prayer of concentration helps you still your unruly thoughts so that one basic thought can rest in your mind. As it rests in your mind, it penetrates, permeates, saturates your thought and feeling nature, going deeper and deeper within, until your whole being responds and begins to work to make that idea a reality. When this happens you are then experiencing the art of concentration.

The prayer of concentration is powerful because it penetrates not only the thoughts of your conscious mind, but also the tremendous feeling nature of your subconscious mind. Since the subconscious supply of latent energy is enormous, the possibilities of concentration begin to assume enormous proportions.

When concentration penetrates the subconscious, it releases latent energies, undreamed-of forces from all phases of the mental world, and suddenly the impossible becomes possible and happens!

As concentration penetrates the enormous latent energies of the subconscious mind, it has the power to get beneath the surface and dissolve all kinds of blocks and obstacles, which simply melt away under its penetrating power. Because of the obstacle-solving ability of concentration, the ancient people had a saying: "The penetrating power of the mind is the freeing power of the mind."

You will find that the times you practice this inner concentration are times of your greatest accomplishments!

Formal prayers of concentration also tap and release powers of the superconscious spiritual nature within those who use them.

HOW TO DEVELOP YOUR INNER POWERS
OF CONCENTRATION

You can begin developing and releasing this tremendous power of *inner* concentration by selecting a time and place where you will not be disturbed. Seat yourself in a comfortable position, or even lie down, loosening and removing items of clothing that restrict you.

Then speak words of relaxation to the mind and body: "RELAX AND LET GO."

When you begin to feel relaxed and at ease, take a definite statement and rest the mind upon it. Keep calling the mind back again and again to that thought. You may wish to begin by writing down a prayer decree, looking at it, filling your mind with it. You may wish to speak it aloud to help you become attuned to it. Then silently rest your mind on that idea.

Confucius said, "I do not talk of God but of goodness." The word "good" might be the subject of your prayer of concentration: "THE GOOD IS ALL THERE IS IN THIS SITUATION. ONLY GOOD SHALL COME FROM THIS EXPERIENCE. LET THE GOOD NOW BE REVEALED. LET THE GOOD NOW MANIFEST AS PERFECT RESULTS."

The decree you concentrate upon might be "GOD IS LOVE." It might be "PEACE," or "PEACE, BE STILL" for some troublesome situation. Any of the attributes of God's goodness might be the subject of your prayer of concentration: "LIFE" for health; "LOVE" for happy relationships; "WISDOM" for guidance, right action, right results; "POWER" for dominion and authority; "SUBSTANCE" for success and prosperity. (The ancient people felt that the word "substance" was one of the strongest words upon which to concentrate because it contains every element of good. Concentration upon this word seems to stimulate that good in all its parts.)

When your whole being has responded with inspired feeling, then let your mind relax, quietly dwell on the idea you are holding, bringing the mind back to it again and again. When you feel a sense of peace and release about it, your mind has become centered and poised upon your idea of good; your mind has accepted and absorbed it, and will go to work to produce a perfect result for you.

The prayer of concentration is all-powerful because it slows the mind down to the point of revelation. Many people miss their good because, after praying prayers of denial, cleansing and decree, they rush off to further outer activity. They do not take time to slow the mind down to the point of revelation and then wait and listen. Through the process of concentration you'll take time to be holy, to become whole in mind, body, affairs, and in every phase of your world.

In his book *Teach Us to Pray,* Charles Fillmore has written:

> We have found that very definite changes occur in our mind and body when we practice concentration in the silence.[3]

Even fifteen minutes a day spent in this practice of the prayer of inner concentration would bring vast improvement in your life within a matter of weeks. Those who practice concentration evolve quickly!

---

3. Charles Fillmore, *Teach Us to Pray* (Unity Village, Mo.: Unity School of Christianity, 1941).

HOW TO CONCENTRATE REGARDING
TROUBLESOME PEOPLE

In regard to troublesome people, concentrate upon this great truth:

Everything and everybody that comes into your life is there for one of two purposes: either to heal you or to be healed by you of some wrong attitude of mind, body or affairs. Everything and everybody in your life is there to press you into more good, or so that you may draw out of them more good. As Emerson said, "A weed is only a flower whose use has not been found."

As you practice the prayer of concentration, you will learn not to try to run away from troublesome situations or people, but to call forth the good in them. As you do, a blessing for all concerned takes place, and then the picture changes. Decree often, "THE GOOD IS ALL THERE IS IN THIS EXPERIENCE. I PRONOUNCE IT GOOD. I AGREE WITH THE GOOD IN THIS SITUATION, AND THE GOOD IN THIS SITUATION AGREES WITH ME."

Such prayers of concentration upon the idea of "good" give you emotional stability and control of your world. With that stability comes every blessing, since most of one's problems have an emotional basis.

THE ART OF CONCENTRATION DEVELOPS SLOWLY

Concentration is a bridge between the inner and outer phases of prayer. Concentration leads you into the mystical phases of prayer: meditation, the silence, and realization. *But concentration must come first since it gives you the mind control needed before meditation can become deep and satisfying.*

Indeed, concentration is the first step in meditation.

The thing you concentrate upon is the thing you draw to yourself. Your prayers will be answered to the extent you can hold to one thought quietly. Developing this ability takes time. Do not become discouraged if at first you do not succeed. Practice makes perfect.

The art of concentration is not acquired in a short time but is a matter of growth and practice. Nevertheless it is worth the effort, because the regular practice of concentration will greatly quicken your powers and enable you to do speedily and efficiently everything you undertake. Both Sir Isaac Newton and Thomas Edison proved this.

Indeed, you gain this interior hold upon the deeper forces of the mind through *continuous practice.* As you continue to practice concentration, you awaken latent forces, develop new talents, and arouse increased power in every faculty and talent you are already using.

Concentration can lead the mind further and deeper in every direction. Concentration gets you ready for meditation and the more interior phases of prayer, which are described in the following chapters.

THE PRAYER OF MEDITATION

— Chapter 9 —

Meditation is one of the most fascinating forms of prayer. The great and near-great have attempted to understand its power. Buddha meditated for seven weeks under the bodhi tree, and Socrates meditated in the marketplace. The novelist Somerset Maugham devoted an entire book to the indescribable power that meditation and its practice can have upon a person's life.[1] And the Eastern practice of meditation has now become popular in the Western world.

Though we have often regarded the art of meditation as a mystical practice, it can also have practical value. A Broadway producer once related how, at the end of the World War II, he was broken in mind and body. He began a spiritual search that led him through

---

1. *The Razor's Edge* (New York: Doubleday & Co., Inc., 1944).

a study of the major religions. He visited Hindu monas-
teries and other shrines around the world. As he learned
how to meditate, his health was transformed and his
career prospered. He found the practice of meditation
both practical and soul-satisfying.

HIS SECRET WEAPON FOR SUCCESS

I first became aware of the far-reaching, yet practical, effects of meditation through a doctor of chiropractic. He was a peaceful man who radiated a sense
of inner power. People often sought him out from long
distances for treatment, and he was sometimes able to
help patients that medical science had given up on.
His secret weapon for success was the daily practice
of meditation.[2]

He spent an hour each morning meditating before
going to his office. In that quiet period, he would ask
Divine Intelligence to direct to him the patients he
could help that day, and to reveal to him anything he
needed to know to help them.

Later, in his office, he would meditate another 15
minutes with his staff. They would begin by affirming
together: "WE FEEL THE PRESENCE OF GOD'S HEALING
POWER GUIDING AND DIRECTING US. WE GIVE THANKS THAT
ALL PATIENTS COME TO US THIS DAY WHOM WE CAN HELP.
WE GIVE THANKS THAT TENSION IS RELEASED, HARMONY IS
EXPRESSED, AND WHOLENESS IS RESTORED. 'THIS IS THE DAY
THE LORD HATH MADE, SO WE WILL REJOICE AND BE GLAD
IN IT.'"

------

2. Also see Chapter 6 of the author's book *The Prosperity
Secrets of the Ages.*

If there was a problem-patient they were concerned about, they took up that person's name in meditation and asked for guidance about his treatment. In quietness and peace, they relaxed and listened for that guidance. It often came through an intuitive hunch or as a flow of ideas. These daily acts of meditation gave this doctor and his staff both inner direction and outer control of their day.

If the atmosphere got hectic during the day, this doctor dropped everything and headed for his "meditation room." There he got renewed in mind and body and regained his poise. When he again felt peaceful — whether it took 5 minutes or 45 minutes of meditation — he returned to the treatment room. He was often able to treat his patients far more effectively in half the time it would have taken had he *not* first become renewed in meditation! He proved the truth written by scientist and doctor Alexis Carrel: "Man integrates himself by meditation just as by action."[3]

MEDITATION PROVIDED GUIDANCE

Not only did he handle his healing practice through meditation, but this chiropractor also conducted his financial affairs through the guidance received in meditation. On one occasion he wanted to trade cars and took the matter into meditation, posing this question: "DIVINE SUBSTANCE, WHAT IS THE TRUTH ABOUT THIS MATTER? SHOULD I TRADE MY CAR NOW?"

It came to him in a flow of ideas that he *was* to trade his car in on the new one he had in mind — but only

---

3. *Man the Unknown* (New York: Harper & Row, 1935).

for a certain cash price. This amount seemed unreasonably low, and he doubted he could get the dealer to accept his offer.

Again he took up the matter in meditation. When the same cash-trading figure was repeated he accepted it as authentic guidance. Quoting this price to his car dealer, the reply was, "I cannot possibly trade with you for that amount. It is far too low." Since he knew that the guidance that came to him in meditation was always right, the doctor released the possibility of a trade.

A few days later his brother visited him and the doctor mentioned the trade-in figure that had come in meditation, stating he was puzzled why it was so low. His brother replied, "I have an extra car I am not using. Why don't you trade it along with your car? That should make your meditation figure come out right." That was the answer! The trade was on.

MEDITATION PROSPERS

Meditation has often been regarded as a mystical phase of prayer that was good for the nerves, but that had little practical value. Yet just the opposite is true: *Meditation prospers!*

The covenant made by Jehovah with Joshua before he led the Israelites over the Jordan River into the Promised Land was that if he would meditate on the law day and night: "Then thou shalt make thy way prosperous, and thou shalt have good success" (Joshua 1:8).

The Psalmist made a similar prosperity promise:

"To those who delight in the Law of Jehovah and meditate on it day and night . . . whatsoever they do shall prosper" (Psalms 1:2, 3).

The result-getting power of meditation is reflected in the story of Isaac, who went out to meditate in the fields at eventide. Looking up after his meditation, he saw his servant bringing his future wife, Rebekah! (Genesis 24:63). No wonder the Psalmist described meditation as "sweet unto him" (Psalms 104:34).

Once the mystical fascination of meditation captures your attention, you will not be satisfied until you have developed its practical power, too. A businessman once made weekly appointments to talk with me about the power of meditation, and also to meditate with me briefly. He spoke of how he had pulled himself up by the bootstraps, both spiritually and financially, after he took up the practice of daily meditation. The prospering power of meditation had taken him from that of a mechanical employee to that of an affluent owner of his own shop.

It was the 17th-century Brother Lawrence who wrote from the workplace:

> Were I a preacher, I should above all things, preach the practice of the presence of God; and were I a director, I should advise all the world to do it, so necessary do I think it, and so easy, too . . . I cannot imagine how people can live satisfied without the practice of the presence of God.[4]

---

4. From the booklet *The Practice of the Presence of God* (Westwood, N.J.: Fleming H. Revell Co., 1958).

MEDITATION HEALS

There is a quip: "More meditation leads to less medication." A man returned to Indonesia from Europe reportedly suffering from a severe case of asthma. He was met at the boat with instructions to proceed to Bourabodour, the most famous Hindu temple in all of southeast Asia. There he was to meditate in the sunshine for one week, speaking to no one.

This diplomat was unskilled in meditation, not much interested, and felt like a fool. But he obeyed those mystic instructions, and during the week his asthma left him never to return. The sacred Hindu text *The Bhagavad Gita* speaks of how meditation can destroy all suffering.

There once was a spiritual healer whose ministry developed through meditation. He had first learned the power of meditation as a businessman: "I was shown by a friend how to meditate in the silence. Through the years I spent much time being still with God. The practice of meditation gave me a wonderful power and strength. It also led me into the constant practice of His presence in my business." After he began to stop each evening on his way home from work to meditate for an hour in a lovely church, his business prospered.

Later, when he suffered financial reverses in spite of his meditation practices, he took that as guidance to make a change. He then went into the ministry of healing on a financial shoestring. He began his healing ministry in a room loaned him by a friend. His first patient was a lady crippled with arthritis in the legs. After they prayed together, she arose completely healed.

Some years later, before his retirement, I had occasion to witness the healing power of this former businessman when he held services at a church where I was serving briefly as a guest minister. After he walked out on the church platform, closed his eyes and began to meditate, his spiritual power was so profound that a hush came over the audience, then a stillness. He breathed deeply several times and shifted into a deeper level of meditation. As I sat observing him, currents of power began swirling around me and flowing through me, and I felt renewed in mind and body.

After he meditated in the silence for a few minutes, he began his healing service audibly. I had never felt such profound spiritual power pour forth from anyone. A number of people were healed during his two-hour service, including a man who had suffered from arthritis for 30 years! The pain and limp simply left him that night.

THE DIFFERENCE BETWEEN CONCENTRATION AND MEDITATION

Whereas concentration is centering the mind upon a single idea, calling the mind back to that idea again and again, meditation is more of a mental analysis, in which one ponders ideas and lets those ideas reveal their truths to the mind. *In concentration, you feed the mind ideas. In meditation, the mind feeds you ideas.* The word "meditate" simply means "to ponder." You give yourself to the practice of meditation in order to receive that which is for your growth and understanding; and also to become a channel of blessing to others in your life.

You can practice meditation in both formal and informal ways. But regardless of whether you use formal or informal methods, *one holy thought meditated upon can become a mighty magnet, drawing to it other holy thoughts, which in their union become so powerful that they sweep away opposition, danger, sickness, poverty or inharmony!* That is the wonder of meditation.

TWO REASONS FOR MEDITATION

You go into meditation basically for two reasons:

First: To commune with the God-power within you, and to enjoy the inner renewal of mind and body which that communion can bring.

Second: To get ideas and guidance from that indwelling Intelligence and apply it in your daily life, as well as using it to help others.

The Indian mystic Tagore wrote: "I cast my own shadow upon my path because I have a lamp that has not been lighted." The goal of meditation is to get your inner lamps lighted! In meditation you pray to a God within, and then let that divine power come alive within you—like a lamp that gradually lights up your whole being. In the process, you make union with your own indwelling Lord, whose only business is to care for you.

This indwelling Lord is "the spirit in man" of which Job wrote; the "Christ in you" of which Paul spoke; and the "kingdom of God within" which Jesus described.[5] Through that warm flow of power and ideas

---

5. Job 32:8, Colossians 1:27 and Luke 17:21.

generated in meditation, you realize what both David and Jesus meant when they said, "Ye are gods, and all of you sons of the Most High."[6]

Whereas some methods of prayer are a means of *getting*, meditation is a means of *letting*.

THE AUTHOR'S MEDITATION EXPERIENCE WITH THIS CHAPTER

It happened to me while I was working on this chapter. I first wrote this material twenty years ago, but most of it was deleted by an editor from the earlier edition of this book. I all but "lost my religion" trying to get him to include this chapter. He had nothing against meditation, but he felt something had to be cut. And being an action-oriented person, he decided this chapter on meditation had to go.

For the next two decades, the material in this chapter got moved from one apartment to another, and from house to house, first in Texas, later in California. Finally, with a change of publishers I felt free to again look at these ideas.

I spent several days perusing this material, meditating upon it and literally "pondering" it in my heart. Finally, after asking for guidance, I dismissed the matter and relaxed. As I did, suddenly a rush of warm power flooded my being, and a gush of ideas revealed to me how to proceed. I knew then that my meditation chapter was finally to be included in this new edition. Meditation had made clear its power to me!

---

6. Psalms 82:6, John 10:34.

FIRST: HOW TO MEDITATE FOR INNER RENEWAL

When you go into formal meditation for the *first* purpose, to contact your own indwelling Lord, the method is simple:

Relax, close your eyes, and turn your thoughts within to the *mental* area between the eyes, or to the *emotional* area at the heart. Then speak words of relaxation, peace, and quietness to your mind and body: "PEACE, BE STILL. RELAX AND LET GO. BE STILL AND KNOW THAT I AM GOD." Use some spiritual word or phrase that brings alive the Infinite Intelligence within you. Such a word or phrase would correspond to the "mantras" used by the meditators of the East. (See later section on Sacred Texts.)

There may be an interval before there is an inner response. However, during this waiting period, movement and expansion of the soul to a higher level of awareness is taking place. As you call the mind back to the spiritual text you are pondering, there finally comes a "click" which indicates an inner contact has been made. This usually generates a flow of life, energy and peace which finally subsides. When it does, you have just experienced the formal act of meditation.

Meditation becomes easier when you remember your attention is not directed "up" or "out" but "in." You are not trying to make anything happen. You are only attempting to contact your own indwelling Lord, and then let ideas and power flow forth from the center of your being.

NO HURRY IN MEDITATION

In the practice of meditation, you do not become anxious nor do you hurry. Instead, you go apart daily for periods of quietness and silence, as a beloved child would go to commune with a loving Father. You relax physically and mentally, and then very gently, often silently, you quiet the conscious and subconscious levels of your mind. You listen to the superconscious or Christ Mind within: "I AM LETTING THE CHRIST MIND EXPRESS PERFECTLY THROUGH ME NOW. I AM! I AM! I AM!" Then you quietly let Spirit work.

When a feeling of peace, power, or serenity comes, you have made the divine contact you sought. New power is then yours with which to overcome life's problems. After you give thanks, then go forth to use that increased power!

The more you practice this quiet time of meditation, the greater and easier will be your ability to make that inner contact—regardless of the outer experiences you are facing in life.

One of the early lady doctors in New York City, Dr. Emilie Cady, suggested the practice of meditation as a prescription for freedom from bondage on all levels of life.

Her prescription:

> Every person should take time daily for quietness and meditation. In daily meditation lies the secret of power. No one can grow in either spiritual knowledge or power without it. Practice the presence of God as you would practice music.

Her diagnosis for those who use it:

No person, unless he has practiced meditation, can know how it quiets all physical nervousness, all fear, all oversensitiveness, all the little raspings of everyday life — just this hour of calm, quiet, waiting alone with God . . . Inharmony cannot remain in any home where even one member of the family daily practices this hour of meditation upon the presence of God.[7]

SECOND: HOW TO MEDITATE FOR GUIDANCE

When you go into formal meditation for the *second* purpose — to receive knowledge and guidance — the proper way is to dwell upon your subject. Then relax, breathe deeply, and ask for knowledge about that subject. Next, wait patiently for your impressions, or for that definite flow of ideas and that inner "click" that indicates you have made contact.

If you have a business problem, close your eyes, relax your body, quiet your mind, declaring: "AS I RELAX IN MIND AND BODY, I AM BEING SHOWN WHAT TO DO." Or you might pose a specific question: "DIVINE INTELLIGENCE, REVEAL THE TRUTH ABOUT THIS SITUATION. MAKE IT SO PLAIN AND CLEAR THAT I CANNOT MISTAKE IT."

Then let the mind analyze, think about, and probe your subject from every standpoint. This questioning power of the mind starts that flow of energy and power that is meditation.

Presently the subject will open up. You will find yourself knowing or "feeling" the answer, without the ordinary efforts of getting information. You will discover the word "let" is a much more powerful word than "get" in meditation.

---

7. *Lessons in Truth* (Unity Village, Mo.: Unity School of Christianity, 1894).

As you are receptive — not trying to push anything in — but waiting, listening for that deeper wisdom to well up from within — a surge of ideas will not only begin to flow. They will also reach a conclusion and run their course.

You do not try to pour ideas into meditation. You use a spiritual thought to calm the mind and body. Then you ask a question, or gently muse upon your subject. Next, you let ideas begin to flow concerning that subject. Last, you let them expand, reach a conclusion, and then subside. This is the process of formal meditation which brings the guidance you desire.

THE MECHANICS OF MEDITATION

Usually there need be no set time or place for meditation. When and where you practice it depends upon your individual temperament, circumstances, and lifestyle. The Hindus like to use a special place for meditation, such as a small room where sacred scriptures are kept. They prefer accustomed physical surroundings which they feel contain a certain atmosphere that helps to induce meditation.

Since meditation is a means of spiritual realization, whatever manner of meditation is most comfortable for you should be used. Just as the Chinese master said that you do not have to sit cross-legged, neither do you have to go to a certain place, nor adopt other rigid rules.

However, a quiet atmosphere is considered best for the practice of meditation. Early morning as well as evening hours are usually appropriate times, since quietness tends to prevail both inwardly and outwardly then. Mohammed advised, "Pray in the morning and

at night, then spend the day in your useful vocation."
In the early morning, after sleep, you are fresher and
freer of the world's vibrations, and are probably better
able to turn within than at any other time during a
twenty-four hour cycle. Your mind is clearer and your
body more relaxed. However, for many years I had to
do my meditating at night, after my mind had been
freed from the day's activities, and the atmosphere in
which I lived was finally quiet.

SACRED TEXTS FOR MEDITATION

The people of the East have long used a "mantra"
or sacred name in meditation. The people of the Old
Testament often used the name "JEHOVAH" as their
sacred word of power. When Isaac went out to meditate in the evening, that was probably his sacred text.

The Hebrews meditated upon variations of the name
"JEHOVAH." Their sacred text for prosperity was "JE-
HOVAH-JIREH" which means "THE LORD RICHLY PROVIDES
REGARDLESS OF OPPOSING CIRCUMSTANCES."

A professional woman found that her financial
affairs suddenly began to prosper after she meditated
daily upon that sacred text, "JEHOVAH-JIREH." She was
able to move into a bright apartment and buy a new
car. She prospered as never before when she continued
to meditate upon this Name.

When Joshua meditated on the Law day and night
in order to become prosperous and successful, he probably used the same sacred text that had been used by
Moses, "I AM" (meaning God indwelling), or "I AM THAT
I AM" (meaning God universal). Moses had learned

these sacred texts from the Egyptians who had felt they were filled with creative power.[8]

People sometimes find it powerful to meditate upon the Name "GOD" or "JEHOVAH GOD."

In any event, *rush around less and meditate more!* This is the way to accomplish great things with ease. Along with gaining specific guidance or an emotional feeling of well-being, the deeper reason for the practice of meditation is to feel the presence of God and to realize that you have access to His power at all times.

THE AUTHOR'S MEDITATION TEXT FOR ACCOMPLISHMENT

The ancients felt that the name "JESUS CHRIST" was the lost Word of power, which, when meditated upon, could restore one's good in an instant. The name "JESUS CHRIST" still stands for colossal achievement along all lines to those who meditate upon its power today. Indeed, you can become attuned to that same supreme success power in meditation.

I once tried a prayer experiment in which a friend and I met daily for an hour to meditate upon the name "JESUS CHRIST." During our many months of daily meditation, powerful ideas for success came to each of us regarding our chosen fields of work. Ideas flowed to me for my writing projects that proved successful. My prayer partner, a businessman, prospered greatly during this period—all because of the guidance that

8. See Chapter 9 in the author's book *The Dynamic Laws of Healing.*

was generated from that name "JESUS CHRIST" in daily meditation.

FOR HEALING, PROTECTION AND FORGIVENESS MEDITATE UPON THE PSALMS

Along with the *formal* methods of meditation where one relaxes, closes his eyes, turns within, and dwells upon a sacred text, there are also *informal* methods of meditation where with his eyes wide open one often ponders ideas or phrases in relaxed contemplation, or studies inspirational books or the Bible.

For *informal* meditation, the Psalms are filled with powerful meditation passages, perhaps the most popular ones being the 23rd and the 91st Psalms. A businessman came through the Battle of the Bulge unharmed in World War II, when those all around him were being killed, as he meditated upon that familiar passage: "Yea, though I walk through the valley of the shadow of death, I will fear no evil: for thou art with me" (Psalms 23:4).

That the Psalmist practiced meditation as he guarded his sheep during the lonely nightwatches is evidenced by his repeated use of the words "meditate" and "meditation." The 119th Psalm mentions those words seven times. In one of those passages, the Psalmist indicated the soul-satisfaction derived from the practice of meditation: "Mine eyes anticipate the night-watches, that I might meditate on thy word" (Psalms 119:148).

The Hebrews often meditated upon the words of the Psalmist because they felt his words not only had great spiritual power but could ward off trouble or deliver them from any predicament. The 30th Psalm was a meditation for healing.

When you feel you have made mistakes and are seeking forgiveness, meditate upon the "Psalm of Cleansing": "Create in me a clean heart, O God; and renew a right spirit within me" (Psalms 51:10).

THE PSALMS BROUGHT FREEDOM FROM A TROUBLESOME JOB

A businesswoman was troubled over a co-worker who seemed determined to try to force her out of her job. Because of the co-worker's purported influence with the boss, she felt it would be hopeless to mention the matter to him. One night when this troubled businesswoman was praying, she felt guided to meditate upon the 37th Psalm: "Fret not thyself because of evil doers."

She realized that entire Psalm was a promise of salvation from trouble, so she decided to meditate daily upon its various passages. As she followed its advice to keep quiet and wait upon Jehovah, within a few weeks she was offered a better job with another company. This resulted in her quick removal from all previous unpleasantness.

DELIVERANCE FROM TROUBLE

When I think about the protecting power of the Psalms, I am reminded of the forty men who had been prosecuted by several hundred men of wealth and power. The larger group of men had $300,000 for legal counsel and prosecution—a formidable amount several decades ago.[9] The forty men being prosecuted had little but their faith in God. But they met regularly and meditated together upon the 27th Psalm:

Jehovah is my light and my salvation; whom shall I fear? Jehovah is the strength of life; of whom shall I be afraid? Though a host should encamp against me, my heart shall not fear . . . I had fainted, unless I had believed to see the goodness of Jehovah in the land of the living. Be strong and let thy heart take courage, yea, wait thou for Jehovah.

These forty helpless men *did* wait upon Jehovah as they meditated upon His goodness. In spite of the $300,000 and the tremendous political influence that had been pitted against them, the court cases were all eventually dropped.

When Jesus was being crucified on the cross, he meditated upon words from the Psalms: "My God, why hast thou forsaken me?" (from the 22nd Psalm). His closing words were, "Into thy hands I commend my Spirit" (from the 31st Psalm).

When you are trying to bring peace, protection, or comfort into your life, meditate upon the Psalms.

WHY SOME PEOPLE CANNOT MEDITATE

You should not be distressed if you are not able to meditate formally when you first try. *Prayer is possible to all, but true meditation is possible only to the men-*

---

9. This situation and its outcome is more fully described in the author's book *The Prosperity Secrets of the Ages.*

tally polarized person. If you have not evolved into the meditative phase of your prayer powers, you should not attempt to force it. To do so could be both frustrating and dangerous. The mystics felt that a person's ability or inability to meditate depended upon his soul development, and that it sometimes took a number of lifetimes before one was ready. They felt that a person who meditates easily may have developed that ability in past lives.

There are three types of prayer: Physical, mental and spiritual. You should practice:

First: *Physical prayer,* where you speak definite words to relax your mind and body. (Chapter 3)

Second: *Mental prayer,* which includes the prayers of cleansing, denial, forgiveness, and prayers of decree. These phases of prayer clear the mind of fear, and other negative emotions, and then make firm the belief in good.

Such verbal methods of prayer are necessary because you have to clear away psychological blocks and emotional conflicts before you can go deeper in consciousness and meditate effectively. It is impossible to meditate properly when you are filled with anger or resentment. Verbal prayers of denial and affirmation help clear away those blocks. (Chapters 4, 5, 6 and 7)

The prayer of concentration is then necessary to stabilize your mind and help focus your attention upon the good you desire so that peace, poise and harmony can result. (Chapter 8)

Third: *Spiritual prayer* includes the more advanced methods of prayer: the practice of meditation and the prayer of silence, which leads to inner realization and outer results. (Chapters 9, 10 and 11)

Success in meditation comes only to the relaxed body

and the controlled mind. When you are ready mentally and emotionally for meditation, it becomes an easy, natural phase of prayer. Something within you draws your attention inward and holds it there, feeding you new energy and ideas. As you make that contact, it connects you with an inner current of power and intelligence.

But until you are ready for it, you cannot develop the art of meditation properly. And the results will be unfavorable, especially to your nervous system, if you try to force it.

DO NOT FEEL GUILTY

You should not let anyone make you feel guilty, if you have not yet developed your meditation powers. Early in my spiritual search, I met a lady who had practiced meditation for thirty years. She scoffed at my simple methods of affirmative prayer.

I had considered my introduction to prayers of decree as a priceless spiritual blessing. They had worked for me at a time when I had known little about effective prayer methods. Affirmative prayers have worked well for many people under similar circumstances. Furthermore, it is a prayer practice that has been used with great success down through the centuries.

Yet I foolishly became discouraged that I could not yet meditate as did this lady. It was only much later that I realized I was just as spiritual as the one who meditated! But the time had not yet come in my spiritual growth for me to meditate—a practice that had taken that lady thirty years to develop!

A friend once conducted a weekly prayer group.

A college student said, "Teach me how to meditate. I want to spend my life in the woods meditating." My friend replied, "What a waste! That would only lead to an unbalanced life. True prayer balances you. Meditation you don't need at this point. Instead, you need to learn and practice the simple methods of prayer: relaxation, denial, and affirmation. When you have gotten your life balanced with these simple prayer methods, then I will show you how to meditate."

This previously penniless young girl soon met and married a well-educated, well-to-do man. After they had a family, she finally returned to say, "You were right. I needed to use simple prayer methods. They have brought every blessing into my life. Too many of my friends tried meditation first. They became discouraged, gave up on prayer completely, and have led lives of confusion and failure ever since."

WHY MEDITATION USUALLY HAS NOT BEEN TAUGHT IN THE CHURCHES

Since the early centuries after Christ there have been numerous mystics in the church. But they were often viewed with suspicion. At best, the Protestant mystical experience has been sporadic. More often it was left to the saints of the Middle Ages, the mystical gurus of the East, or the metaphysical religious/philosophical groups of the last century to reintroduce methodical meditation into our lives—even though the philosophies of the world have taught its practice for centuries.

Sadly, the church's apparent lack of understanding of the true nature of prayer in its deeper facets has a historical basis. It is a carry-over from primitive times when religious man went to his gods in prayer only under special circumstances, or on the occasion of regular public worship. Prayer was a public, rather than a private practice, with the priests and spiritual heads of the congregation officiating. When I first began to search for effective prayer methods in the denomination in which I had been raised, I found a similar attitude: "That's the preacher's job. Leave the praying to him."

Although the prayers of the Israelites, the prophets, the Psalmist, the early Christian leaders, and the mystics of the early church all clearly revealed a personal prayer fellowship with God, this type of prayer tended not to be as prevalent after the Reformation of the 16th century. Instead, historians feel more emphasis may have been placed in religious practice on the *second* commandment: of loving one's fellowman through service to others and in outer good works. Following the *first* commandment of loving God by communing with Him in prayer tended, too often, to become secondary in spiritual emphasis.

Thus, it is understandable why prayer — which should be the essential element in the life of spiritually-minded people — has sometimes been sadly lacking. In some of our seminaries, ministerial students have spent years learning Greek, Hebrew and theological doctrine. Yet they often were inadequately trained in the practice of prayer and meditation.

Also, in the Western world where we tend to be so result-oriented, we may have discounted the power of meditation, because we felt its origins were in the East. There meditation has often been practiced amid ignorance, disease, and poverty. With our logical Western minds we may have judged meditation by its lack of *outer* results rather than realizing its *inner* benefits.

Nevertheless, when spiritually searching people first learn of the deeper phase of prayer known as meditation, they have often been fascinated with its possibilities. They may have even rushed into this phase of prayer first, totally uninformed and unprepared. *To attempt meditation before you have mastered the simpler phases of prayer can be both disappointing and inappropriate.*

THE DANGERS OF MEDITATION

Centuries ago, seers of India pointed out the fundamental law governing meditation: "Energy follows thought."

Because of the tremendous energy generated, both consciously and subconsciously, in meditation, it would be unwise for a person to have deep meditation powers that had not been developed gradually. The mind and body need to be slowly refined over a long period of meditation practice in order to first receive, and then properly assimilate, the powerful vibrations set up in true meditation.

The Hindu philosophers known as the Vedantists say that one may stumble into superconsciousness sporadically, without previous disciplines, but that it is an impure and dangerous practice.

In the *mental* type of person, who centers his attention in the head during meditation, the brain cells can become over-stimulated, leading to a sense of fullness, tension and headaches.

In the *emotional* type of meditator, who centers his

attention at the heart, the reaction often stimulates the solar plexus region. Nervous conditions of irritation, anxiety, worry, even nausea, can result.

A problem for both types of meditators can be excessive sexual stimulation. Another danger is that of becoming too receptive to the thoughts and moods of others, thereby unconsciously taking on their problems. Also, if depression and negative emotions take over, the meditator may even become subject to psychic obsessions from the astral planes of life.

The remedy is to meditate for only short periods daily during the first year. If you suffer from any of the above reactions, you should reduce your meditation time. If you find yourself becoming overly sensitive to the psychic plane, you might want to suspend your meditations temporarily, then relax and deliberately externalize your attention.

A little consistent, faithful meditation practiced every day over a long period of time will bring infinitely greater results than will enthusiastic but spasmodic efforts. A few minutes of meditation practiced regularly will carry you much further than hours of effort spent meditating only occasionally.

Usually the dangers of meditation can be avoided if you use some of the sacred names suggested in this chapter as the subject of your meditation. They contain both spiritual power and protection.

Once your meditation periods are over, get busy releasing that energy in constructive ideas and action. "Put feet on your prayers." It is the energy received in meditation that is not used constructively that can become dammed up in the nervous system, leading to unfavorable reactions.

TO MEDITATE UPON EVIL IS DESTRUCTIVE

All of us have meditation powers, but unless we grow into their use gradually, we tend to meditate upon problems instead of dwelling upon the good we wish to experience.

So cease to dwell upon injuries, troubles, hurts, or poverty in your own life or in the world about you. What you meditate upon, you draw into your life. If it is already there, your attention only multiplies it.

When negative moods try to take over the meditation periods, say to them, "I NEVER KNEW YOU. GET THEE HENCE." To all memories of injuries, hurts, and wrongs of the past or present say, "BE THOU DISSOLVED."

To meditate upon evil is to invite troubles. Our mental institutions are filled with people who became upset by meditating upon the ills of life, instead of using their mind powers to meditate upon good. This is why the use of prayers of cleansing are necessary in your spiritual development first. They release the mind from the belief in evil and its detrimental effects.

WHY A HOUSEWIFE GOT NEGATIVE RESULTS FROM MEDITATION

I once knew an attractive young housewife whose mental and physical health was adversely affected when she tried to practice meditation before she was ready for it. She had not cleansed her mind of hostilities through prayers of denial and affirmation, nor had she learned to relax her body in prayer.

When she tried to meditate, she got tense and rigid,

and the only things she was able to meditate upon were all the conditions of her life that she disliked. She became emotionally disturbed and mentally ill. In her confusion, she had psychic obsessions and decided she was "too spiritual" to be married. This brought great suffering upon her husband and children.

When people appear to become unbalanced because of religion, it is often because they have gotten involved in sin-oriented beliefs, regarding God as wrathful and man as sinful. You need never fear becoming unbalanced through your spiritual studies when you dwell upon the goodness of God and the divinity of man.

THE PAST AND FUTURE CAN BE SEEN
IN MEDITATION

Meditation is an active mental process. There's nothing passive about it. Your *conscious* mind makes contact with either the *superconscious* or *subconscious* activities of the mind, as the need arises.

When the *conscious* mind makes contact with the *superconscious* in meditation, not only can you get flashes of intuitive guidance or a flood of divine ideas. But your extrasensory powers such as telepathy and clairvoyance may be activated.[10] As your deeper mind powers are tapped in meditation from the *superconscious,* you may know things that are occurring at a distance in the present or foresee things that are to happen in the future.

A long-time meditator once described experiences

---

10. See chapters on your "genius powers" and your "special powers" in the author's book *The Dynamic Laws of Prosperity.*

from my past that he had no way of consciously knowing. Another long-time meditator said, as she was leaving to summer elsewhere, "Don't bother to write. Through meditation, I will know what you are doing."

A young man asked a prayer group to pray about a certain job he was trying to obtain. When its members began to meditate on his situation, they "saw" certain problems he had, which he and his family had long concealed. He was startled to learn that his secret had been revealed in meditation, but he agreed it made him unsuitable for that job. He decided to use his abilities in more appropriate ways.

In meditation you may also tap deep within your *subconscious* mind the memories of the past. People who practice meditation for a number of years have sometimes related what they considered to be glimpses of past lives which they first "saw" in meditation. They felt those scenes from the past explained certain problems they were trying to resolve in the present.

THE FRUITS OF MEDITATION

Every time you consider a subject and listen to the flow of ideas that follows, you are meditating with your eyes wide open. Business people with disciplined minds easily learn the art of formal meditation, because they have already used the principles of meditation in informal ways.

However, the act of formal meditation is a deeper, more soul-satisfying process than merely meditating in a surface manner. Casual meditation usually penetrates no further than the *subconscious* level of the mind. Whereas, spiritual meditation penetrates *super-*

consciousness, or the spiritual phase of the mind which can release miracle power.

"DRY" PERIODS IN PRAYER ARE NORMAL

Since the soul is pivotal in action, there will be times when you will be able to meditate deeply and with satisfaction. Yet at other periods in the development of your prayer powers, you will experience those dry periods which the mystics described as "the dark night of the soul." Such dry periods are a normal process for keeping you balanced.

When you have completed a cycle of practicing deep meditation and can no longer do so, do not try. You may wish to practice the prayer of silence, then wait for realization, as described in the following chapters. Or you may wish to return to the more verbal methods of prayer, described in earlier chapters.

A friend said, "I was beginning to have numerous human relations problems, and realized that I needed to change my prayer methods. I had grown stale, and my meditation periods no longer generated spiritual power. So I returned to the verbal use of denial and affirmation. And these simple prayer methods began to solve my problems."

Be assured that when you are again ready for meditation, you will feel that inner pressure calling you back to it.

THE PRECIOUS BALM OF PRAYER

As St. Francis of Sales advised, "After prayer, be careful not to agitate your heart, lest you spill some of the precious balm you have received."

Learn to enjoy the different seasons of prayer to which you are called in your soul growth. The various prayer methods — both simple and advanced — can bring balance to your over-all growth and understanding. Since there is nothing dull about prayer, they are also necessary for experiencing a satisfying and exciting life!

THE PRAYER OF SILENCE

— Chapter 10 —

There once was a country banker who practiced the prayer of silence. His bank needed to borrow what it considered a large sum of money and he went to New York City to negotiate for the loan, but without success.

While he was talking over the matter with a city bank executive, his customary "silence hour" approached and he was puzzled about what to do. He finally decided to be honest, and in the midst of the apparently unfavorable discussion, this country banker quietly announced that he always devoted a few minutes to prayer at that hour, and begged to be excused.

The attitude of the city bank executive immediately changed. He recognized in his client something he did not have: peace, poise, and trust in the face of defeat. The city banker haltingly replied that he also liked to observe daily periods of prayer and would be glad to join in.

Together these men entered the silence and experienced a strong realization of God's presence and power. At the conclusion of their prayer period, the city banker informed his country client that he was satisfied with the securities offered and that the loan would be granted without delay.

THE SECRET OF ALL ATTAINMENT

There is an occult formula for success: *Think. Act. Wait.*

Many prayer people dissipate their prayer powers because they think and act, but do not complete the last part of the formula *by then waiting*. The prayer of silence *helps you to wait*.

In my book *The Prosperity Secrets of the Ages*, the importance of this silence period of waiting is discussed in connection with the Sabbath, or seventh day of creation, in which God finished His work and rested. It was thereafter that it manifested as a visible result.[1] The success symbology is that you should do all that you can mentally and visibly to make a situation right. Then you should "let go" and let it work out completely in God's own way. While it is working out in God's own way, you observe a silence. And unless, and until, you observe a silence, it never works out, because you haven't released it to do so!

---

1. See Chapter 3 of *The Prosperity Secrets of the Ages*.

Why is the silence so powerful? Why is waiting necessary in order to get your prayers answered? Why did everything change for the country banker after he practiced the silence?

Everything changed because the silence creates. The reason the silence creates is because in it you still your surface mind, so that the deeper levels of the mind may be free to function. In the silence, when your conscious mind becomes quiet, then the subconscious phase of the mind, which is the seat of memory and feeling, is free to function. In the silence as you are still, the highly sensitive superconscious phase of the mind begins to function, revealing fresh inspiration and new ideas. *Though the silence appears to be a "do nothing" state of prayer, plenty happens in that state, so that it is one of the most powerful and creative. Indeed, everything comes out of the silence!*

The silence is the simplest operation of which the mind is capable. There is no mystery about it. *In the silence you gather together your spiritual forces and creative energies necessary for the expression of your good.* Within you is a mighty quietness in which lies all power. By going into the silence, you tap that power.

The silence is the workshop of God. "Silence is the element in which great things fashion themselves together," explained the Scottish writer Carlyle.

The silence is the key to greater power, dominion, harmony, health, to perfection of every phase of your world. *Whatever your heart craves, whatever your life needs, may be contacted in the silence. Practicing the silence is the secret of all attainment, because it is the secret of all creative power.*

WHY THE LACK OF SILENCE IS ABNORMAL

Most people think that unless you stay busy every minute, something is wrong with you. Just the opposite is true: It is only *if* you stay busy every minute that something is wrong with you! People usually seek outside themselves for the calm, peace, and creative power that can only be found within themselves, in the silence.

People who condemn the practice of repose, stillness, quietness do not realize that the silence is the "power behind the throne" of all results. Meister Eckhardt, the 13th-century German mystic, described the silence as "that immobility by which all things are moved." People who sit with folded hands, apparently doing nothing, may not be lazy or idle but just may be in the process of bringing forth a great and wonderful stillness out of which new good will be created. The difference between laziness and quiet contemplation is that the contemplator is taking time to be holy, or to become whole.

Unfortunately, a number of our useless daily activities arise from the erroneous belief that we must be doing something all the time and that, if we are not busy, something is wrong with us. Yet the practice of the silence is a more powerful cause of results than many of the activities we see about us that have no principle.

In his book, *Commonsense about Prayer,* Lewis Maclachlan explained:

Many people imagine that they are serving God when they are doing far too much and working far too hard. . . . People who work themselves to death, or very near it, for the sake of God have surely misunderstood what God requires of them. This passion for overwork, when it is not caused by conditions that call for the help of a psychiatrist, is usually due to an unconscious desire to expiate unworthiness and obtain merit and distinction. . . . Overwork continues to do so much harm largely because it is considered the mark of devoted and saintly character. . . . Overwork is usually a failure both in faith and in self-discipline. It deserves more blame than praise. Far from being heroic it is often quite selfish and instead of being encouraged as a virtue, it should be reproved as a fault.

The worst feature of excessive *busy-ness* is that it deprives us of that calm and unhurried waiting upon God which is one of the means that He uses to communicate His mind to us. Many people in their prayers, as in their whole attitude to life, are far more conscious of what they are doing for God than of what God is doing for them. . . . Prayer is not so much something that we do as something that God does in us. Our excited self-importance must subside before God can use us. It is not as though we were labouring in prayer to produce some result. We are quietly putting the matter into the hands of God and leaving Him to do what we cannot do ourselves. *It is in rest that we receive much of God's answer to our prayers.*[2]

It has been estimated that a person who practices the silence can accomplish more in thirty minutes than the average person accomplishes in eight or nine hours. Though this may be an overestimation, one thing is sure:

---

2. Lewis Maclachlan, *Commonsense about Prayer* (London: James Clarke & Co., Ltd., 1962).

Too much talk, too much action often wastes your powers and scatters your forces, whereas through concentration, then meditation on holy things, your mind is cleansed and becomes uncrowded. It can then listen, hear, and follow the guidance given it in the silence. Just as in the silence the tiny sapling gathers strength to become a mighty oak, so do you gather immense strength in the silence to carry forward into your daily life. Carlyle advised:

> Hold thy tongue for one day; on the morrow see how much clearer are thy purposes and duties. What rubbish within thee has been swept away!

Achievement is not always the result of struggle and strife. Sometimes the greatest rewards are won by the leisurely expectant. Strife does not win anything but temporary results. Knowing how to wait is always more permanently effective.

WHAT HAPPENS IN THE PRAYER OF SILENCE

In the prayer of silence, you are not trying to rest the mind on a single idea, as in the prayer of concentration. You are not trying to consider freely many ideas and let them unfold their meaning to you, as in meditation. In the prayer of silence, you cease trying to think, be, do, get or have anything.

You simply become mentally quiet, physically still, and make contact with your own indwelling Lord. Prayer has been described as communion with God. In the practice of the silence, you make common union with your indwelling Lord.

In the silence you may hear or receive new ideas and guidance or you may not. *Nothing may seem to happen in the silence.* Yet you are always helped through practicing the silence, because it feeds your inner being.

In the silence you are not reaching out. You are turning within; then resting, listening, waiting, trusting. In this "do nothing" state of mind, you become completely open and receptive to the flow of divine power from deep within. You become an empty vessel which the Holy Spirit is then able to fill anew.

When you first begin to practice the silence, you may feel a bit like George Bernard Shaw felt when asked his opinion of prayer: "Many people have prayed for me and I have not been any worse for it."

You may not feel that anything is happening when you first begin to practice the silence, but you will find that you are not any worse for having done it! As you continue the practice, you will begin to enjoy it and may finally find yourself looking forward to its "sweet stillness."

HOW ONE BOY GREW UP TO REALIZE
THE POWER OF "SITTING IN THE SILENCE"

Once upon a time there was a lively little boy who accompanied his parents to the midweek prayer service at their church, though he personally considered it a waste of time. His objection was that nothing seemed to happen at these services: There would be a prayer, a few songs, and the minister would say a few words about prayer and healing. But most of the hour would be spent by the minister and congregation "sitting in the silence."

This little boy thought it foolish for his parents to come so far and sit for an hour with these people doing nothing. After everyone had been in silent prayer for a long time one night, this child could stand it no longer. He jumped up and yelled: "Wake up, everybody! It's time to go home!"

Years later, this man realized the great power that had been generated in those prayer periods in his childhood, and he seriously took up the practice of the prayer of silence. He became so fascinated with its power that he finally became a minister. The day even came when he, too, conducted prayer meetings in his church which consisted of "sitting in the silence" —where nobody seemed to do anything!

HOW TO GET SPIRITUALLY READY
FOR THE SILENCE

Prayer is effort, then becomes effortless. The silence is the effortless phase of prayer.

These "do nothing" prayer times can be among the most fruitful and rewarding of your life, once you are ready for them spiritually. Too many people try to be "advanced" in prayer, scoffing at the prayers of relaxation, denial, affirmation, concentration, and even meditation.

They state that they have gone "beyond" these types of prayer, and that they practice the silence only. *The prayer of silence, however, is creative, satisfying, productive only for those people who are ready for it spiri-*

tually, for those who have already worked their way through the other phases of prayer, and for those who readily use the other types of prayer.

The average person has many old negative memories and psychological blocks that must be cleared up through prayers of relaxation, denial and affirmation, before he can possibly practice concentration, meditation, and the silence. *If one attempts to practice the silence before mastering the other types of prayer first, he will only meet with frustration.* He has not cleared the way to make contact with the innermost part of his being, out of which the silence comes.

In due time, as you practice the other types of prayer, you come to a period in which you are ready to practice the silence. When you reach that point in your spiritual unfoldment, you will know it because you will find that other forms of prayer no longer satisfy you or meet your spiritual needs. There will be an inner longing that turns your attention within in a waiting, receptive manner.

When you reach this point in your prayer development, you may find that your prayers are no longer being answered. No lesser method of prayer than the silence satisfies. It is then that you are ready to launch forth into the prayer of silence.

In his book entitled *The Silence,* E. V. Ingraham has written about its rewards:

In the silence, man brings himself to a realization of the good for which he has long sought in vain.[3]

---

3. E. V. Ingraham, *The Silence* (Unity Village, Mo.: Unity School of Christianity, 1922).

THE TRULY GREAT PEOPLE IN HISTORY
PRACTICED THE SILENCE

Practice of the silence clears away trivial thought and opens an inner channel through which results can then flow forth from infinite mind within. This method has been used by every genius, inventor, and philosopher of note throughout the ages: Buddha, Moses, Jesus, Mohammed, St. Benedict, Spinoza, Thoreau, Carlyle, Emerson — all of them knew that the power of solitude was among the most important practices in the art of fulfilled living.

The mystics of old described it as the art of "holy indifference." Brother Lawrence regarded the silence as a "holy inactivity."

Plotinus, the greatest philosopher of the Neoplatonist school, wrote in the 3rd century: "We can pray only when we come alone to the Alone." St. John of Damascus described solitude as "the mother of prayer." The individual nature of the prayer of great religious souls expressed itself in this solitariness.

There is a theory that great people often have a "period of obscurity" and that those "lost years" are times in which they gain wisdom, strength, and emotional stamina for the periods of intense activity and great achievement that lie ahead.

Jesus apparently observed an eighteen-year period of silence and obscurity prior to beginning his public ministry. His greatest works in his public ministry were always performed after He went up into the mountains and observed creative periods of silence.

Moses spent forty years in the silence of the Midian Desert tending sheep, in creative preparation for leading two million people out of bondage. Both

David and Paul went into periods of obscurity after realizing they had divine missions to accomplish — David into the wilderness of Southern Judah, and Paul into Arabia. Those obscure periods prepared them for the work that lay ahead. Both later wrote of the importance of the silence: David, when he said, "My soul, wait thou in silence for God only, for my expectation is from him" (Psalms 62:5); Paul, when he advised the early Christians, "Abound more and more . . . study to be quiet" (I Thessalonians 4:10, 11).

It was in the silence of the temple that little Samuel first heard Jehovah's call. He responded, "Speak, for thy servant heareth" (I Samuel 3:10). Out of the silence Samuel soared forth to become the foremost figure of his age.

Many of the prophets and leaders of Israel were prepared for their work by the discipline of fasting from speech. The voice in the wilderness was felt to be a clearer revelation of God than earthquake, fire or storm to the prophet Elijah, who described God as "a still, small voice" (I Kings 19:12).

In almost all periods of religious history, in every part of the world, silence has been suggested as a preparation of the soul for spiritual contact. A 14th-century A.D. Chinese philosopher put it succinctly: "If a man keeps his mouth shut, his words become powerful."

The Greek essayist Plutarch stated: "In sacrifices, religious mysteries, and ceremonies of divine science we receive by tradition the command to keep silent. Silence is a mythical secret and a divine virtue."

The unspoken word was both center and circumference of the ancient Hindu religions and philosophies, as it was also of Buddhism. *Persian, Arabian,*

Greek, Hebrew and Christian mystics have all preached the discipline of silence as a way to find God. Egyptian mystical worship called God "the Lord of the Silent."

The ancient Hebrews substituted the vowels of "Adonai" (Lord) and "Elohim" (God) for those of the sacred name Jahweh (Jehovah), so as to avoid uttering carelessly the name of the Almighty. The tradition among the ancient Druids of Wales, known as "the All-Knowing Ones," was to guard in silence the things that they had learned about their God who was "forever sacred and secret."

Socrates practiced silence as a means of inner culture, while the Greek philosopher Pythagoras required that his disciples observe an absolute silence for as much as from one to five years.

A number of the early Christian mystics spent several years alone practicing the silence, before ministering in powerful ways to the people of their era. Among the Christian Fathers, St. Augustine in particular insisted upon solitude and silence for one who would find God, and this practice descended to the various monastic orders. St. Catherine of Sienna spent three years alone in her house practicing the silence, and then went forth to pour out her spiritual power to the world. Her tremendous influence was felt among the heads of state as well as among the leading priests, soldiers, artists, merchants, lawyers and politicians of her day. They were all attracted to the serenity and wisdom she had gained from her years alone in the silence.

A well-known sect in modern times which practices the silence is the Society of Friends, popularly called Quakers. To them God is an "inner light." It is interesting to note that, during the two hundred years of our early colonial history when thousands of our colonists were attacked and killed by the Indians, the Quakers, who numbered more than any other group of outlying pioneers and who differed from the rest in an outer way only in that they never pulled in their latch strings at night and never carried a gun by day, were always left untouched. Not a child, man or woman of the Quaker faith was hurt by the Indians! Their secret weapon was doubtless their knowledge and practice of the silence.

In his booklet *The Lord's Prayer,* Glenn Clark reminds us that present-day religion needs to rediscover the power of the silence:

> When one experiences a thing, he does not talk about it. He grows still and rests in it. The bane of our churches today is their much talking. A Chinese philosopher was once asked what he thought of the Christian religion. "Well," he said slowly, "it is a very talky religion."
>
> The first thing required, then, for a deeper outpouring of the spirit, first in our individual lives, and then in the lives of the world, is for us to *get still.* American churches cannot Christianize the world until they themselves have learned how to be still.[4]

SILENCE IS IN EVERY ELEMENT OF NATURE

We see the principle of the silence operating in every element of nature: The night quiet after the day; the quiet going out of the tide after it has noisily come in;

---

4. Glenn Clark, *The Lord's Prayer* (St. Paul: Macalester Park Publishing Company, 1932).

the bare silent winter after the profuse and bustling growing time of spring and summer, and then fall's harvest; the creation story of six days of activity followed by the spiritual silence of the Sabbath.

Fisherman have a saying: "There is a time to fish and a time to dry the nets." We all need to "dry our nets" occasionally. Periods of silence are periods of "drying the nets."

Have you ever watched a ship going through a lock? When it moves into the lock, it cuts off its own power, it rests, it stands still. If the ship is going upstream, the water in the lock slowly rises and lifts it to a higher level, and then, when the gate is opened, it moves forward again at that higher level. Just so with man, when he "cuts off his engine" and dares to be silent.

The farmer knows about the power of silence in connection with the soil. He calls it "crop rotation," a form of soil conservation. A good farmer refuses to plant any piece of land with the same crop year after year. He knows this depletes the soil. He will often plant that area with rye, then plow it under to enrich the soil. He knows *there must be an "inworking" before there can be an "outworking."*

Philosophers of all ages have taught that a person of no silence is like a tree with no roots, which is turned to leaves and boughs, and must eventually wither and die. The Chinese philosophers have a saying: "In returning to the root is rest."

THE HEALING POWER OF THE SILENCE

The silence is to the soul what food is to the body. Incessant talk and activity give the soul no chance to express normally and stifle it, whereas the silence is a healing balm. Carlyle said, "The highest melody dwells only in silence — the melody of health."

Incessant talk and incessant activity cause the most marvelous of all mechanisms, the body, to get thrown out of balance, fly off at a tangent, and cause all its delicate organs to set up war against each other. On the other hand, in quietness the soul is given a chance to inaugurate its recuperative powers and send its vital, regenerative influences flowing through the complex system of nerves, veins, and arteries of the body.

When you give yourself up to the practice of the silence, the soul comes into its own again, and channels are opened for its rhythmic vibrations to restore hurried, discordant nerves to normal action.

It is then that this health jingle seems appropriate:

> Joy and temperance and repose,
> Slam the door on the doctor's nose!

SILENCE HEALED THOSE WHO HAD BEEN HOSPITALIZED

A busy woman found herself in the hospital. She mentally resisted thinking, "What have I done to cause this? I have too much to do to be here. I just cannot waste my time in this way."

Since she worried, fretted, and remained in an agitated state, she did not get well. Then a minister came to visit her and in a quiet moment he said, "It is so restful to sit here. Just to be still, to be very, very still, and to know that God is here healing."

After the minister's visit, this lady meditated on the idea of stillness. She practiced the silence by stilling her mind with the words of the Psalmist, "Be still and know that I am God" (Psalms 46:10). When thoughts of agitation tried to take over, she said to them, "Peace, be still."

In this stillness, her mind and body began to relax, and a great sense of peace finally came, followed later by a sense of joy. She "let go" every care. In relaxed stillness, she slept without medication that night. When she went home two days later, she realized it was only in stillness and silence that her healing had come.

There is an Oriental proverb: "The flower of Truth blooms in the stillness, after the storm and stress of effort."

Another woman once went to a hospital for just the opposite reason—not because she was sick, but to keep from getting sick—by getting away from her noisy family!

During the hospital stay, she was freed from contact with an embittered relative who had had an unhappy love affair. This relative had poured out her bitterness upon this woman, who then entered the hospital to get peace, quiet, and freedom from the poisoned emotions of her unhappy relative. As she quietly relaxed, rested more physically, and calmed her mind emotionally, doing inspirational reading and spending long periods in quiet meditation and silence, she realized the value of Longfellow's healing formula:

> Let us labor for an inward stillness,
> An inward stillness and an inward healing.

INFORMAL METHODS OF PRACTICING
THE SILENCE

Informally there are several simple ways you can begin to practice the silence and reap its unlimited benefits:

First: By being still and quiet: listening in prayer.

Second: Through the act of self-control as you keep quiet in daily living.

Third: Through the act of withholding criticism, condemnation, judgment of others.

Fourth: Through the act of refusing to talk idly, to chatter needlessly.

Fifth: Through the act of saying in prayer, "It is done," when you have prayed for a season and perhaps have witnessed no visible results. This should be a time of "letting go and letting God."

The following stories relate how others have used these simple methods of practicing the silence in daily living with rewarding results.

AN ADVERTISING EXECUTIVE REAPED
THE REWARDS OF SILENCE

You can take up the practice of the silence informally by making a practice of being still and quiet: listening in prayer.

A man in the advertising business said he used to sit down at his typewriter in the morning and try to turn out so many ideas in so many hours. He often strenuously produced the ideas, but felt dissatisfied about their content.

Then he learned to sit for about fifteen minutes each

morning, waiting in the silence, before starting his work. He thought of God as the source of all ideas and as the creator of everything, and he asked that divine ideas be expressed in his work. As he quietly waited, out of the silence feelings, ideas, and phrases would come to him and he found himself eager to put them on paper. Practicing the silence each morning before beginning his work proved to be the turning point to his success.

The practice of the silence leads to power and increased productivity. Whatever you have to do, whether it be housework, farmwork, factory work, office work, handwork, or brainwork, you can get much more done in far less time if you take time out every day to do nothing but sit in silent communion for a time.

As you daily practice the silence, you will find confusion leaving your mind; you will feel a sense of inner peace and power, and you may even hear the "still small voice" of God as did Elijah.

I have found that my clearest guidance about personal and professional matters often comes when I have seasons of just being silent, open, receptive, listening.

First comes a sense of peace, followed by a sense of power. Next, a flow of ideas is often followed by a flow of energy which wells up from deep within. Isaiah had doubtless had this same experience when he wrote: "They that wait for Jehovah shall renew their strength" (Isaiah 40:31).

Edward Everett Hale told a story of the little girl who had a habit of running into a chapel near the field where she played to talk to God. After she talked a bit she would get perfectly still for a few minutes, "waiting," she said, "to see if God wanted to say anything" to her. Though she did not hear literal words, often a great happiness welled up within her, and her life seemed richer and fuller after these waiting periods.

THE PRACTICE OF THE SILENCE CAN
BRING MORE FRIENDS

The *second* way you may informally begin to practice the silence in daily living is through the act of self-control, of keeping quiet in daily activities.

A housewife recently said:

> I used to pride myself on being what I like to call "frank." But I was always in "hot water" with relatives and friends because I never hesitated to give them my honest opinion, which wasn't always complimentary. People seldom appreciate that kind of frankness because it is usually a form of disapproval or criticism. I finally learned if I cannot say something kind and constructive, I had better hold my tongue. Now I get along better and have more friends.

James Watt, Scottish engineer and inventor, is said to have conceived the idea of harnessing the power of steam through watching the rise and fall of the lid above the boiling water in his mother's teakettle. *Uncontrolled, steam is only a noisemaker.* Under control, it can drive trains across the continent, propel great liners across the ocean, generate electricity to light homes and cities and to run the wheels of industry.

When you are tempted to listen to the futile chatter around you, or to dissipate your own mental and spiritual forces in idle talk, remember the proverb: "Whosoever keepeth his mouth and his tongue, keepeth his soul from troubles" (Proverbs 21:23).

THE TRIUMPH THAT ONLY SILENCE CAN BRING

The *third* way that you can informally practice the silence is through the act of withholding criticism, condemnation and judgment of others.

There once was a housewife who was noted for her sharp tongue and scolding, nagging personality. Her husband tried to escape from it by drinking, and her children retaliated with very bad behavior. There was no harmony or cooperation in this home.

Finally this woman's health was affected, and she sought medical relief, to no avail. In desperation she sought out a spiritual counselor, who quickly informed her that her own sharp tongue was the cause of all her problems, both in her health and in her home. The counselor stated she would be helped only if she bridled her tongue, practiced harmonious thinking, and became silent in her speech.

With effort, this desperate woman became quiet and stayed quiet. When her husband arrived home drunk at night, she reacted only with silence. As she refrained from endlessly reprimanding him and the children an amazing thing happened: Gradually her husband's drinking diminished and finally ceased. One by one the children became more cooperative. Finally order and harmony were restored to the home. Peace and joy came into the atmosphere, and even the health problems disappeared.

One day when they could finally communicate

again, her husband asked what had brought about all these pleasant changes. This formerly "nagging wife" quietly replied, "Practicing the silence has transformed me and our lives."

In his book, *Honey and Salt,* Carl Sandburg wrote:

By the gong of time you live.
Listen and you hear time saying you were silent long before you came to life and you will again be silent long after you leave it.
  Why not be a little silent now?
  Hush yourself, noisy little man. [5]

THE PROSPERING POWER OF THE SILENCE

The *fourth* method for informally practicing the silence in daily living is through the act of refusing to talk idly, to chatter needlessly.

"I was struggling and striving like mad, running in circles, and talking my head off, trying to make a go of my trucking business," a young man said, "until my nerves went to pieces and I was in an accident. Flat on my back, I had to be quiet for a while. I had time to think and got on the beam. Since then, I no longer struggle.

"I have learned to relax and listen to the voice of God within. *I never dreamed there could be such power in quietness! I have found that it is only when I'm still that God gives me the answer to my problems and shows me what to do.* He runs the universe without a lot of fussing and fuming, and He knows how I

---

5. Carl Sandburg, *Honey and Salt* (New York: Harcourt, Brace & World, Inc., 1963).

THE PRAYER OF SILENCE285

should run my business better than I ever did. I have a bank balance to prove it. But I have something even better: satisfied customers, appreciative employees, and inner peace."

This man had discovered what the athletes meant by "pressing." When athletes try too hard they call it "pressing." They lose rhythm and fall short of peak performance.

He also discovered that if you do not willingly practice the silence, you may be forced to do so through negative circumstances that result from lack of quietness. When this happens it can be a blessing in disguise. There is an old mystical saying: "Darkness is but the mantle which closes round about to bring stillness to the soul."

KNOW WHEN TO REST YOUR CASE!

The *fifth* method of informally practicing the silence in daily living is that of "letting go and letting God" after you have tried in inner and outer ways to make things right in your life. Just get silent with God and man. *Let go and let God.*

This method of the silence is very much like a lawyer "resting his case," after he has presented it to the judge and jury. It is in this state of "resting his case" that he awaits the decision of the judge. *It is only after he "rests his case" that the processes of law begin to operate.* At this point, all concerned withdraw their efforts and wait to learn in what manner the law itself will move.

How do you let go and let God at this point? How do you rest your case?

One woman had remarkable answers to prayer only

after she released her prayers to God saying, "Father, I'm trusting." Whenever fear or doubt would try to creep in she would reaffirm, "Father, I'm trusting!" Her prayers were always answered.

A very discouraged woman had spent five years running a boardinghouse. It was a job filled with long, hard hours and strenuous work which she had been forced to take after her husband's death. One day, feeling she could stand it no longer, she sought out a spiritual counselor and poured out her unhappiness.

The counselor quietly replied, "Nothing was ever gained by fighting. What you fight always fights back. Before you can be free of this distasteful job, you must learn to love the place where you are and know that you are doing God's work, even if it is only washing pots and pans in a boardinghouse. Then you must pray and trust God to lead you to something better."

The prayer she was given to use was this: "I PLACE MYSELF AND ALL MY AFFAIRS LOVINGLY IN THE HANDS OF THE FATHER, WITH A CHILDLIKE TRUST. THAT WHICH IS FOR MY HIGHEST GOOD SHALL COME TO ME."

During the long hours of the days and nights that followed, this previously embittered woman declared over and over amid the pots and pans, mops and cleaning utensils, "LOVINGLY IN THE HANDS OF THE FATHER."

At first nothing happened, nothing changed in an outer way, though much was changing within this woman's thoughts and feelings. Then two real estate men appeared one day and said they were looking for someone to manage a large, luxury hotel nearby.

This woman's heart sang because this had been her dream—to work amid beautiful surroundings where she could meet interesting people. As she continued affirming "LOVINGLY IN THE HANDS OF THE FATHER," she was offered the job and took it.

These words then became her secret text for success in her new assignment. Many times a day she declared, "LOVINGLY IN THE HANDS OF THE FATHER." One day the owner of the hotel said, "The whole atmosphere has changed since you took over managing the hotel. It is what I have always desired it to be. Now we never have an empty room and the class of people we are attracting is the kind I've always wanted here." She thanked him and as she walked away she said again, "IT IS LOVINGLY IN THE HANDS OF THE FATHER."

If there is some challenge in your life that has not been resolved after diligent prayer, like this woman you may need to "rest your case." Try practicing the silence. *Stop talking about the problem.* Place it "lovingly in the hands of the Father." Declare, "FATHER, I AM TRUSTING." Then do so! Let go and let God.

Many people's prayers are not answered because they do not practice the silence. Did you ever notice how impossible it is for you to help the person who loves to rehearse his difficulties? He cannot receive the answers to his prayers until he gets quiet and listens, because his mind is too crowded with the problem to receive the answer. Quiet listening is the only assured way one can receive answers.

HOW TO FORMALLY PRACTICE THE SILENCE

In order to experience fully the results of the silence, there comes a time when it is wise to have daily periods of practicing the silence in a more formal way than previously described.

Indeed, there comes a time in your prayer development when you must learn to let the mental, reasoning side of your nature alone. You must learn how to be still and listen to that which a loving Father would say to you through the intuitional side of your nature. The guidance you crave will come out of the deep silence within you, if you will get still and listen for it there.

Most people do not realize that they have this powerfully silent area within them, that this silence is nothing new or foreign, but a part of them. When they turn within and become attuned to it, they find it their greatest power.

The steps in practicing the prayer of the silence are these:

1. Relax your mind and body. "I RELAX AND LET GO. I LET GO AND LET GOD."

2. Turn your attention within, closing the eyes and quieting the mind. "I AM RELAXED IN MIND AND BODY."

3. Dwell upon the nature and presence of God, thereby establishing contact: "THERE IS ONLY ONE PRESENCE AND ONE POWER, GOD THE GOOD. GOD'S GOODNESS IS RIGHT HERE WITHIN ME AND AROUND ME NOW."

4. Continue to still your random thoughts by saying to them: "PEACE, BE STILL."

5. Then listen. If no conscious revelation or impression comes, give thanks for perfect results, and when you have experienced an inner feeling of peace, satisfaction, serenity, and a sense of well-being, conclude your silence period. Inspiration and fulfillment may come later, since you have made inner contact.

6. Conclude your silence periods with a word of thanks for divine fulfillment: "FATHER, I THANK THEE THAT THOU HEARDEST ME, AND I KNOW THAT THOU HEAREST ME ALWAYS." Or, "IT IS DONE. THE PERFECT FINISHED RESULTS NOW MANIFEST." Or, "NOT BY POWER, NOR BY MIGHT, BUT BY GOD'S SPIRIT, IT IS DONE." "THIS IS A TIME OF DIVINE FULFILLMENT."

Then get busy in an outer way, with your daily activities. You will carry with you into your world of activity the stored-up energy, inspiration, and sense of tranquility gained from the silence, thereby having achieved your purpose. Achievement will follow.

7. Make your beginning silence periods short—only two or three minutes.

Practice the silence more and more often: early in the morning, last thing at night, at odd moments during the day. The silence is not a spectacular time for seeing lights, hearing voices, or having unusual experiences. It is simply a time of quiet, peaceful, inner renewal.

8. Do not be discouraged if your silence periods do not yield anything in particular. Only by practice can you develop a consciousness of spiritual power that you seek in the silence. Practice makes perfect.

Often you will discover that it is after these silence periods that your greatest revelations come—through thoughts that flow into your mind, through words you read in a book, through something someone says that seems to contain special significance for you, or perhaps through dreams. In countless ways, the rewards of the silence will be gradually revealed to you.

THE FRUITS OF THE SILENCE

Though nothing definite or spectacular may happen in your silence periods, you will find some quietly rewarding results taking place within you after practicing the silence.

You will develop a strange new consciousness of serenity and quiet, a feeling that something has been done, that some new power to overcome is yours. The hard things in life become easier, the troublesome things will no longer have as much power to worry you, the rasping people and conditions of the world will lose their power to annoy you.

When you have learned how to abandon yourself to infinite spirit and have sessions of doing this daily, you will be surprised at the marvelous change that will be wrought in you without any conscious effort on your part. It will search far below your conscious mind and root out things in your nature of which you had scarcely been conscious.

As you continue practicing the silence daily, you will stop being so humanly strenuous. (There is a proverb: "*Hurry* is the devil.") The feeling of being so important, of having so much to do, will leave you.

The petty personality problems will begin to fall away from you: anger, fear, jealousy, impatience, depression. You will let go trivial things, activities, people. You will learn to say "no" to the lesser. You will have clearer insight about everything and will dare to follow that insight unhesitatingly. You will clear the clutter out of your life.

Previously, through intensity and hurry you may have shut off the divine power within you. Through practicing the silence you will now find yourself rising out of this state of tension, into one of living trust. It is in this new state of quiet trust that the highest work is done in prayer. *There are some things which you are to do for yourself in your prayer experiences, but there are others which God does not expect you to do!*

For instance, with your conscious mind you are to speak the word of life, truth, abundance, health, peace, and you are to act as though the words are true. But the bringing of them to pass is the work of that Higher

Power. *Its ability to work depends on your trusting by getting very still inside. It is when you get beyond the point where you try to do it all yourself and let God do His part, that you get the desires of your heart.*

There are ten direct references in the Bible to "stand still" in the face of challenging circumstances, beginning with Moses who instructed the children of Israel concerning how they were to escape from Egyptian bondage:

> Fear ye not, stand still, and see the salvation of Jehovah which he will work for you today; for the Egyptians whom ye have seen today, ye shall see them again no more forever. Jehovah will fight for you, and ye shall hold your peace (Exodus 14:13, 14).

Just prior to being anointed king, Saul was instructed by Samuel to "stand thou still first, that I may cause thee to hear the word of God" (I Samuel 9:27).

The turning point from destruction to restoration of all God's blessings came in Job's life only after he followed the instructions: "Hearken unto this, O Job. Stand still, and consider the wondrous works of God" (Job 37:14).

These promises clearly reveal that one of the rewards of the silence is that the Lord can produce perfect results in your life, too, but only after you learn to hold your peace.

The anonymous 14th-century mystic who wrote *The Cloud of Unknowing* explained that there are two kinds of "life in the spirit": One is the active life and the other is the contemplative life. He states that the active life is lower, and the contemplative life is higher.

Dr. Robert Russell has explained that "the way to

immunize ourselves from the lesser things of life and to open ourselves to the greater ones is the way of the silence."

The possibilities and rewards of practicing the prayer of silence are great. This practice can help you to develop the contemplative life, which is considered among the most important phases of the spiritual way of life. Indeed, the practice of the silence can bring the most satisfying results to both the inner and outer phases of your world!

THE PRAYER OF REALIZATION

— Chapter 11 —

The prayer that gets results is the prayer of realization. The word "realization" means "a feeling." To realize is to feel, make real, accomplish, to acquire as a result, to conceive vividly as real.

This is what you are trying to accomplish as you study the various phases of prayer described in this book. You have sought to get the feeling of inner contact, the feeling of accomplishing results, or just a vivid feeling of peace, serenity, and that all is well.

Many people's prayers are not answered because they never get such an inner realization. *They do not work in prayer long enough or often enough to attain the feeling of answered prayer.* They observe short periods of verbal prayer or the silence, and then rush

off wondering why their prayers have not been answered.

HOW A HUMAN RELATIONS PROBLEM
WAS RESOLVED

A businessman faced complex human relations problems. To outer appearances there was nothing he could
do. The power to produce satisfactory results seemed
to be controlled by other people, who were hostile to
him. In spite of this, he realized that if he could gain a
realization of answered prayer, the good would manifest regardless of what others were doing or saying.

He began to declare with authority: "WITH GOD
THERE IS ALWAYS A WAY. GOD IS NOW OPENING THE WAY
TO PERFECT RESULTS IN THIS SITUATION. I AM IN TRUE
RELATIONSHIP WITH ALL PEOPLE AND ALL SITUATIONS
NOW. THE GOOD IS NOW VICTORIOUS!"

He persisted in this declaration until he gained an
inner realization of peace, and a vivid feeling that
all was well. When he got that realization, he gave
thanks for perfect results, dismissed the matter, and
kept re-releasing it every time the troublesome subject
entered his mind.

Suddenly the tide turned and his good began to
work through the very people and conditions who had
seemed hostile to him. Without knowing or caring
what his desires in the matter were, these people
began unconsciously to fulfill them anyway! His own
prayer of vivid realization had opened the way.

HOW TO IDENTIFY WITH THE PRAYER
OF REALIZATION

The prayer of realization is the prayer that gives you a good feeling. That good feeling may come as a sense of peace or it may come as one of electric excitement. But it produces a vivid feeling that all is well.

Charles Fillmore has explained the prayer of realization in his book *Atom Smashing Power of the Mind.*[1]

Spiritual realization changes things. In scientific prayer, realization is the high point of attainment.

HEALING OF BREAST CAME THROUGH
REALIZATION IN PRAYER

Many more people would experience answered prayer if they would just persist in prayer long enough to attain that vivid feeling of realization. Prayer can only do for you what it can first do through your thoughts and feelings. *Effective prayer works from the inside out.*

You do not have to get a spiritual realization in order for your prayers to have power, but realization is a sure indication that you have made inner contact, and that your prayers *will* be answered. Even though you can be helped—things can improve through prayer without your experiencing realization—usually the matter is not completely cleared up until you get a vivid feeling

---

1. Charles Fillmore, *Atom Smashing Power of the Mind* (Unity Village, Mo.: Unity School of Christianity, 1949).

about it. Therefore, *realization is worth working for in prayer, because it produces completed results.*

A young businesswoman feared cancer of the breast. She had been under doctor's care for some time but medication had rendered no improvement. Finally the doctor informed her that she should go to the hospital within a week for a biopsy and further tests. He tried to prepare her for the worst.

After returning from the doctor's office, this young woman wrote two letters: The first was to *Silent Unity* requesting their prayers for her healing. The second was to a friend who had been a powerful prayer partner in the past.

There was no noticeable improvement until the day before she was scheduled to go to the hospital for tests. Then she noticed that some activity was occurring in the troubled area. By the next morning the lump that had been the size of a pecan was no larger than a pea. When the doctor examined it, he explained that what remained was nothing more than harmless scar tissue that probably would remain indefinitely. (It later disappeared, too.)

Her prayer partner later wrote a letter saying:

"I usually sit in my big chair and pray for about fifteen minutes each night just before retiring. Last Thursday night (the night before you were to go to the hospital), I started to pray but somehow all I could think about was your healing, that it had begun and would continue. I knew then that our prayers for your health were being answered."

SPIRITUAL PREDICTION COMING TRUE

Perhaps you think such experiences are "unusual" in these times when we hear so much about poverty, war, crime, and disease. They are not unusual, as reported in my book *The Dynamic Laws of Healing*. But such good news is rarely shouted from the house-tops nor does it get headlines in the press.

In the late 1890's the Canadian medical doctor Richard Bucke predicted that the spiritual consciousness in man, which he called "cosmic consciousness" (also the title of his book),[2] would soon become common thinking for everyone.

When Dr. Bucke spoke to the British Medical Association in Montreal in 1894, he told those physicians that this divine phase of man's being known as "cosmic consciousness" was even then becoming increasingly common and that it would eventually become general. Dr. Bucke also predicted that the development of the spiritual phase of the mind would soon lift the whole of human life to a higher level.

Dr. Bucke was a medical doctor who had had a spiritual awakening and dared to tell the world about it. He even dared to predict the spiritual evolution of mankind. He stated that the human race was in the process of developing a new kind of consciousness, far in advance of the present one, and that this new kind of consciousness would lift the race above and beyond the fears, ignorance and brutalities that beset it.

In recent decades, Dr. Bucke's predictions have been coming true. More and more people have quietly taken

2. Richard Maurice Bucke, *Cosmic Consciousness* (New York: E. P. Dutton & Co., Inc., 1901).

up a spiritual quest and have begun to develop their innate spiritual powers.

You may not hear much about them. You may hear just the opposite — that the world is "going to the dogs." But in spite of such reports, more people are quietly seeking spiritually in this age than at any time since the 1st or 2nd century after Christ! They are doing so through a private search and they are keeping quiet about it. But the inner world of spirit is being discovered, explored and contacted as Dr. Bucke predicted it would be.

This is not unusual but follows a pattern:

History reveals that the great periods of mystical activity tend to correspond with the great periods of artistic, material, and intellectual civilization. As a rule, great periods of spiritual activity come immediately after and seem to complete such other periods. When science, politics, literature, and the arts have risen to their height and produced their greatest works, the mystics have then appeared and carried on, as though to give spiritual balance to these various areas of achievement!

Between the 1st century A.D. and the 19th century, this curve exhibited three great waves of mystical activity, besides many minor fluctuations. They came at the close of the Classical, the Medieval, and the Renaissance Periods in history, reaching their highest points in the 3rd, 14th, and 17th centuries.

We can see why there has been so much spiritual searching in this present era, which has also been a period of much scientific and intellectual discovery. Dr. Bucke's heartening prediction about man's spiritual evolution is in the process of quietly coming true!

REALIZATION: THE PRAYER OF HOLY TELEPATHY

Prayer has been described as "holy telepathy." *Surely the prayer of realization is the prayer of holy telepathy.*

You have heard much in recent years about "mental telepathy," where you become attuned in thought to some other person. But holy telepathy is an even higher activity of the mind, because in holy telepathy you become attuned in thought to a divine power and its indwelling presence within you.

That is the main purpose of prayer anyway. Not to get something but to be something, to find and express your indwelling divinity. Through the prayer of realization you make contact with the God power within you. This results in "holy telepathy" which, in turn, always brings appropriate results.

How does one get a realization in prayer that will assure results? Sometimes just by (1) asking for an inner assurance of answered prayer; (2) dwelling upon the subject you need guidance about; (3) affirming guidance and a realization of answered prayer. Any of these acts may result in a flash of "holy telepathy" that will reveal the answer to you. The following will indicate how you can develop the foregoing three methods.

ASK FOR INNER ASSURANCE OF
ANSWERED PRAYER

At a time when I was overworked and underpaid in my first ministry and was suffering from near exhaustion from which there seemed no relief, one night while working late in my study, in a moment of despair, I placed my head wearily on my desk and thought: "If this is what the ministry is all about, I won't last. I cannot believe that working so hard for so little and reaching so few people can be a loving Father's will. Surely there is a larger plan for my life and for my ministry than this."

Finally, I remembered to ask, "Father, what is the truth about this? What is the divine plan of my life? What is it that I am supposed to be doing in the ministry?"

Quick as a flash, on the inner plane I saw a stack of books, placed one on top of the other in a rather casual way. The stack was high. The books were big. Just as suddenly the vision was gone, though I can still see it mentally.

At that time I was writing magazine articles, but had no plans for writing books, nor any idea of what I would write books about. At first I was puzzled, then overwhelmed, because I realized how much work goes into writing. Nevertheless, within a year, through an orderly sequence of events, I was busy on my first book. Later, through another orderly sequence of events, a change in ministries gave me much more time to devote to writing. A far more balanced way of life with adequate time for rest and relaxation unfolded, too.

That first book and others of mine have since stacked up on my coffee table, just as they did in that inner flash several decades ago. There is still a large stack of books on the inner plane, though. I often see them. They are like unruly children, all clamoring to get my attention, impatient to be "born."

Often our prayers are answered in flashes of realization similar to this one, after we ask for guidance.

RECEIVE GUIDANCE BY DWELLING
ON THE SUBJECT

Sometimes a realization of answered prayer comes just by dwelling casually upon the subject you need guidance about and then by releasing it.

Once when I was planning to fly to Canada to lecture, one night late I was thinking that I must get my lecture notes made for that trip within the next few days. That night after turning out the light and relaxing, the main lecture for that trip, a banquet talk, came to me in three parts. The first part of the lecture started flowing in ideas to me so strongly that I turned on my light and made several pages of notes. Again the light went out and I prepared to sleep. Again, a flow of ideas started, which was the second part of the banquet talk. And the third part flowed forth an hour later, after I had again attempted to sleep. This time, the banquet talk was complete — at least in rough form. Thereafter, making final notes was a simple matter.

One spring during a yearbook deadline, an editor prayed for guidance about how she could have more time in her personal and professional life. Two mornings later, after dwelling for several days upon the truth that there should be time for everything, she awakened at 5 A.M. and a complete and workable plan for the next year's yearbook unfolded as rapidly as she could write it down. Exactly what to do in each section of the book was revealed. The end result would be a saving of time, energy, supplies, printing, and it would be a far better book, which it later proved to be.

AFFIRMING GUIDANCE GETS RESULTS

Sometimes just by affirming guidance and a realization of answered prayer, it comes.

It is wise to assert, decree, and declare it. Then you should stand fast in the vivid feeling that there is a right solution to every problem, a right answer to every prayer.

One lady often had amazing answers to prayer just by asserting over and over in the face of challenging experiences: "Prayer works!"

If you will begin to declare, affirm, decree this, you will find it coming true. For any situation that concerns you, begin now to declare, "THERE IS A RIGHT SOLUTION TO THIS SITUATION. THERE IS A RIGHT ANSWER TO THIS PRAYER."

Decreeing it over and over will give you a sense of peace and that is what you want. When you get that, the problem is well on the way to being resolved.

Repetition of truth has a tendency to open up the inner recesses of your mind to infinite power, and to allow it to flow forth as perfect, complete results.

AN INNER FEELING IS THE SECRET
OF EFFECTIVE PRAYER

There was a period in the history of religion when there arose a division of thought as to the use of verbal prayers. Some said that prayer should be expressed silently, and, in the 17th century, there existed those groups called the Pietists and the Quietists who believed in quiet communion with God as the only method of prayer. But the school of though that was popular prior to the 17th century continued to proclaim that prayer was not prayer unless it was put into oral form and spoken. The majority of mankind during that period continued to believe that prayer should and must be uttered aloud in definite words. So fixed prayers were formulated and people were taught to recite them. They were instructed to "say" their prayers.

The problem with just "saying" prayers was that the act of prayer became automatic with no feeling in it. *When the feeling was gone out of prayer so was its power, because only prayers with feeling or inner sensing have the necessary power in them to produce permanent, satisfying answers.*

Both schools of thought were right. Silent prayer and verbal prayer are both necessary. *The prayer method that helps you induce feeling is the one to use. The prayer with feeling is the prayer that brings realization, and realization produces results.*

You may have tried to solve your problems when you had not first gotten the right thought and the right feeling about those problems. The good works from within your God-nature outward.

If you have tried to master your problems without having first mastered your own thoughts and feelings about them, nothing much happened and frustration set in.

The creative activity of good must first take place within you before it can work for you, through you or round about you.

Knowing this, you stop trying to make things right in an outer way. Instead you get down to business spiritually within your own thoughts and feelings. You begin to work within yourself until you get a feeling that all is well within. When you have mastered the problem there, the good manifests.

When you learn of the power of realization, you stop fighting your problems. You stop trying to force your good. You know that the only place you ever have to work out anything is on the inner plane of your own thoughts and feelings. When you have worked it out there, it is done. You can then let it alone and watch it come about in an outer way.

This kind of realization in prayer changes things. This kind of vivid feeling of well-being in prayer is result-getting. Such realizations are the high point of attainment in prayer. The lecturer and writer known only as Neville wrote that "feeling is the secret," that a good feeling that comes in prayer is an inner assurance of outer results.

Regardless of how your realization comes, it is priceless. During the 17th century, George Fox, founder of the Quakers, had a tremendous realization at the age of 24. He described it as an "opening" and stated: "In one quarter of an hour, I saw and knew more than if I had been many years at a university."

VARIOUS PRAYER METHODS CAN BRING REALIZATION

Any of the prayer methods described in this book can give you a realization or feeling of answered prayer. Sometimes one prayer method will give you that feeling; sometimes another.

First: *The Prayer of Relaxation,* where you relax your mind and body and turn your attention within, can bring a realization of God's indwelling presence and power. Often realization comes as you breathe deeply and relax into this prayer: "I AM RELAXED IN MIND AND BODY. I AM OPEN AND RECEPTIVE TO MY HIGHEST GOOD WITHIN AND WITHOUT NOW."

Sometimes it is the relaxed attitude toward a problem that brings the realization of answered prayer.

A man wrote from England: "Not long ago I had a flat to let. It had been occupied for some time by a charming couple, and my wife and I were reluctant to advertise the vacancy lest we get tenants who would disappoint us. We decided to relax and leave the matter 'lovingly in the hands of the Father,' to let Him bring the right tenant knocking at the door.

"A week or so after we made this decision the telephone rang. It proved to be a wrong number, but before I could ring off, the voice on the other end of the wire said, 'I'm looking for a flat.' I asked him to come to see me, and he proved to be the tenant we were waiting for."

Second: *The Prayer of Cleansing* may be the one that brings a realization of answered prayer, as you dissolve negative appearances with the thought, "NO, NO, NO. I DO NOT BELIEVE THIS." Or "NO, NO, NO. I DO NOT ACCEPT THIS," or such outright denials as "MY GOOD CANNOT BE LIMITED!" Also the prayers of forgiveness and release dissolve fear and bring a realization of peace and power.

One woman had so much trouble that she felt she was losing her mind. Then she began to declare over and over, "I DO NOT BELIEVE IT IS GOD'S WILL THAT I SHOULD BE IN TROUBLE, AND SO I DO NOT ACCEPT TROUBLE AS NECESSARY OR REAL IN MY LIFE." Over and over when troublesome thoughts or situations tried to take over

her feelings she would declare Isaiah's promise: "THOU
WILT KEEP HIM IN PERFECT PEACE WHOSE MIND IS STAYED
ON THEE" (Isaiah 26:3). She was saved from her troubles, not only mentally and emotionally, but literally
as conditions adjusted themselves.

Third: *The Prayer of Decree* for many people is the
one that brings realization. Positively asserting words
of truth releases tremendous spiritual power.

A lady who was sitting by her husband's sickbed suddenly realized that he appeared to be dying. Knowing
that he was needed and wanted to remain on this earth
plane, she began declaring over and over, "GOD IS LOVE,
GOD IS LOVE, GOD IS LOVE!" That was the only prayer
she could think of at the moment. It worked, as it gave
her a sense of peace and harmony. Soon her husband
rallied and he later completely recovered.

Another woman and her family were in great trouble. She knew that they could not endure much more
strain. She could think of no words to decree except the
name, "JESUS CHRIST." That became her secret text.
As she used it many times daily, her family came
through to safety.

Both of these women had proved the words of E.V.
Ingraham in his booklet, *The Silence.*[3]

> To be true to the fact that there is but one Presence
> and One Power is to be possessed of the key to a correct
> solution of life's problems.

Fourth: Sometimes it is *the Prayer of Concentration*
that gives you the feeling of answered prayer. In con-

---

3. E. V. Ingraham, *The Silence* (Unity Village, Mo.: Unity
School of Christianity, 1922).

centration, you keep resting your mind on an idea; often by holding to one idea, that idea opens up its secrets to you. Then you find yourself suddenly realizing the truth about that idea, which you had not been able to see before. That is the quiet power of concentration. A marvelous prayer statement to use for this purpose is this: "TRUTH, TRUTH, TRUTH, MANIFEST THYSELF IN THIS SITUATION NOW. THAT WHICH IS HIDDEN SHALL BE REVEALED."

THE AUTHOR ATTAINED REALIZATION THROUGH THE PRAYER OF CONCENTRATION

Once when I had been trying for many weeks to gain a realization of answered prayer about a troublesome human relations problem, it finally dawned on me that I needed to invoke the prayer of concentration; to get very emphatic in prayer about the situation because all lesser methods had failed.

I asked a prayer partner who knew of this troublesome situation to join me in an afternoon session in the prayer room at the church. We spent an entire afternoon trying to gain a realization of answered prayer. Finally when all lesser prayers had not given us a sense of peace and well-being that we sought, we asked in a sense of quiet concentration: "TRUTH, TRUTH, TRUTH, MANIFEST THYSELF IN THIS SITUATION NOW. THAT WHICH IS HIDDEN SHALL BE REVEALED."

As we kept our minds on this idea, the thing that was revealed was that we should pray over and over the Lord's Prayer. We realized that the Lord's Prayer was filled with power from on high, having been given by Jesus as a result of His own strong spiritual realizations.

We also realized that this prayer, perhaps above all others, was all-powerful because it had been used by praying people for twenty centuries.[4]

We decided to boldly assert over and over in a loud voice the Lord's Prayer in an effort to gain a realization of victory in the face of this troublesome problem. The ancient people often spoke their prayer decrees over and over fifteen times when trying to gain a feeling of answered prayer. They believed that the number fifteen had a mystical power for breaking up hard conditions. Jesus had effectively spoken forth in a loud voice the decree, "Lazarus, come forth!" with amazing results (John 11:43).

As we slowly but loudly decreed each phrase from the Lord's Prayer over and over with authority, the troubled feeling within us began to diminish. Then as we said the Lord's Prayer the ninth time, we both stopped right in the middle of it as we gained a tremendous feeling that the problem had just been "broken up" within our thoughts and feelings. It was in great relief and thanksgiving that we continued decreeing the Lord's Prayer and concluded it after fifteen times.

Our realization proved right. When the block was resolved inwardly, the outer block was gone, too. All involved quickly responded with right action. The hard condition had been dissolved. However, the turning point had not come until we had gained a vivid realization of peace about it. In this instance, it had taken an emphatic prayer method to bring that about.

The prayer through which realization comes is not the prayer that begs or beseeches God to do anything.

---

4. See Chapter 5 of the author's book *The Millionaire from Nazareth.*

The prayer that brings results is the one that asserts the truth positively, confidently.

Fifth: *The Prayer of Meditation* may bring your realization of answered prayer, as you take one basic idea, hold it in mind, let it begin to come alive, giving you other ideas or feelings related to it.

I have found it particularly powerful to meditate upon the name "JESUS CHRIST," when I am trying to get a realization of answered prayer. When you take the name "JESUS CHRIST," breathing it in and out a number of times with your eyes closed, and then begin to meditate upon that name, it will come alive within you and go to work for you in any situation or condition that concerns you. Often you can feel when the Christ consciousness has completed its work in your thoughts and feelings, because it subsides and that inner activity is terminated. All sense of hurt, confusion and concern dissolves and subsides, and peace returns. You know then that the work is done, you feel at peace, and all is well.

On one occasion I encountered a difficult situation that did not seem to clear up. There was one troublesome personality involved, who was causing many unnecessary problems for himself and countless other people.

I had prayed and blessed the situation and the person, decreeing that "THIS PERSON IS A DIVINE IDEA IN THE MIND OF GOD AND IS NOW GUIDED INTO HIS TRUE PLACE," but I had not been able to get any clear feeling that this was actually happening. Things remained troubled; this person did not fade out of the picture nor conform to it.

One night when the situation had come to my attention again and something obviously needed to be done I thought, "If I can just get the right feeling about this situation, it will begin to clear up. The feeling is the thing. No one has gotten the right feeling about it yet."

I went to the church chapel and sat there alone in the dark for a long time trying to get into a peaceful, prayerful state of mind. Finally I decreed aloud that "JESUS CHRIST IS IN CONTROL OF THIS SITUATION, NOT PEOPLE OR CONDITIONS, BUT JESUS CHRIST. AND JESUS CHRIST IS HEALING THE MATTER IN HIS OWN WAY." After that I relaxed and meditated on the name "JESUS CHRIST," over and over, breathing it in and out.

In a little while there was an inner click and it was as though the Christ consciousness had come alive within me. There was a feeling of vibrating power at work, as I kept meditating upon that name.

Previously there had been a sense of burden about the problem; it felt like a lump of hurt, concern, anxiety. But now as I meditated upon the name "JESUS CHRIST" and it came alive within my feeling nature in the area of the lungs and breath, it was as though the hurt, concern, anxiety and the pulsating power of the Christ consciousness suddenly met there in consciousness. Later in my meditation it felt like that Christ consciousness had begun to surround, enfold and dissolve the burdensome problem, right there within me.

Finally the problem of hurt and concern seemed to have been completely dissolved by the tremendous vibration of the Christ consciousness as it worked deep within my meditation. Then the meditation gradually subsided, so that there was only a feeling of peace and quiet remaining. I knew then that the work was done in consciousness.

Very soon the outer picture changed. The trouble-some personality found his true place in life, to every-one's relief and satisfaction.

Sixth: It may be through *The Prayer of Silence* that your realization comes, as you join the prophet in knowing that "in quietness and confidence shall be your strength" (Isaiah 30:15). In the prayer of the silence, you stop, look and listen.

Some of the world's greatest spiritual realizations came to those who went into the solitude of the silence. Every new creation in the sphere of religion had its origin in the prayer of silence. The silence has been the birthplace of most of the world religions, as well as the source from which have come great religious refor-mations.

It was on the lonely mountain of Sinai that Jehovah revealed Himself to Moses. It was in the stillness of prayer at the baptism by the Jordan that this same spirit came upon Jesus of Nazareth and revealed to Him the secret of His divinity and messianic task. It was in the lonely sojourn in the desert that Paul, who had been laid hold of by Christ at Damascus, realized he was to become an apostle to the Gentiles, an unheard-of-thing in those days.

It was on a solitary mount near Mecca that Moham-med was called to be the messenger of Allah. It was on the remote crags of the highlands of Alverno that Francis of Assisi was visited by the resurrected Christ as he was in the solitude of prayer. It was in private struggles in prayer that Luther won at Worms that unshakable strength and assurance with which he became the great reformer. Even Buddha, the gentle,

self-renouncing sage of India, whose message of salvation to Asia became a world religion, through the
prayer of silence became the founder of a religion.

Everything that has been great, new and creative in
the history of religion rose out of the depths of silent
prayer. And everything that is great, new and creative
in the life of man began sometime somewhere in the
silence. It was to such creative periods of the silence
that Paul might have been referring when he advised,
"Be ye transformed by the renewing of your mind, that
ye may prove what is the good and acceptable and
perfect will of God" (Romans 12:2).

REALIZATION MAY COME CASUALLY

*Realization may not come through the formal act
of prayer.*

Sometimes in a more casual way—on the golf course
or while driving your car, or just before dropping off
to sleep at night, or early in the morning before arising,
as you are in a relaxed, receptive mood—realization
may come. However, the formal act of prayer usually
induces that realization and starts it on its way into
your conscious mind where you can recognize it.

Realization may come while you are reading a book,
studying the Bible, attending an inspirational class or
lecture, in a church service, or while you are talking
with others along inspirational lines. There is also
something powerful about getting into a group of like-
minded people when you are trying to get a realization
of answered prayer. For several decades I have had
prayer partners for this purpose (see next chapter).

HOW PRAYER WAS TESTED
IN SCIENTIFIC EXPERIMENTS

Some years ago Dr. William R. Parker was director of the speech clinic at the University of Redlands in California. There he conducted a scientific experiment in prayer which he later wrote about in his book entitled *Prayer Can Change Your Life*.[5]

The experiment was conducted as a test by psychologists to determine what part prayer might play in improving a person's life. The usual psychological tests were given. Then those tests were separated into three groups:

Group I were those receiving individual psychotherapy with no mention of prayer or religion.

Group II were the random pray-ers, those who prayed on their own every night at home without benefit of psychological insight or group prayer support of others.

Group III were the prayer therapy group, which met once a week for a two-hour session of psychological therapy and group prayer.

Two significant things came out of these experiments:

The first group, which received individual psychotherapy with no mention of prayer or religion, made some progress.

The second group of random pray-ers who prayed at home on their own made no progress.

The third group, the prayer therapy group, made the greatest progress!

---

5. William R. Parker and Elaine St. Johns, *Prayer Can Change Your Life* (Englewood Cliffs, N.J.: Prentice-Hall, Inc., 1957).

Dr. Parker concluded from these experiments that *prayer is the most important tool in the reconstruction of a man's personality and way of life.*

The thing that interested me in Dr. Parker's experiments was the power of group therapy in prayer.

You are a part of a similar technique every time you attend a church service, or an inspirational class or lecture. You pray together and sit together considering uplifting ideas. There is tremendous power released in this procedure, because *two agreed tune in on a third power.* There is multiplied power in group therapy along spiritual lines. Psychology has placed much emphasis upon this method.

HOW OTHERS GOT RESULTS
THROUGH REALIZATION

Often you will get a realization by sitting in a group of people who are considering uplifting ideas, when nothing else has given you that realization. Because there is a multiplied spiritual consciousness being generated by the group, you tune in on that multiplied power and get a realization.

A lady who always attended the midweek services at her church was in trouble one Wednesday. The bookkeeper could not find an item of thousands of dollars, which had been wrongly entered on the ledger so that nothing balanced. All day they looked for the mistake. As the time drew near to attend church that night, she considered breaking her rule of never missing a service, but decided against it.

When she entered the church chapel and relaxed for the first time that day, a sense of peace and relief enveloped her and she went into a deep meditation that renewed her mind and body. Suddenly she "saw" in a flash the bookkeeping entry and where it had been posted on the wrong ledger sheet. In an instant her problem was solved; but only after she got to church and joined in the uplifted unified consciousness she found there, and then got quiet, still, and listened.

To please his wife, a young bridegroom attended a lecture on healing that his father-in-law, a prominent church layman, was giving. The young son-in-law, who had never been interested in spiritual subjects, became fascinated with his father-in-law's talk. On the way home from the lecture he was noncommittal, but he spent the night awake, considering all he had heard. Later he made a plane trip to a distant state to talk with a minister he had once met and admired. From that point on he was on his way spiritually. But his awakening had come at his father-in-law's lecture.

A woman was in much pain. Though medical aid had helped, it had not healed her. One day she attended the midday healing service at her church. She wondered if she would be able to sit through the service because of the pain. But as the congregation rose to sing, "I'm healed! Praise God, I'm healed!" her whole body responded to that idea. By the conclusion of the service her pain was gone and never returned. She had gotten a realization of healing by hearing others sing about it in church.

AFTER REALIZATION, THEN WHAT?

Regardless of how your realization comes, remember this:

First: Keep quiet about it so that you do not dissipate it.

Second: Remember that you may get a realization on the inner plane long before it works out as a visible result. In some instances, I have waited years for my realizations of answered prayer to manifest, but always they have come at the right time in the right way, when all the pieces of the puzzle were ready to fit together for the good of everyone involved.

Once you get that vivid feeling, or that inner flash of answered prayer, just hold to it mentally. Do not disturb yourself if it is a long time in coming forth as a visible result. That realization came to encourage, inspire and assure you of further good. It will manifest as a result at the right time in the right way, if you keep quiet about it.

As Stella Terrill Mann has explained in her book *How to Live in the Circle of Prayer:*

> There is a spiritual law which says "Tell no one," when you are working in prayer for anything.[6]

Perhaps the hardest part of the assignment is to keep quiet after you have gotten a realization of how things are to be, far in advance. The realization that I was to enter the ministry came a number of years before it actually happened. That realization was made clear to me one day when I opened my Bible asking for guidance and these words stood out "For to this end have I appeared unto thee, to appoint thee a minister and a witness" (Acts 26:16). For several years

6. Stella Terrill Mann, *How to Live in the Circle of Prayer* (Marina del Rey, Calif.: DeVorss & Co., 1959).

thereafter I would open my Bible, look at those words and then quickly shut my Bible again. This had been the call into the ministry to Paul from the Christ Himself. With Paul I later found that I, too, could not be "disobedient unto the heavenly vision" (Acts 26:19).

Third: Be sure to recognize your realization when it comes:

It may appear as an excited, electrifying, uplifting feeling; or it may come as a quiet, peaceful feeling of power, harmony, bliss. It may come in a flash of ideas, or you may suddenly "see" the pictured result. To receive a realization is an exciting, satisfying experience usually. But later when its vividness and the assured feeling of results that usually accompanies it have faded, you may doubt that what you experienced had power.

Once when I was trying to get a realization concerning ministering to more people in the first church I served, in a flash I saw hundreds of people and assumed my prayer had been answered. All those people never appeared in that ministry, but I was soon traveling around the country lecturing to hundreds of people in church and convention groups.

REALIZATION MAKES RESULTS REAL

A realization makes real. It accomplishes results on the spiritual and mental planes first. You conceive vividly as real a feeling or a flashed mental picture. That is your realization that makes real. It is the highest form of prayer.

Such a realization will banish every ill. It is the light that reduces darkness to nothingness. Prayer expands the mind to receive. Realization is receiving. Realization is answered prayer. You can help bring about such realizations by declaring often:

"THERE IS A TRUE SOLUTION TO EVERY SITUATION. THERE IS A TRUE ANSWER TO EVERY PROBLEM. I HAVE FAITH THAT EVERY NEED IS FULFILLED NOW. THERE IS DIVINE FULFILLMENT FOR EVERY NEED. I GIVE THANKS FOR THAT DIVINE REALIZATION NOW!"

Realization changes things, people, situations and events for the better. The prayer of realization is the one worth working for, because it is all-powerful in its assurance of answered prayer.

PRAYER PARTNERS CAN MAKE THE DIFFERENCE

— Chapter 12 —

Someone has said that the most successful people in this world are praying people — or relatives and friends of praying people! I believe it. Through years of searching out and experimenting with the various facets of prayer, I am convinced that prayer partners and prayer groups can make the difference between prayers that get answered and those that don't.

Jesus pointed out the power of having prayer partners, or participating in prayer groups, when He promised:

> Again I say unto you, that if two of you shall agree on earth as touching anything that they shall ask, it shall be done for them of my Father who is in heaven. For where two or three are gathered together in my Name, there am I in the midst of them. (Matthew 18: 19, 20)

319

THE AUTHOR'S INTRODUCTION
TO PRAYER GROUPS

I became interested in the possibilities of having prayer partners, or being part of a prayer group several decades ago when I heard about a man who had done so during World War II, while serving at a military base in Morocco.

He began meeting there in the Senior Officer's Quarters every week for prayer and Bible study. The lives of the men attending were profoundly improved by those prayer meetings. A number in attendance went into the ministry after the war; some even returned to Africa as missionaries.

The man who started that prayer group eventually became a minister. He soon found himself engulfed in all the problems that one can face in the ministry: too little time to meet too many demands; being understaffed, underpaid, with countless "people problems" to cope with.

It was at that point he remembered the power for good generated in that prayer group in Morocco. He mentioned this first to his wife, then to his staff, and finally to his congregation. He gathered what material he could find on the power of prayer groups, passed it around, and started such a prayer group in his church. Though it was a small group (which prayer groups should usually be), things immediately began to smooth out in his personal life and in his church.

An alcoholic joined this prayer group and was healed. He brought others who were also helped. This church came alive, as its members got busy and did many things that had long needed to be done, both for the church and its minister. Within a year, six "prayer cells" were functioning successfully.

Through these prayer groups, this minister proved what Dr. Evelyn Underhill once wrote:

> All the effective things in the history of the church have been begun by individuals and done by small groups. The Holy Spirit has always worked through the minority.[1]

THE AUTHOR'S EARLY PRAYER PARTNERS

While still in the business world, I tried to find a prayer group to join. Finding none, I went to members of my Sunday School class, hoping to find someone there with whom I could pray. But this fine group of active young adults, comprised of many of the town's prominent people, were not interested. Though some of their lives were problem-filled, their attitude was: "That's the preacher's job. Leave the praying to him."

They suggested, instead, that I join their square-dancing group. I noted that the leaders of this dance group were a couple who had opposite personalities. He was outgoing, rather vocal. She was introverted, rather quiet. I went on my way in search of someone with whom I could pray.

A few months later, the townspeople were shocked to learn of the tragedy that had come into the lives of this couple: The introverted wife had quietly commited suicide, and her vocal widower was left bereft. I could not help but feel that less emphasis on socializing and more emphasis upon the power of prayer to right things might have saved her life. (There is nothing

---

1. *The Mount of Purification* (New York: David McKay Company, 1960).

wrong with square dancing. It is a healthy form of recreation, but it is no substitute for prayer.)

Then and there, I vowed to learn all I could about the power of prayer groups, and to pass that information along to others of "like mind" of whom Paul spoke. (I Peter 3:8, 9)

During that period of my life, I was secretary to the mayor of our town, who was also a prominent attorney. I soon discovered that the most unlikely people could make wonderful prayer partners! The maid who cleaned the office building where I worked was the one destined to become my first prayer partner. Often I would send her into the cleaning closet at the end of the hall to pray when things got hectic in our office. At other times I would sneak away from my desk and join her there amid the vacuum cleaners, mops and disinfectant. Together we would speak our affirmative prayers.

Our joint prayers never failed to get results, though one of our closet prayer sessions could have cost that maid her job. In a tense moment I had asked her to literally go into the closet—as the Bible commands—and pray until I notified her an answer had come. Her prayers worked and the problem was soon resolved.

But the answer came so naturally that I forgot about that praying maid in the hall closet. It was only several hours later, when her mystified supervisor came looking for her, that I remembered her whereabouts and rushed forth to rescue her.

One of the town's leading matrons became my first prayer partner outside the office. I met with her at her home one night a week where she prayed with me from her wheelchair. I suspect that her fervent prayers helped pray me into the ministry, though at the time neither of us realized what was happening. Later, a friend I had known since childhood became interested in spiritual subjects and served as a prayer partner.

Upon entering the ministry, a businessman in my first church became my prayer partner. I am convinced that his prayers, united with mine, got me through those first demanding years in the ministry. He helped pray my first book into print. Still later, there was a housewife who met with me in the church prayer room one afternoon a week, and there was a busy saleswoman who met with me one night a week, after the midweek service, to help with extra prayer projects.

With each change of ministries, my first project always was to locate a new prayer partner. Over the years my prayer partners have helped to smooth out life's difficulties every step of the way. When I hear of ministers, churches or individuals who are experiencing continuing difficulties, I can't help but think, "It's too bad they don't have prayer partners or participate in a prayer group."

THE POWER OF PRAYER PARTNERS

Perhaps you are thinking that having prayer partners could become a "crutch." If so, what a heavenly crutch! We are all human beings on the way to becoming divine, and any constructive help we can get along the way should be welcomed.

If you know how to worry, you know how to pray, because worry is prayer-negative rather than prayer-positive. The effectiveness of prayer partners is that they help you turn from prayer-negative (worry) to prayer-positive (constructive thought and action).

Prayer partners are powerful because they lift you up when you are down. They help carry the load psychologically until you are able to release it spiritually to a Higher Power. You become attuned to their faith when your own is low. Their spiritual power combined with your own opens the way to much faster results.

Among the great people of the Bible who benefited from the help of prayer partners was Moses. He defeated the warlike Amaleks in the wilderness only after he was assisted by Aaron and Hur, who affirmed "strength" for him.[2]

I was once serving as guest minister at the Unity Temple in Kansas City, Missouri. My lectures had been well advertised and I was speaking to capacity audiences. But in a cold wet winter climate, to which I was unaccustomed, I had gotten a sore throat which hung on. One rainy day I was sitting in the minister's study looking at my busy calendar of appointments, scheduled lectures, and social engagements, wondering how I was going to meet them all successfully with that throat.

The telephone rang with a long-distance call from a member of my out-of-state prayer group. "Catherine, what is wrong? We have been praying for you for two days, but what are we praying about?"

When I told her, she replied, "THERE IS NOTHING TO FEAR. THE HEALING POWER OF JESUS CHRIST IS POURED OUT UPON YOU NOW. EVERY LECTURE WILL BE GIVEN, AND EVERY APPOINTMENT WILL BE FULFILLED." And they were. After that call I relaxed in the assurance of answered prayer.

---

2. See chapter entitled "Your Secret Weapons for Success" in the author's book *The Millionaire Moses*.

WHY PRAYER GROUPS ARE POWERFUL

Christianity got started because of a small prayer group that met in an "upper room" in Jerusalem. Yet the results of that humble prayer group have been spreading around the world for twenty centuries.

Many people's prayers are not answered when they pray alone, because they are not willing to discipline their thinking and their lives enough to make contact with a Divine Intelligence, then let its answers come through to them. Yet such people, who have a sincere desire to know how to pray, can find vast help in a prayer group that slows them down, and quiets them down to their good. In such a prayer group they catch the spirit of prayer. Effective things can be done in and through a prayer group, without fuss or strain, that you might not be ready to accomplish alone. Such joint prayer power can be survival power.

HOW PRAYER GROUPS FUNCTION

There need be nothing mysterious or complex about the way these small groups function. Usually the members come together bringing their prayer lists, which include a list of their own problems and the names of others for whom they are praying. They get quiet, and speak forth affirmative prayers. People sometimes think this method is too simple to work. Yet those who use it regularly find it not only works but brings deep, indescribable soul-satisfaction. *The simple way is the powerful way in prayer.*

There are both public and private prayer groups. One of the most effective prayer groups I ever led, to which the public was admitted, was a morning prayer group held in my ministerial study. The ladies sat in a circle, and for an hour they discussed ideas on prayer from an inspirational book or from the Holy Bible. We would then place our hands on our prayer lists, blessing the names silently and with joint verbal affirmations, but not discussing the names or needs.

Next, we would bless the church, its trustees, staff, financial ministry, each room of the building, and any special projects. We did not discuss any of these, so no confidences were made or broken, and no gossip was generated. The results were phenomenal. Troublesome church matters were resolved, the financial ministry was revived and thrived, new church members appeared, and those in the prayer group were enthusiastic about the results they personally experienced.

One wealthy matron was driven by her chauffeur one hundred miles each way to attend these weekly gatherings. When she arrived, her driver would follow her into the church, carrying huge silver trays filled with blooming flowers out of her garden or green-house, often in the dead of winter. These were distributed to the ladies in the prayer group, with an abundance left over for decorating the church. Her presence in our group reminded me that just as she added a touch of glamour to our lives, so the act of prayer can add a touch of glamour to the daily life of those people who pray.

THE POWER THAT COMES FROM PRAYING
WITH OTHERS

Your prayers will often be answered by being a part of a prayer group when you will not get them answered any other way! Why? Because by being part of such a group you begin to think about and pray for someone other than yourself. You get your mind off your own problems as you release your prayer power to help others. *If a person would have his own prayers answered, he must be willing to be a channel through which the prayers of others can be answered.* Job was healed of all his problems only after he prayed for his friends who had been such a trial to him: "The Lord turned the captivity of Job when he prayed for his friends." (Job 42:10)

As you pray for another, knowing he is a radiating center of peace and serenity, that peace and serenity is usually first felt by you. This opens the way for your own prayers to be answered!

As spiritual healers have discovered, people have been healed in their services when they asked them to rise and pray for some person whom they found standing nearby. Scientist-doctor Alexis Carrel wrote about the power of being healed while praying for another:[3]

> Generally the patient who is cured is not praying for himself, but for another.

He also described how someone else's prayers could heal the patient:

> Certain spiritual activities may cause physical, anatomical, as well as functional modifications of the tissue and organs, including the state of prayer . . . There is no need for the patient himself to pray, or even to have religious faith. It is sufficient that someone around him be in a state of prayer.

---

3. *Man the Unknown* (New York: Harper & Row, 1935).

PRAYING FOR YOUR ENEMIES

The importance of praying for others, including one's enemies, was once expressed by the Aramaic Bible scholar, Dr. George Lamsa:

> Some of the prayers I heard as a child were vehement supplications to God to speed the coming of the Russians to deliver my people from the Kurds. When hopes for Russian intervention on their behalf vanished, I heard them pray for the coming of the British to deliver them from the Turks. Eventually the British did take over, but our prayers were still unanswered and our difficulties multiplied. The people are now refugees scattered everywhere; poverty and suffering are even greater than in former days.
>
> We now realize our mistakes in prayer, and we know why our conditions are not bettered. Our prayers were in our own selfish interests. We should have prayed for the Kurds and the Turks as well. They were our neighbors, and could have helped us better our conditions if our attitudes toward them had been changed. Instead we trusted in the arm of man, which often errs.[4]

SELECT PRAYER GROUPS WITH CARE

You should take your time in choosing prayer partners or in joining a prayer group. It is usually not wise to join a group that includes people with whom you are out of harmony. Persons who are attuned to each other can pray together more effectively. If necessary, form

---

4. *The Kingdom of Earth* (Unity Village, Mo.: Unity Books, 1966).

your own group. Jesus loved to retreat to Bethany for prayer and fellowship with three kindred souls for whom he had a special affinity. (John 11:5)

This explains why large, formal prayer groups can be ineffective, even boring. They contain too many conflicting states of mind which can neutralize each other's prayers with their secret thoughts.

Prayer groups should be small, preferably "closed" groups that do not want any fanfare. Such meetings should not be talky, pious, or "churchy." There is nothing more deadly to a prayer group than to try to "organize" it.

A prayer group should be a place where people can join together in a relaxed, intimate atmosphere to share the things nearest their hearts, or to pray about those situations they dare not to discuss openly.

Generally the rule should be "little talk" and "much affirmative prayer." This is a time to set aside for talking to God, not to man, through earnest affirmation. It should not be wasted in too much spiritual theorizing about prayer, or even given too much formal Bible study. *A prayer group should be just that: a group that prays.* Such a group knows that prayer is where the action is and will settle for nothing less! (There is, of course, nothing wrong with inspirational study groups or Bible study groups, but their purpose and function are usually somewhat different from prayer groups.)

Conversely, prayer meetings that observe only silent prayer seem to lack something, too. I once attended such a meeting, whose method was to practice the silence with only the leader speaking affirmations, or mentioning Bible promises occasionally during the entire hour of prayer. I found my mind continually wandering.

How much more effective it would have been had those in attendance been asked to join in verbal affirmations with the leader occasionally during that silence hour, thereby raising their consciousness quickly through the spoken word. I suspect that most of those in attendance spent a large part of that silence hour doing what I attempted: To bring my wandering thoughts back into that prayer period. Had we been invited to join the leader in verbal affirmations, from time to time, that would have been accomplished.

PRAYER PARTNERS VERSUS PRAYER GROUPS

For the sake of confidentiality, I generally prefer prayer partners to prayer groups. Perhaps there is more real "soul therapy" connected with meeting one or two prayer partners, where you feel completely free to talk about and then pray about whatever is on your mind, whereas in a larger group you may wish to be more cautious.

I have had prayer partners over the years whom I never publicly identified. The words "sacred" and "secret" have the same root meaning. Taking a lifetime oath of silence should be a requirement for all prayer partners or members of prayer groups.

One advantage of having either prayer partners, or participating in a prayer group, is if it stirs you up emotionally or arouses antagonism for you to pray for another, you can release that one to someone else's prayer list rather than trying to pray for them personally.

When attempting to locate the right prayer group or prayer partner, ask God to send you your own true prayer partner or prayer group. They will hear your call through the ethers and respond. Either you will find them or they will search you out.

When forming a new ministry, my first concern was always for appropriate people with whom to staff my prayer group. Through the ethers my call was always heard. In one instance a professional woman whom I hardly knew said, "I have a feeling there is something I am supposed to be doing spiritually. Do you know what it is?" Indeed I did! A housewife also asked, "What have I got to do to get into your prayer ministry?"

"Just ask," was my reply. Again she was the Holy Spirit's choice.

It is only as your prayer consciousness grows that you can successfully grow in other ways, too. Prayer partners and prayer groups can assist you in this expansion. Also, *two people agreed in prayer seem to tune in on a third Power. Their joint agreement can then produce miraculous results!*

LETTING GO BRINGS FULFILLMENT

A businessman, who became successful through prayer, described what happens when you have prayer partners or are part of a congenial prayer group:

> What do you do when you relax and pray? You let go of strain, of pushing and shoving, of self-assertion, of determination to have things your own way. You cease fighting, struggling, swinging your fists, or even reaching out for your good. You stop striving, and leave everything to the Power that is ready to flow into and through you.

But relaxing, letting go, quitting the struggle, giving up the fight, surrendering, trusting, leaving it all quietly to God, content to be just what you are, one with God—does that concept scare you?

Do you imagine that nothing can come of that but failure, loss, frustration, maybe even punishment? What happens when you give up effort and accept what comes? Over and over what comes is fulfillment of the very desires of which you had let go!

BEING ON A PRAYER LIST BRINGS PROMOTION

An employee had been considered for the position of assistant fire chief. But when a new fire chief was hired, he did not want this man assisting him because he had been a close friend of the former chief. Instead, the new chief chose as his assistant a man far inferior in experience and ability to the one who wanted the job.

The one who wanted it was disappointed, resentful and became restless about this slight. His wife mentioned his bitterness and disappointment to a relative, who was part of a small prayer group. The relative asked to place his name on her prayer list. At the next meeting of her prayer group, they blessed this man and affirmed that God was guiding him into his true place in life.

The prayer group met on a Tuesday night. On the following Thursday morning, this man was called in by the new fire chief and given the job of assistant chief! His boss declared that the man originally designated for the job just did not meet the job requirements, and this man did. The tide turned quickly and this man's dreams came true, when a small group had confidently prayed for him.

The apostle Paul must have had a remarkable prayer list! He often spoke of "making mention of you in my prayers" (Romans 1:9, Ephesians 1:16 and I Thessalonians 1:2). Although Paul was a great thinker, theologian, missionary and writer, he was also a powerful intercessor in prayer. His prayer consciousness was doubtless one of the secrets of his greatness.

THE PERSONAL BENEFITS OF PARTICIPATING IN A PRAYER GROUP

Dr. William Parker, a professor in Southern California, had ulcers and was on the verge of a nervous breakdown when he resorted to prayer. Within a few months he had been healed. He then formed a Prayer Clinic. Of the three groups formed (as mentioned in Chapter 11), he found that the Prayer Therapy Group made the most significant progress — a strong indication of the power that prayer in groups can sometimes have over that of individuals praying alone in an uninspired way.

Prayer partnerships bring spiritual growth to each of the partners. One learns from the other, and each one feels more secure, confident, and daring in prayer. Jesus said, "Hitherto have ye asked nothing in my name. Ask and ye shall receive, that your joy may be made full" (John 16:24). Others participating often receive help through joint prayers that they would not attempt to attain alone. When we help others in prayer, we also help ourselves because the process expands our own consciousness of asking and receiving. The good that prayer groups can accomplish is endless.

A PRAYER GROUP'S EXPERIENCES
WITH DIVINE LOVE

I know of a group of people who once experimented with the power of divine love in a prayer group and found it to be the greatest thing in the world for solving both personal and business problems. One evening a week these people met for an hour and together affirmed statements on divine love. They brought to this prayer group their private prayer lists containing the names of people and situations they wished to bless. No one else saw these prayer lists nor were the people and problems on these lists mentioned.

Instead, each person quietly placed his hands on his own list while the group affirmed together various statements on divine love: "DIVINE LOVE IS DOING ITS PERFECT WORK IN ME AND THROUGH ME NOW," they affirmed for themselves, for their own health, prosperity and happiness. "DIVINE LOVE IS DOING ITS PERFECT WORK IN YOU AND THROUGH YOU NOW," they affirmed for others.

In a quiet, peaceful way amazing things began to happen to the various members of that prayer group and to the people for whom they prayed. One businesswoman was out of harmony with a number of her friends. As she began dwelling on affirmations of love, these people began appearing unexpectedly at the prayer group, and reconciliation quickly took place.

Another businesswoman had been troubled for some time because of a misunderstanding that had arisen months previously between her and some friends. She had made every effort to apologize and bring about harmony again, but she had been coldly rebuffed through her letters, telephone calls and personal attempts to reestablish good will.

One night during the prayer time, as the group affirmed divine love for the names on their prayer lists, this woman and one other heard a tremendous popping noise in the air. One of the ladies discounted it, thinking it was the product of her imagination. But after the session ended, the second lady came to her and confidentially said, "Did you hear that popping sound in the air? That wasn't your imagination. It really happened! That was the hard thoughts that have existed between me and my friends being broken up. I am convinced that through our spoken words here tonight, divine love dissolved the inharmony that has existed."

From that night on, this lady had a completely different feeling about the previous inharmony, and quietly gave thanks that divine love had healed the situation. It proved to be so. Some weeks later, she felt led to contact her friends again. Instead of rebuffing her, this time they reacted as though nothing had ever been wrong between them. The previous cordiality was reestablished and continued.

Prayers of divine love are a force that can dissolve all opposers of true thought and can put your affairs or that of others in divine order, as this prayer group discovered.

THE HELP THAT PRAYER GROUPS AND PRAYER PARTNERS CAN GIVE ORGANIZATIONS

What prayer groups can accomplish for a church or other organization is just as powerful as their prayer results for single individuals or families. A minister's wife once described the work she and members of a small prayer group accomplished over a thirty-year period. They met fifteen minutes before services and sat in silent prayer, asking that the power of the Holy Spirit fill that church. Not only did healings occur, but personality conflicts that plague so many churches just never occurred in that place of peace and power. Praying people in prayerful environments seem to become charged with an aura of peace and power that can dissolve inharmony, lack and limitation, and produce miracles.

I once watched a minister raise up a new church from financial scratch through the use of weekend prayer partners. Two people met each hour, day and night, at the church over a concentrated twenty-four-hour period. This minister met with them and they all prayed for the church's growth, financial income and expansion on all levels.

As this formerly penniless minister persevered with her weekend prayer vigils, a small group of people grew into a prosperous throng. They progressed from a small, rented hall into the purchase of beautiful property and church buildings. She did not have fund-raising campaigns, or emergency meetings to thrash out problems. Instead, she stuck to her weekend prayer vigils at the church. This prayer method dissolved all problems as it expanded the consciousness of both the minister and the members. Prayer not only raised the needed funds for that church. It also attracted a number of millionaires as members and staunch supporters. Hers soon became one of the most prominent churches in that city, after she initiated her weekend prayer sessions.

THE SUCCESS SECRET OF FIRST-CENTURY
PRAYER GROUPS

If you had lived in the early part of the 1st century after Christ and had gone out searching for a prayer group, you would have found an amazing thing: Small groups of people meeting in secret who witnessed dramatic results. More people were raised from the dead and healed during that era than during the entire ministry of Jesus!

How?

One method they used was to decree repeatedly in unison the Lord's Prayer, slowly and with feeling. For them, repetition of the Lord's Prayer had a certain energizing effect, like eating and drinking. It fired their whole being with energy and power from on High.

They knew Jesus had made big claims on God. His prayers had consisted of one strong affirmation after another. And His Lord's Prayer consisted of a series of determined affirmations. The early Christians felt that when they affirmed His Lord's Prayer over and over, they called the living Christ into action.

They also felt that the fifteenth time they affirmed the Lord's Prayer, all manner of tribulation and disease began to subside, then dissolved. (Fifteen was considered the mystical number for breaking up hard conditions.) Centuries later, a number of healings were reported at the healing shrine of Lourdes by those who had been taught to declare the Lord's Prayer fifteen times while entering the healing waters.

The 16th-century German physician, Paracelsus, was recognized as a miraculous healer. He spoke of the healing power of the Lord's Prayer, and how he caught flashes of genius through declaring it repeatedly.

Decreeing the Lord's Prayer in a small group, or with your prayer partner, is one of the most powerful ways you, too, can pray! If you need inspiration or guidance about anything, this prayer method can generate it for you. This prayer can attune you to the same miraculous, all-knowing power that Jesus had for multiplying the loaves and fishes, producing money with which to meet financial obligations, and healing both mental and physical illnesses. The mystic St. Teresa said she found in the Lord's Prayer the whole art of contemplation — from its simple beginning to its transcendent conclusion. It can prove so for you, too.

SHOULD FAMILIES PRAY TOGETHER?

It was Father Patrick Peyton who reportedly first made the statement that became famous: "The family that prays together stays together."

Family groups sometimes wonder if they should attempt praying together. If they are in accord and of one belief, yes. But where there is an emotional conflict that makes it hard for them to be impersonal enough in prayer to be effective, it is often wiser for them to have impersonal prayer partners, certainly at first: A neighbor, business associate, or spiritually-oriented friend. Later, as they become inwardly harmonized, it may be easier to pray with others connected by strong emotional ties.

A businessman once went to his minister for counsel. He was in poor health, had financial problems, and had quarreled repeatedly with his wife. Though they attended an inspirational class together, they had never prayed together. They had one child who was failing in school, and another child by a former marriage was not allowed by this man to live with them.

Their minister convinced this businessman that if he and his wife would begin praying together for a short time each day, using specific affirmations aloud, their problems could be resolved. The minister also suggested they pray short affirmative decrees with the young son who had been failing in school.

When this man returned weeks later with his wife, their minister hardly recognized this couple. Their quarreling had diminished, their young son was improving in school, the husband had welcomed the stepson into their home, and both health and financial problems were being resolved!

It makes the load lighter and the way easier when you have someone with whom to pray.

PRAYERS FOR SPOUSES CAN BRING RESULTS

When it is not wise to pray *with* marriage partners, that does not preclude praying *for* them — sometimes with phenomenal results.

A businesswoman was stopped on a city street by an old acquaintance. When the second woman identified herself, the businesswoman was amazed. Because of the vast improvement in her friend's appearance, this businesswoman had not recognized her. The friend explained that improvement had come in her appearance after she started praying for her husband's success!

"A praying wife can add mightily to her husband's success, whether he knows about it or not," she explained. "My husband is now happy in his work, earns an excellent income, and has developed a wonderful prosperity consciousness. Have I slowed down in my prayers for him? Certainly not! He now knows about them, and has come to depend upon my spiritual support."

Prayers had not only brought success to this husband, but peace and beauty to his wife.

THE EFFECTIVENESS OF PRAYERS
AT A DISTANCE

It can be effective to have someone pray with you, even at a distance. A school principal had been discharged from his job, even though he was considered the best principal in that school system. But the superintendent of schools seemed jealous of this man's popularity, so he had not renewed his teaching contract. When this dismissed principal said to my sister, a schoolteacher, "I think prayer is the only thing that can straighten out this situation," she telephoned long distance to enter his name in our Prayer Ministry. He had a wife and four children, and needed work.

Within forty-eight hours after we began quietly praying for him and his family, the city superintendent suddenly appeared at his house, apologized for his previous behavior, and renewed this principal's contract! He also gave him four new teachers. This was needed in that crowded school, but it also meant increased income for this principal—another answered prayer.

My late father once wrote saying that an employee who worked with his company was having so much marital trouble that his wife had taken legal action against him. He had asked my father to appear as a character witness for him in court.

Being a long-time friend of both this husband and wife, my father did not wish to take sides. Instead, he asked this man's permission to enter his name and that of his wife in our Prayer Ministry. Though this man had no religious affiliation, he gladly consented to our prayers. My father then told his friend that once prayers were offered, he felt the court case could be called off and no testimony would be necessary. After we began praying, my father's prediction came true: The court case was dropped and the couple were reconciled.

Prayers at a distance can be effective, because there is no time or space in the spiritual world. God's goodness is omnipresent, and because prayer is creative, active, forceful, its action can tap and release that goodness anytime, anywhere.

HOW TO MEET "DRY PERIODS" IN PRAYER EFFECTIVELY

Most of us experience "dry periods" when we seem either in a slump unable to pray, or too upset to do so. At such times prayer groups and prayer partners are invaluable.

The ones praying must first heal their own views of the matter before their prayers can become effective for others. This is often the first indication of answered prayer: someone praying begins to feel better about the situation. Speaking aloud the name of the person being prayed for often helps to focus prayer power on him. Also, the one being prayed for tends to unconsciously hear and respond when his name is called. Writing out a person's name, making a prayer wheel ("wheel of fortune") that pictures his good, can also be effective methods — especially when one feels too upset to pray formally.

A family had experienced extreme inharmony. The father and one of his sons had quarreled violently. The son had packed his clothes and left home. A week had passed, yet no one had heard from him. When relations became strained among family members, the mother asked her two prayer partners for help explaining, "I've become too upset to pray."

Her prayer partners affirmed that love, order, harmony, peace and understanding were being reestablished in that household. The first indication came when the mother no longer felt that the situation was hopeless. She began to feel it could be healed. Next, she realized she was thinking about other things, and had released the problem. Several times a day she spoke prayers of protection for the entire family, and then relaxed. Later she noticed that her husband was beginning to act in his usual affable manner again. She was not really surprised the following week when her son returned home acting as if he had never been away. It was as though the quarrel had never occurred.

A prayer partnership not only helps those who are too distraught to pray, but such prayer activities can bring spiritual growth and increased understanding to all involved.

WHEN TO CONCLUDE A PRAYER GROUP

Perhaps you are wondering if prayer partners or prayer groups ever run their course?

Yes. Like other relationships in life, they can grow stale and begin to wither. If so, let them go. After a recess, you may wish to pray for a new arrangement, or you may wish to "solo" in prayer for a while.

Usually quiet, unassuming people make the best prayer partners. Yet quiet introverts are the type most prone to have deep psychological disturbances or neurotic behavior that can make them unstable prayer partners. Either they will grow restless and want out of the arrangement, or they may try to bind you too closely to them emotionally. If either happens, give and claim freedom: "CHRIST IN ME NOW FREES ME FROM ALL LIMITATION. I AM UNFETTERED AND UNBOUND." Bless your prayer partner with that same freedom.

You should not feel guilty if you grow into and out of prayer relationships just as you grow into and out of other relationships in life. That an association in prayer is no longer needed or productive can be a healthy sign indicating that growth and expansion in consciousness has taken place.

THE GREATEST STRENGTH OF OUR TIME

The greatest blessings in life often come as you pray for and with others. A businessman had long prayed for more recognition in his work, yet had constantly been bypassed for promotions. It was at this frustrating point that he formed a prayer group and became its weekly leader. Within three months he was given a promotion and a raise in pay that far exceeded any of the others that had passed him by.

The mail I have received from around the world for several decades convinces me that prayer partners and prayer groups are among the greatest strengths of our times. Although no one knows how many prayer groups there are in the world today, you can be sure there are far more than anyone realizes. There are many more outside our churches than in them. We have no idea how many people we personally know belong to such groups, since most people wisely keep quiet about such private spiritual activities.

But of one thing you can be sure: Much of the unexplained strength you find when you need it most may be the result of someone, or some group, holding you up in prayer. Just as in Biblical times, the greatest victories in life are still won by "prayer warriors."

Conclusion . . . .

AFTER PRAYER, THEN WHAT?

A sage once said: "He who rises from his prayer a better man, his prayer is answered."

You start out to get a problem solved. That's usually how you get "hooked on prayer." And you discover that prayer *is* problem-solving power. Sometimes the results are immediate. At other times, the answers may be slower in coming. However, in that interim period, something else happens: You find yourself contacting an inner world of mind and spirit you never before dreamed existed! That experience alone is enough to keep you going back for more.

After the sweetness of prayer fades, however, you discover that from the mountaintop of prayer you must descend into the valley of outworking. The act of prayer is the *inworking*. What you do afterwards is the *outworking.* This is the time to "put feet on your prayers."

THE PRICE OF ANSWERED PRAYER

You should begin to "put feet on your prayers" through the act of thanksgiving.

Why?

Because thanksgiving is the price of answered prayer. Once you have gained a realization of answered prayer, you should begin to praise and give thanks. Even if you have not yet gained such a realization, the smartest thing you can do is to praise and give thanks anyway! "THANK YOU, GOD, FOR ANSWERED PRAYER," should be your constant refrain.

Words that express thanks, joy, gratitude, or praise release certain potent energies within and around you not otherwise tapped. The act of thanksgiving carries the mind far beyond the region of doubt into the clear atmosphere of faith and trust where all things are possible! Thus, the prayer that expresses praise and thanksgiving is the miracle prayer.

HOW TO "SEAL" YOUR GOOD
AND MAKE IT PERMANENT

However, in Bible times the act of giving thanks was not just done verbally. It also took definite financial form. The people of the Old Testament had a special success formula for getting their prayers answered:

Before embarking on a journey, going into battle,

or facing any challenging situation, they gave "thank offerings" to their priests and temples in the faith that their mission would be successful.

After returning from any challenging experience, they went directly to their priest or place of worship and gave a "thank offering" in appreciation for the blessings received, and in order to seal their good and make it permanent.

If you have been able to demonstrate greater good, but couldn't hang on to it—or if you've had a hard time getting your prayers answered in the first place—this may be the reason:

When was the last time you gave a "faith offering" in anticipation of answered prayer? When was the last time you gave a "thank offering" in appreciation for blessings already received, in order to seal that good and to make it permanent?

Did such generous giving deplete the Hebrews? On the contrary! The more they gave, the more they thrived on all levels of life. Furthermore, they never complained about their acts of giving. They gave graciously with "holy joy" in the assurance of answered prayer. They knew that the purpose of such giving was to keep them in touch with God as the Source of all their blessings.

They proved that *giving thanks beforehand gets your prayers answered. Giving thanks afterwards keeps them answered!*

PRAY, THEN PAY

Along with giving many special offerings, including those just described, the Hebrews also practiced a special success method known and used by all great civilizations since primitive times.

The word "tithe" means "tenth." The ancient people felt that "ten" was "the magic number of increase," and they invoked it through giving their systematic tithes to God's work and workers. *There has never been a nation, however remote or ancient, among whom the practice of tithing has not prevailed!*

Often we have been inclined to tell God what we wanted Him to do for us, then selfishly stopped there. Or we may have been inclined to tell God what we would do for Him later, *after* He had met our demands. If so, we did not go all the way by recognizing God as the Source of all our good, and in appreciation, return to Him on a regular basis a tenth of all He gives to us. To practice tithing is a fascinating and mystical method for getting your prayers answered, since it puts your life on a spiritual, faith-filled basis.

Problems result from lack of balance in our thinking and in our lives. The act of systematic giving tends to restore a harmony and balance in the mind, body and affairs of man. Thus, the act of consistent giving to God's work opens the way to consistent receiving in your own! It is a practice that is businesslike, orderly, scientific, practical and spiritual. If the farmer refused to give back to the soil a certain percentage of the crops which the soil has given him, he would eventually have no crops.

This explains why life-long problems have been overcome by those who regularly recognized God as the Source of all their blessings, and made consistent tithing a way of life.

A businessman observed: "I have two kinds of friends who study along inspirational lines: *First,* those who complain, 'This philosophy sounds good, but it doesn't work for me.' They think they can't afford to tithe. *Second,* those who feel they can't afford *not* to tithe, and do so gladly. They are the ones who rejoice over the bountiful blessings that constantly come their way."

You should pray and then pay, since consistent giving and sharing is the beginning of increased good on all levels of life!

HOW TO GAIN FREEDOM FROM A NARROW, PINCHED EXISTENCE

Does it startle you to think of giving in connection with prayer? It no longer will when you realize that the act of giving has always been a required part of spiritual worship, as well as a requirement for spiritual growth. Thus, the act of consistent giving is an important part of the spiritual process that opens you up to answered prayer. *The practice of putting God first financially can lead you out of a narrow, pinched existence into a more expanded way of life!*

Those who practice tithing testify that it leads them into an understanding of the relation of God to the affairs of man that they can get in no other way. Keeping the law of giving and receiving is recognized as a great step in your spiritual development.

In Biblical times, the act of tithing was considered to be so powerful that it was believed to purge one of sin, sickness and even death; whereas, to withhold tithes was considered a form of robbery which stopped one's good. *If some unpleasant experience has come into your life, ask yourself what you have withheld that you should have given.* Then get busy sharing it.

One businessman declared: "You'll never find a tither in the poorhouse."

"That's true. I have had money in my pockets, for the first time, since I began to tithe," replied another.

A third person stated, "I would have been 'picked clean' had I not begun to put God first financially. Tithing is survival power."

It is true. Life can become ten times easier for the person who shares the sacred tenth with God, since he opens himself up to the spiritual power, protection and guidance that tithing can bring.

THE VAST BENEFITS OF TITHING

After they returned from exile, the prophet Malachi described to his followers the vast benefits that tithing could bring to all levels of life:

First, he described the cause of the non-tither's problems:

From the days of your father ye have turned aside from mine ordinances, and have not kept them. Return unto me, and I will return unto you.

But ye say, Wherein shall we return? Will a man rob God? Yet ye rob me. But ye say, Wherein have we robbed thee?

In tithes and offerings. Ye are cursed with the curse; for ye rob me, even this whole nation.

Second, he described the lavish blessings due the tither:

Bring ye the whole tithe into the storehouse, that there may be food in my house, and prove me now herewith, if I will not open you the windows of heaven, and pour out a blessing, that there shall not be room enough to receive it.

Third, he promised divine protection to the tither:

And I will rebuke the devourer for your sake, and he shall not destroy the fruits of your ground; neither shall your vine cast its fruit before the time in the field.

Fourth, he promised personal happiness and universal prestige to the tither:

And all the nations shall call you happy; for ye shall be a delightsome land, saith Jehovah of Hosts.

(Malachi 3:7–12)

THE POWER OF A SUCCESS COVENANT

Jacob, who became one of the Bible's early millionaires, had a specific method for putting God first financially and reaping life's bountiful blessings. He made a success covenant with God at the lowest point in his life, when he was out of favor with God and man. He asked God for what he wanted. He vowed in return: "Of all that thou shalt give me, I will surely give the tenth unto thee." He then got busy invoking his part of that covenant, trusting God to do the rest. *All* that he asked for was given him: wealth, position, peace of mind, reconciliation with his family, and increased spiritual understanding. Jehovah even renamed him "Israel" meaning "prince of God" (Genesis 28:20-22).[1]

Jacob's success covenant consisted of two parts, which you can use, too:

In *Part I,* tell God what you want Him to do for you:

(1) List what you want Him to help you *eliminate* from your life.

(2) List what you want Him to help you *manifest* in your life.

(3) List what you now have to be *thankful* for.

In *Part II,* write out what you are going to do for God, such as:

(1) Spending a specific amount of time each day in prayer, meditation and inspirational study.

(2) Putting God first financially by tithing a tenth of your income to His work on a regular, consistent basis, at the point or points where you are receiving spiritual help and inspiration.

(3) List any other things you plan to do for God.

Next, get busy invoking your part of the success covenant in Part II: "Of all that thou shalt give me, I will surely give the tenth unto thee." You will find that the practice of putting God first in your time and

---

1. See the chapter "How to Make a Success Covenant" in the author's book *The Millionaires of Genesis.* Also see the chapter on Jacob in the author's book *The Prosperity Secrets of the Ages.*

money provides you with a sense of security, protection, and guidance that nothing else can.[2]

One businessman reported, "The success-covenant prayer method works! As a result of using it, everything I have asked God for has come to pass."

DISCIPLINE PERFECTS

People sometimes object, "But I am a New Testament Christian, so I am not required to tithe." The Hebrews never repealed the powerful tithing law. It continued as a required Temple practice in the time of Jesus and, later, Paul. In fact, the tithers of the early Christian era contributed greatly to the rapid spread of Christianity throughout the ancient world.[3]

Does it surprise you that such inner and outer disciplines are needed in order to get your prayers answered? Not when you realize that the word "discipline" means "to perfect." However, nobody can place those disciplines upon you but yourself. Ignorance or enlightenment, bondage or freedom: the choice is up to you!

AN INVITATION FROM THE AUTHOR

You were divine before you were human, and to that divinity you must return. The development of your

---

2. For a personalized copy of the author's Success Covenant, write her requesting it.

3. See Chapter 9 of the author's book *The Millionaire from Nazareth*.

prayer powers can help you to make that "return trip" in triumph, garnering the rich blessings of life every step of the way.

I am but one of many fellow-travelers silently journeying with you on the pathway of prayer. Together, let us travel toward a divine destiny of increased health, wealth, happiness and spiritual enlightenment. May the practice of prayer, as described herein, make easier your journey every step of the way!

CATHERINE PONDER

SPECIAL NOTE:

See the author's tithing chapters in her books: *The Dynamic Laws of Prosperity*, Chapter 10; *The Dynamic Laws of Healing*, Chapter 13; *The Prosperity Secrets of the Ages*, Chapter 9; *Open Your Mind to Prosperity*, Chapter 6; *Open Your Mind to Receive*, Chapter 7; *The Prospering Power of Love*, Chapter 7; *Dare to Prosper!*, Chapter 4; *The Millionaires of Genesis*, Chapter 3; *The Millionaire Moses*, Chapter 7; *The Millionaire Joshua*, Chapter 6; *The Millionaire from Nazareth*, Chapter 9; *The Prospering Power of Prayer*, Chapter 6; and her book *The Secret of Unlimited Prosperity*.

A SPECIAL NOTE FROM THE AUTHOR

Through the generous outpouring of their tithes over the years, the readers of my books have helped me to financially establish three new ministries — the most recent being the global, nondenominational *Unity Worldwide*, with headquarters in Palm Desert, California. Many thanks for your help in the past, and for all that you continue to share.

You are also invited to share your tithes with the churches of your choice — especially those which teach the truths stressed in this book. Such churches would include the metaphysical churches of Unity, Religious Science, Divine Science, Science of Mind, and other related churches, many of which are members of the international New Thought movement. (For a list of such churches write The International New Thought Alliance, 5003 E. Broadway, Mesa, AZ 85206.) Your support of such churches can help spread the prosperous Truth that mankind is now seeking in this New Age of metaphysical enlightenment.

To contact Catherine Ponder or her UNITY CHURCH WORLDWIDE ministry for prayer help, literature, or other reasons, you may reach her at P.O. Drawer 1278, Palm Desert, CA 92261 USA.